CREATIVITY:
Paradoxes & Reflections

Also by Harry A. Wilmer

Huber the Tuber: Lives and Loves of a Tubercle Bacillus

Corky the Killer: A Story of Syphilis

This is Your World

Social Psychiatry in Action

The Mind: First Steps

The Correctional Community (co-editor)

Vietnam in Remission (co-editor)

Practical Jung: Nuts and Bolts of Jungian Psychotherapy

Facing Evil: Light at the Core of Darkness (co-editor)

Mother Father (editor)

A Dictionary of Ideas: Volume 1, Closeness

CREATIVITY:

Paradoxes & Reflections

edited by
Harry A. Wilmer
with the assistance of Elizabeth Juden
The Institute for the Humanities at Salado
Preface by
LINUS PAULING

Jacques Barzun • Isaac Bashevis Singer • Naomi Nye • Lee Marvin • Linus Pauling • Joseph Henderson • Anthony Stevens • Norman Sherry • Peter Ostwald • Douglass Parker • Edward Albee

Chiron Publications • Wilmette, Illinois

Acknowledgment is gratefully made to Breitenbush Books, Portland, Oregon, for permission to reprint poems which first appeared in Naomi Shihab Nye's books, *Different Ways to Pray, Hugging the Jukebox,* and *Yellow Glove.*

Library of Congress Catalog Card Number: 90-25470

Printed in the United States of America.
Copyedited by Siobhan Drummond.
Book design by Michael Barron.

Library of Congress Cataloging-in-Publication Data:
Creativity : paradoxes & reflections / edited by Harry A. Wilmer : preface by
    Linus Pauling.
        p. cm.
    Includes bibliographical references.
    ISBN 0-933029-44-6 : $14.95
    1. Creation (Literary, artistic, etc.) I. Wilmer, Harry A., 1917-   .
BH301.C84C73   1991
153.3'5 — dc20   90-25470
ISBN 0-933029-44-6   CIP

Cover art: painting by Maisi Sirois, Georgetown, Texas.

Dedicated
to John Wilmer

Contents

Part I: Paradoxes

Part II: Reflections

Preface

The enjoyment of life by everyone is enhanced by learning about novel aspects of the world discovered or invented by creative persons. In this book about creativity, eleven authors present their ideas. Their ideas, originally given to appreciative audiences in the rural village of Salado, Texas, are presented here for the reading pleasure of others.

The perception of creativity that is revealed relates to a concept that I presented in a talk to the Third World Congress of Psychiatry — the "Genesis of Ideas." The following paragraphs are excerpted from that speech since they represent well my feelings of ideas on creativity.

From my own experience, I have come to the conclusion that one way for me to have a new idea is to set my unconscious to work on a problem. This is probably what the Persian philosopher Avicenna also did a thousand years ago when he was unable to solve a problem. He would go to the mosque and pray for his understanding to be opened and his difficulties to be smoothed away; he probably had fixed the problem in his mind before going to the mosque, and his nature was such that his unconscious could then set to work on it.

I doubt that the unconscious can be directed to work on a problem. But the problem can be suggested to it, and if it is interested in it, something may result.

Herbert Spencer has written that it was never his way to set himself a problem and puzzle out an answer; that instead, the conclusions at which he had from time to time arrived had been arrived at unawares, each as the ultimate outcome of a body of thoughts that slowly grew from a germ.

I could mention many examples of important discoveries in the fields of physics and chemistry that have resulted from the effort of a scientist to satisfy his or her curiosity. It is, of course, possible to be curious about trivial matters — as Poincaré said, a good mathematician has an intuition that leads him to select a significant field about which to be curious. During the years just before 1900, Max Planck became curious about the observed distribution of intensity with wavelength of the light given out by a heated body. His curiosity led him to discover the quantum of action, Planck's constant — one of the most important discoveries ever made. It is unlikely that Planck would have made this discovery if his interest in the radiation had been a practical one; instead of discovering the quantum theory, he might well have developed an improved pyrometer, permitting high temperatures to be measured with greater accuracy than before, and the world would have suffered accordingly.

It is possible to train the unconscious to help in the discovery of new ideas. I reached the conclusion some years ago that I had been making use of my unconscious in a well-defined way. I had developed the habit of thinking about certain scientific problems as I lay in bed, waiting to go to sleep. Sometimes I would think about the same problem for several nights in succession, while I was reading or making calculations about the problem during the day. Then I would stop working on the problem, and stop thinking about it in the period before going to sleep. Some weeks or months might go by, and then, suddenly, an idea that represented a solution to the problem or the germ of a solution to the problem would burst into my consciousness.

I think that after this training, the subconscious examined many ideas that entered my mind and rejected those that had no interest in relation to the problem. Finally, after tens or hundreds of thousands of ideas had been examined in this way and rejected, another idea came along that was recognized by the unconscious as having some significant relation to the problem, and this idea and its relation to the problem were brought into the consciousness.

As the world becomes more and more complex and the problems that remain to be solved become more and more difficult, it becomes necessary that we increase our efforts to solve them. A thorough study of the general problem of the genesis of ideas and the nature of creativity may well be of great value to the world.

Linus Pauling

Introduction

The storyteller and poet of our time, as in any other time, must be an entertainer of the spirit in the full sense of the word, not just a preacher of social and political ideals. There is no paradise for bored readers and no excuse for tedious literature that does not intrigue the reader, uplift his spirit, give him the joy and escape that true art always grants. . . .

I am not ashamed to admit that I belong to those who fantasize that literature is capable of bringing new horizons and new perspectives—philosophical, aesthetical and even social.

Isaac Bashevis Singer[1]

The essays in this book, *Creativity: Paradoxes & Reflections*, are adapted by the authors from lectures they presented at the Institute for the Humanities at Salado, Texas, an autonomous, nonprofit corporation for public programs in the humanities.

The book is divided into two parts. The first, titled "Paradoxes," presents role-oriented perceptions from inside out. The second, "Reflections," consists of reflections from the outside in. Since inside out and outside in are more or less thresholds or mirrors, we can discern different points of view of perception from within and reflection from without.

Part I: Paradoxes

Jacques Barzun views creativity in contemporary culture as becoming what divine grace and salvation were in former times. He addresses the ambiguity of the use and meanings of the words *creative* and *creativity*, from cult and advertising to the soul and creations of artistic geniuses. The layers of meaning of creativity are unfolded to reveal the paradox of creativity.

Nobel laureate Isaac Bashevis Singer's lecture at Salado, at age eighty-three, was one of his last formal public addresses. Singer was quite frail; it was necessary to cancel his Saturday seminar and it seemed uncertain whether he could give his lecture on Sunday. When we got to the lecture room, I helped him up to the podium. One or two pages of his lecture notes floated to the

[1] Isaac Bashevis Singer, Nobel lecture (New York: Farrar Straus, Giroux, 1979), p. 5

floor. His secretary retrieved them and stood by him at the lectern. Then Singer spoke. His voice was strong, his lecture composed and animated. We laughed and cried. One could feel the audience's awareness of a precious and precarious moment. It seemed as if everyone in some empathic mood was helping him to the completion of his lecture.

Naomi Shihab Nye points out that we imagine creative people to be producing all the time, making things and sending them out into the world, while in actuality creative people are those who are taking *in* as much as possible in a continuous receptive gesture.

Lee Marvin talked with me about Fred Astaire's ALCOA Premiere film, *People Need People*, which starred Lee Marvin and was adapted from my book, *Social Psychiatry in Action*, about my work with Korean War veterans at a U.S. naval hospital. Lee was a man of sensitivity, intelligence, and poise and was profoundly stirred by his unruly creative muse.

Linus Pauling's chapter is a tour de force, weaving together threads that reveal the pattern of mind and dedication that led him to win a Nobel prize in chemistry and a second Nobel prize in peace. Linus Pauling, blunt, imaginative, charming, is an ultimate model of exuberant creative genius.

Part II: Reflections

Joseph Henderson, dean of American Jungian analysts, explains how the inner world of imagery symbolizes the meaning of religion, archetypes, and mythology in dream analysis.

Anthony Stevens, a British Jungian analyst, writes of war and creativity in a stunning essay that blends the analyst's insight and social and historical awareness with biology. Stevens shows that it is necessary to know that war is the activity *par excellence* of which people pool their creative powers in the service of destruction, in order that we might understand peace.

Norman Sherry describes his literary detective work and research in preparing a biography of Joseph Conrad in the manner that he also used to create his famous of biography of Graham Greene. Sherry dives headlong into the exciting pursuit of the real-life mysteries — spying and tracking in the world and in his mind one of the most creative novelists of this century. His strategy reveals a Scotland Yard detective's cunning, a bloodhound's persistence, and a scholar's intelligence.

Psychiatrist Peter Ostwald's essay on the life and music of Robert Schumann is an exemplary psychological investigation of the inner voice of creativity. Schumann's creative genius and tormenting shadow are unearthed and reconstructed. Ostwald is an accomplished violinist, and his wife, Lise Deschamps, is a concert pianist. They played a duet of Schumann's music at the Salado Institute to reveal a sense of the consuming creative power of both

Robert and his wife, Clara. Schumann's tragic madness is presented in relation to his creativity.

Douglass Parker is the originator of the field of parageography—the creation of imaginary worlds. In recounting his story of discovery of fantasy worlds such as Oz, Narnia, Middle-Earth, and Shangri-La, Parker keeps his feet on the ground. Parageography is the name of Professor Parker's course at the University of Texas where he takes his students on a creative journey that introduces them to such writers as Dante, Plato, Spenser, Homer, and Herodotus and teaches them to create their own imaginary places.

Edward Albee, with wit, charm, and biting candor, recounts highlights of his life as poet and playwright. Thoughts, intuition, and angst percolate in this essay revealing Albee's own creative spirit in the interplay of the inner and outer worlds.

Harry A. Wilmer

Part I: Paradoxes

CHAPTER ONE

Jacques Barzun

A TEACHER CRITIC

Jacques Barzun, well-known teacher, author, critic, and translator, was born in Creteil, France, on November 30, 1907. He entered Columbia College in New York at the age of sixteen and graduated four years later at the head of his class. Appointed a lecturer in history at Columbia that same year (1927), he began his career as a teacher. By 1945, he was a full professor in the field of cultural history of the modern period. He became Dean of the Graduate Faculty and Provost at Columbia University. He was appointed Extraordinary Fellow at Churchill College, University of Cambridge, England. In 1967, he was named University Professor—the highest honor at Columbia University. At the same time, he served as special adviser in the arts to the president. He retired in 1975 to become literary adviser to Charles Scribner's Sons. Since his retirement, he has lectured widely.

Professor Barzun has been twice president of the American Academy of Arts and Letters. He is a director emeritus of the Council for Basic Education (Washington) and is on the Board of Editors of *Encyclopaedia Britannica*.

He has contributed to many learned and general periodicals. And he has published ten books in history and biography and seventeen books of criticism. He has translated eleven books, including *Berlioz's Evenings with the Orchestra* and Flaubert's *Dictionary of Accepted Ideas*. His latest books are *Critical Questions* (a collection of his essays from 1940 to 1980), *A Stroll with William James*, *A Word or Two Before You Go*, and *The Culture We Deserve*.

Jacques Barzun is married and lives in New York.

The Paradoxes of Creativity

The first paradox of creativity resides in the very idea of creation. To most people that idea means producing something where nothing was before — making a thing out of nothing. The same people who take that meaning for granted, however, also believe from common sense and from the teachings of science that nothing can be made from nothing. Every object or creature is only the transformation of some preexisting thing. In science, of course, that is the law of conservation governing matter and energy.

By a further twist of thought, the question arises: How did anything whatever come to be for later conservation and transformation? The idea of creation *ex nihilo* returns full force. Believers in the Bible's literal truth are sure of an answer, which is that an all-powerful being performs what none of us can do. Unfortunately, the well-named Book of Genesis is also of two minds. It contains not one, but two stories of creation. In the first chapter, the world and its denizens come out of chaos, which is nothing. In the second, they are made out of the ground, which already exists as in most primitive cosmogonies. Biblical scholars tell us that the more majestic creation-from-the-void was, in fact, a later, more sophisticated version that was put ahead of the other. The vast majority of church fathers and Catholic believers as well as all good Protestants have believed in creation out of nothing. This concept is so strong that it influenced the King James translators who in strict grammar should have said that God *gave form* to the earlier chaos.

These differences and distinctions occur again, as we shall see, in theories of artistic and scientific creation. The present-day conflict between creationists and evolutionists exemplifies this dualism. To create species, evolution needs material on which to work as do human beings or beavers. This situation is paradoxical because there seems no way to escape seesawing between the two ideas. It is virtually a form of thought. We encounter it even on the humblest level. Take that useful household book called *How to Make Something Out of Nothing*. The title is catchy, but makes one suspicious — hence the subtitle provided is *Newel Posts into Candelabra*. With this double view, we get creation and evolution. The one excites our love of miracles, while the other reassures common sense — and also invites us to perform with the aid of a recipe.

To return for a moment to creation on the large scale, however, what does the latest science say about the genesis of the cosmos? The so-called Big

3

Jacques Barzun

Bang theory of the astrophysicists states that it came out of the void in a sudden explosion. Is this creation from nothing? The answer is "Yes," or rather "Yes but," because if you ask "Explosion of what?" you are told that a vacuum is not altogether empty. It contains sweet nothings called "quantum fluctuations," which can somehow coagulate into something. Nothing happens until, according to calculations, the nothings add up to twenty-two pounds. Then comes the Big Bang. It is clear that Paradox Number One has science in its grip, too. What is more, the do-it-yourself book about candelabra has its scientific counterpart: A Dr. Guth at Stanford has declared that, given the right equipment, he could get a universe going in his laboratory. Here, surely, is a man who can call himself gifted with creativity.

In contemporary culture, no idea is so appealing, no word put to more frequent and varied use than *creativity*. In a new reference book of contemporary quotations, there are fifteen entries for *creativity* and only three for *conversation*, two for *wisdom*, one for *contemplation*, and none for *serenity* or *repose*. The magic of the word *creative* is so broad that no distinct meaning need be attached to it. The word fits all situations, pointing to nothing in particular. Its sway extends over all of art and science, naturally, and it takes us beyond these to the basic conditions of modern society, to education, to our view of the human mind and what we conceive to be the goal of life itself.

Obviously, I can only sketch the relation of these big subjects to the modern passion for being creative and for the kudos attached to the idea. First, however, I must document my impression that creativity has become what divine grace and salvation were in former times. It is incessantly invoked, praised, urged, demanded, hoped for, declared achieved, or found lacking. I take this last complaint from the most recent presidential campaign, in which a leading Democrat called Mr. Dukakis "lacking in creativity"—no further details given, the charge apparently self-explanatory.

The assumption is that creativity is an inborn quality that colors everything one does. It is no longer a rare power found in few people and concentrated on one particular skill. Indeed, it is often attributed to whole groups, as when the head of a dating agency said: "I wanted to attract the professional, the creative," or when a New York newspaper announced: "New Wave of Creativity in East Village." It is in business and education, though (both formerly thought rather humdrum), that the thought of creation is most obsessive. Not only do several best-sellers teach "creativity in business," but corporations also have "creative departments" and "directors of creative services." Schools advertise "creative continuing education" or define education itself as "helping to live creatively through changing times." Simultaneously, critics complain that schools "do nothing for creativity, because they are institutionalized."

What else they could be we are not told, but we get an inkling when we hear that "after kindergarten, schools do not draw on creative ability." Kindergarten gives the child a freedom in learning that is close to play but that comes

4

to an end in later grades. This is a clue to what concerns us here. Creation and creativity have come to mean simply release from compulsion and regimentation. This inference is confirmed by the now familiar demand for a "creative job," that is, one in which much is left to individual initiative. A remark by the notable baseball player Ozzie Smith underscores this point: "The first time I played shortstop, I felt there was no other place for me on the field. It gave me the freedom to create as I feel." Clearly, he enjoys not being tied down to any of the bases. He roams at will and makes his own decisions. He is indeed a free agent.

It is the sense of being hemmed in by the job and the world that has caused the general yearning for something labeled creativity. The word is a condemnation of modern life, especially of modern work — organized as it is in vast networks, themselves parts of still larger systems. Rigid interdependence has long been cited as the cause of alienation on the factory assembly line. The same controls now hobble mental workers whose education and self-esteem make them resent faceless coercion more than an arbitrary boss. *Create*, then, means to do one's own thing, to perform by choosing means and opportunity at will.

Systems imply another feature, equally galling. Like industry, business and the professions now cut what is to be done into pieces assigned to different hands. No one produces anything whole, the effort having a beginning, a middle, and an end. Everyone being a specialist means repetition without completion, so that no object ever emerges as the fruit of one's labors. Nothing feeds the sense of accomplishment. Teamwork is much touted — by the organizers — but its satisfaction is indirect and loses its savor when the "team" is an anonymous mass in the hundreds, as happens not only in corporations but also in broadcasting networks, publishing empires, research laboratories, large foundations, and other supposedly intellectual establishments.

To sum up, the cult of creativity springs from the hatred of abstractness, dependence, repetition, and incompletion in work. The blight cannot be called drudgery, for this has always existed. The independent craftsperson endured it cheerfully as a tested means toward the goal — a finished product, *his* or *her* product. Even the serf on the soil could look forward to a result, the harvest. The very ditch digger has a reward: that person has created a hole from start to finish, whereas the truck driver who collects the tools of the diggers has only an endless round.

Under these conditions, it was perhaps natural enough to borrow the term *create* from the artists, who preeminently make objects — whole objects — at their own pace and according to their own ideas. Widespread as the feeling of deprivation in modern work may be, however, it is not evenly distributed. Some people in business, industry, and the professions must be what *they* call creative, or the evil that a psychologist has called "career malaise" would not be curable by what is also called a "creative work dimension." We are bound to glance at these dimensions. As it happens, a "study of creativity in daily life"

5

has recently been made, complete with an index of creativity by which to measure oneself and others. It ranges from minor creativity to exceptional. Here is an example of minor: "a secretary who sometimes edits books on the side." Exceptional is: "the amateur botanist who strictly limits hours at his regular job and often spends twenty-hour days to complete botanical experiments." This study is said to "illuminate the creative life." I find that it illuminates just the opposite. It confirms what I have said about the distaste for modern work, and the antidotes it names imply no more than the desire for autonomy and continuity of effort. That is not zeal for creation. Even the botanist who skimps on duty to an employer and exemplifies the decline of the work ethic only makes amateur science into an absorbing hobby.

People who use avocations to fill the void left by their jobs and then stick the label "creative" on these sidelines are quite ingenuously debasing the meaning of the term. One tells us that "the home is a document to one's individuality and creativity." Another speaks of the "bold creativity" displayed by the chairperson of a Senate subcommittee. A third, who is a foundation official, praises a plan as being "the most creative, effective, and integrated for the development of faculty, students, and curricula." Here creative simply means practical. The low point of nonsignificance was probably reached by the woman who, in recommending ways to make friends with strangers in a supermarket, said: "The secret is to be a little creative—think before you speak."

Such remarks show how far creativity has drifted from the idea of creation. You can measure the distance if you change the phrase "a creative life" to "the life of a creator." This last phrase makes one think at once of Michelangelo or Beethoven or Einstein. The other is a thought-cliché or else a label not to be taken literally, as when we say that an actor creates a role or a freshman takes creative writing. In this academic usage, creative denotes poetry or fiction. No one could tell you why the essays of Montaigne and the Gettysburg Address were not creative writing. In any case, a creative writing course, being instruction, calls mostly for imitative writing.

This conventional usage was harmless, but now that the adjective has been trivialized, the idea of creativity has actually turned into its opposite. Far from promising the extraordinary and unheard of, it has come to signify a feature of employment that everybody once had a right to expect.

This new paradox was noted by a writer who deflated the claims of an advertising executive.

"Creative," he said, "is industry jargon for words and ideas that go into an ad."

One welcomes the translation, but must not conclude that the abuse of *creative* is only a verbal fault. Rather, it is rooted in our conception of the human being. Democratic theory favors individualism (even though democratic practice may repress it) and the theory posits that being by definition different, individuals possess originality and the urge to show it. Self-expression is promoted throughout the culture from infancy onward: be your-

6

self, have a mind of your own, despise convention, speak up and protest, develop your unique abilities. These injunctions are expected to yield social benefits in the form of new perceptions, ideas, or devices. The word *innovation* is on everybody's tongue almost as often as the word *creative*. Rewards in prestige and promotion await the innovative person with a creative plan — or vice versa.

Looking back over the past five hundred years, one may question whether the true creators of our civilization have ever needed this urging and coaching to become their remarkable selves and to make something really new. Most often their work has been hampered or ignored by the very society that now keeps boosting innovation. *This* paradox takes the form of saying, in words or by actions, "We want what is new and wonderful, not the strange and repellent thing that you offer." The people who are thought original and get pampered are those who bring familiar things titivated by touches of novelty. Think of the tricks that gain attention today in any of the arts. Look at those who express themselves by tampering with what others have made — script writers, directors of plays and operas who cut and transpose and change settings, adapters of all kinds. Shakespeare, whom everybody supposedly worships, is thus regularly mutilated by creative minds that know how to improve him.

When we speak soberly of creation in art or science, we surely mean something quite other. We have in mind a concept of art and intellect that developed in Western civilization beginning in the Renaissance and reaching its present form only in the early 1800s. The workers and craftspeople of earlier ages did not worry about self-expression and did not talk of creativity. On the contrary, the best craftsperson was the one who reproduced the traditional model most exactly. Innovation came in the form of new technical processes — e.g., for firing clay or designing an arch — or it arose out of religious decisions to use or not to use certain motifs or imagery. The great independent creator, the genius whom we affect to revere today, is a new social type who became the central figure in the cult of art when the rise of science brought on the decline of religion.

According to Shelley, it was Tasso who, in the late 1500s, first said that only God and the poet deserve the name of creator. Voltaire probably picked up the idea from Tasso and made a single casual use of it in the mid-eighteenth century. By that time, the words *create* and *creation* had filtered into critical writing, although with a very limited sense. Poets were said to create when they introduced into their work fanciful, unreal beings and events. Thus, Shakespeare's *Tempest* was called his most creative work, because of Ariel, Caliban, and the enchanted isle. It would have surprised everybody to hear that *Hamlet* was a creation, for it only held up the mirror to nature. Johnson's *Dictionary* of 1755 gives no instance of the term *creation* in the modern sense, nor does the four-volume enlargement of 1818. The only uses cited are: the king's creation of a peer, death creating a vacancy (or similar sequences), and lastly, an illusion leading to a false belief, as when Shakespeare in *Macbeth* calls the dagger "a creation of the mind."

The application of the word to a work of art coincided with a parallel change in the use of the word *genius*. In ancient and medieval times, a genius or demon was a person's guardian spirit, giving good or evil advice in daily affairs. Then it came to mean a knack of doing a particular thing—a gifted person was said to "have a genius" for calculation or public speaking. It gradually acquired a more honorific sense. By the 1750s, it was defined by the poet Young as "the power of accomplishing great things without the means generally reputed necessary to that end." This notion fit Shakespeare's case, for he was thought lacking in discipline, learning, and art. He had a wild, untutored genius.

In the next generation came the subtle shift from "having" to "being" a genius, with no limitation such as Young included in his praise. A genius was now a fully conscious, competent, and original "creator," and only two classes of artists were recognized: the geniuses and the nongeniuses, the second group being dismissed as "talents." Unable to create, they followed the path blazed by the geniuses.

The genius being seen as a creator gave art a new meaning. It was no longer a careful imitation of nature or observance of established rules. It was discovery, revelation, invention in all realms—new aspects of nature, new insights into character and social life, new and astonishing technique. The genius fashioned masterpieces that startled by their form and substance, thereby proving all rules wrong or futile. They also shocked by telling truths previously hidden behind convention and stupidity.

All this bore hard on the public and the merely talented. The art lover must now continually learn new habits and steel against the shocks, while every aspiring artist must strive for novelty at any cost. Since the works of genius, being born of a unique imagination, do not resemble one another nor those made earlier, each seemed a world complete in itself. The analogy with God's creation became obvious and inevitable.

Equally obvious is the fact that this new conception of the genius-creator has become for the modern world the prime model of human existence. The students who rioted in Chicago twenty years ago included in their platform "the abolition of money" and "everybody an artist." As for adults, many now find the former patterns of glory—the soldier, the politician, the divine—no longer on par with the artist and the scientist. These are the new heroes, because they seem the only selfless and beneficent members of society. Indeed, they exemplify the scorn for money as well as the life that ordinary work precludes: no thought of gain, no routine, no orders from above or below, no bourgeois conventions—continual creativity and eternal fame.

The popularizing of such ideas came with the spread of public education and the diffusion of culture through libraries, museums, and the mechanical means of reproducing books, art, and music. The result has been that more and more people are tempted — indeed encouraged — to write novels, poems, and plays, and to paint pictures, compose, and perform. It has begun to look as if artistic ability were universal and only stunted or repressed in those who do not become artists. Creativity, in short, is everybody's birthright. It is this democratizing that has produced the glut of acceptable works of art and with it the perpetual shortage of money for the support of artists and their well-wishers, even though modern society is the most generous on record in its eager consumption of cultural products.

Pondering all these facts suggests that the blanket term *creativity* has at least four layers of meaning. At the bottom is the commonplace quality of initiative illustrated above from workaday sources. Next comes the ordinary widespread knack of drawing, singing, dancing, and versifying, modestly kept for private use. Above this level we find the trained professional artist, including the commercial, who supplies the market with the products in vogue. At the top is the rare bird, the genius, whose works first suggested the idea that a human being could be called a creator.

It seems to me to make no difference whether this scale denotes one quality bestowed in increasing amounts, or two, three, or four distinct powers. What is important is to maintain in private and public opinion the awareness that there is a scale. One might call that effort "quality control." It should prevent one from believing, as many reviewers and other good people do, that the masterpieces touted in the journals every week or month are actually such, and — at the other end of the scale — that the painting done by Johnny and Susan or the picking up of driftwood on the beach, or the spraying of graffiti on the wall are creative acts in any reasonable sense.

A very able journalist recently wrote of a woman giving birth as the "ultimate act of creation." If that is an acceptable view, then we must find some other word to describe God's performance and that of the great artist or scientist. The appreciation of true creators (and their early recognition) depends on remembering that even if their abilities are simply abundant, at some point quantity suddenly turns into a difference of quality. It behaves like the critical mass in physics, which sets off a chain reaction in otherwise placid material. Colloquial speech records this same surprising sort of event when it uses *create* to mean whipping up a tantrum out of little or nothing.

The leap of creation tantalizes curiosity and prompts close scrutiny in hopes of an explanation. Some of the distinguishing traits of genius have long been noted. Plato wrote two dialogues on the ways of poets to show that they work in a kind of frenzy for which they cannot account. That is the reason the philosopher wanted to exclude them from his ideal republic: they are not rational, responsible people. Like the prophetess at Delphi, they are mad — and bad poets if they are not mad. He made a pun on the subject — μαντικε (*prophecy*) is much the same as μανικε (our word *manic*).

This observation is linked with the belief in a resident genius or demon whose urgings may inspire great deeds or great wickedness. With the emer-

9

gence of "the artist," the connection between genius and strange, abnormal behavior was often taken for granted and served as an explanation. Shakespeare was only half joking when he described the poet with eyes "in fine frenzy rolling" and Dryden meant seriously his line about "great wits to madness near allied." Yet another piece of theorizing along this line was published only five years ago.

Indeed, the systematic study of genius has swung between this assumption of the crazy artist and the idea of common ability rising in regular gradation to uncommon heights. Intelligence testers actually give to high scorers the name of genius. It is a standard classification. Earlier, Darwin's cousin, Francis Galton, had gathered statistics on what he called human faculty that proved to his satisfaction how it was distributed. It seemed to him a law of nature that geniuses should be at one end of the curve to balance the idiots at the other.

Those investigators who, as it were, put their money on madness, have gone about proving their case by studying the parentage and diseases of artists. Cesare Lombroso, who found a criminal type, also found a genius type of warped physical and mental constitution. But the man who made the greatest splash with that idea was Dr. Max Nordau with his book *Degeneration*, a bestseller that alarmed and delighted readers at the turn of the century. It asserted that nearly all contemporary masters in every art were degenerate or diseased: Zola, Wagner, Ibsen, Tolstoy, the Impressionists, were all hospital or asylum cases.

In a stunning refutation called "The Sanity of Art," Bernard Shaw established the paradox that poets and other artists are called great only when their works show the rest of the world some new and profound truth about people or society: Geniuses, said Shaw, are "masters of reality." If they are mad as well, it follows that it takes the mad to teach the sane.

Of course, the madness theory is unfounded. Some geniuses have been mad: Tasso, Van Gogh, and Sir Isaac Newton showed symptoms of mental aberration, as did Dr. Johnson. But (like Samuel Johnson himself) Byron, Goethe, Rubens, and Berlioz were among the sanest men who ever lived—able managers of complex worldly enterprises and models of elevated common sense.

What is true is that when Nordau was making his diagnoses by remote inspection, a number of poets and artists were dragging out lives of disease, alcoholism, drug addiction, and psychosis. W. B. Yeats, who was strong and healthy, was appalled at the extent of the evil and wondered what curse had befallen his generation. The social and economic conditions of the time suffice to explain the curse—that is, the pressures that sensitive and often destitute human beings failed to withstand.

There is, moreover, what might be termed the biographical fallacy. Books about the lives of the great fill our minds with anecdotes of their odd behavior, but these are oddities only because the comparable acts of ordinary people are never written up for the world to read. Thus, when we learn that to compose his poems Schiller wanted a drawer of his desk open and full of overripe apples, the impression is given of a not quite normal character. Again, we shake our heads on reading that Dickens had to have certain ornaments in a certain pattern on his writing table. No one ever hears of the bank manager who has to doodle, however, and must have a colored pencil to do it or he cannot think financially. Yet all three are merely using a sensory stimulus to trigger the habit of work.

The specific traits of creative genius have never been ascertained, nor any correlation with genetic, medical, or environmental factors. I have read more studies of genius in English, German, Italian, and French than I care to remember, and I think their findings would leave any reader unconvinced and uninstructed. For a sample, turn to the article, "Creativity," in the *Encyclopedia of the Social Sciences*. It starts out with the usual confidence of people armed with method and faith in science. It winds up pathetically with a list of characteristics that covers the full range of human abilities — necessarily so, since the world's great performers have been of every kind and temperament.

It is wiser and more entertaining to read good biographies, and, even better, memoirs, letters, and diaries. If one guards against the fallacy of "How odd!" they will be found to disprove every cliché, including the definition of genius as an infinite capacity for taking pains, or as they say in French, "a protracted patience." Ruskin, writing to Rossetti, repeatedly urged him not to draw and rub out and draw again, adding on one occasion: "I am not more sure of anything in this world than that the utmost a man can do is that which he can do without effort." Shaw put it succinctly when he said: "Great art is either easy or impossible." When Dickens was asked to account for the stroke of genius that changed *Pickwick Papers* in chapter six from a set of rural mishaps for comic illustration into a masterpiece, all he said was: "Then I thought of Mr. Pickwick."

No sooner do we conclude that inspiration is all, however, than we bump into Flaubert who toiled at his desk like a digger in a coal mine. Of course, his output was four novels and three short stories, not Dickens's fifteen novels, plus innumerable tales, travel notes, and historical sketches — all this done while editing periodicals and giving public readings.

To Flaubert, great art was not impossible, but neither was it easy. Nor was it to Beethoven, whose notebooks testify to the very effort that Ruskin advised against — try and try again until the theme, the development, the form satisfy. Many others have recorded their life-and-death struggle with the material of their art. As Goethe said, "Blood sticks to the work."

As for people of science, they have touted unwearied persistence as the chief condition of their creativeness. They have also spoken of sudden illumination — Gauss idly gazing at the hills outside his window and Poincaré finding the solution to intractable problems on arising from sleep. Chalk up another paradox.

11

It is not the last. Far from creativity being a permanent trait that varies only in intensity, it can disappear totally—and sometimes reappear. Hugo Wolf and A. E. Housman are notorious cases in point. Both had two periods of creative energy separated by a long, fallow interval. The saying that poets die young carries a double meaning in the word *die*: the body survives, but the genius has gone, as is frequently true of mathematicians and chess players. At the opposite extreme, we find long-lived poets such as Wordsworth and Victor Hugo, who keep on producing genuine poetry to the end. They go to work, as somebody has said, like bureaucrats, writing day in and day out. The quality fluctuates, but the power never vanishes.

Still more puzzling in its variations is the occurrence of creative historical periods. Why the crowd of great painters and thinkers in early Renaissance Italy, and then the migration of the art to the Netherlands? Why the Elizabethan dramatists and musicians? France, Spain, Germany, Austria, and Russia also have their high moments in one or another art, which relapses into the worthy regularity of the talented, until the next outbreak of the creative epidemic. No correlation is to be found between these bursts of genius and peace or war, freedom or tyranny, prosperity or decline, let alone with climate or race. The only feature present every time is the crowding of the gifted on one spot. This is a kind of tautology, though, since creative period means a cluster of creators, which soon attracts to its center other eager artists from all over. Here again, the critical mass changes the character of the preexisting elements.

Baffled in the search for something like a genius type, modern psychologists and critics have pursued another entity they call the creative process. It is characteristic of a technological age to imagine that creation is a series of steps that can be discovered and analyzed, like digestion or photosynthesis. The public, too, accepts the idea when librarians exhibit writers' manuscripts and bid everybody observe the "process" by which the poet got to the final draft. Well, manuscript corrections may be interesting, but as explanation they are illusory. What impelled dissatisfaction with a bad line may be guessed, but not the leap from it to the perfect phrasing. Besides, great writers have often spoiled some of their work by late revisions—Dryden, Wordsworth, and Henry James, to name a few. Is that a process of decreation?

If creation were a process, its operation would, by this time, have been reduced to formulas or recipes, which intelligence and method could apply to produce great art and great science. Those who come nearest to seizing the secret are the immediate followers of the innovators—and followers, by common consent, rank second best. For what they have caught from the creators is technique, and technique is not enough. Something more is needed—and perhaps something less. Take the music of Saint-Saëns. Here was a precocious, enormously gifted musician; he could turn out pieces that seemed as if written by Mozart or Beethoven or anybody he wished. But as Berlioz, who was his mentor, regretfully remarked, the young man lacked inexperience. Courses in fiction writing may have a number of top-notch students, yet not turn out Chekhovs and Henry Jameses, although people here and there may in time become — themselves. Similarly, laboratories all over the globe are run by scientists who probably deserve to be called brilliant without being of the breed of Newton, Faraday, Pasteur, and Einstein. In short, creation does not proceed, it occurs.

If so, what is the conceivable source of the creative power? Could one discover it, at least one paradox would be removed — the apparent contradiction of great art achieved with ease or else with anxious toil. One could say that some artists must dig a deep well to tap the source, whereas others have a spring that bubbles up on its own. Or, to put it differently, the creative moments are what matter, and they come at different intervals during the work, which is always long and laborious. The ever-inventive Dickens spent long mornings in front of a series of false starts, and Balzac rewrote again and again on one set of proofs after another.

We are thus brought to the final paradox, the one inside the mind. For the past fifty years, the characteristics of creators have been attributed to the Unconscious with a capital "U." Depth psychology posits that the instincts drive the mind, and that individual thought is shaped by the way in which those drives are handled. In human society, the vicissitudes of growing up as well as the permanent focus of culture create inhibitions or repressions. These modify the interplay between the parts of this machinery and hence determine its products. According to one interpretation, great artists are like children, who, unsocialized, heed the imagination and speak out freely. The conscious mind of the adult artist and the acquired techniques merely organize the spontaneous voices from the Unconscious. Geniuses keep in touch with this creative force while the rest of us bottle it up by conventions and neuroses. Through this unusual freedom, the creator is able to express fundamental reality and teach us to see it as it is.

It is true that some artists have likened themselves to outspoken children, but this diagram of the psychologists is open to objections. In the first place, it supposes the mind to be a sort of gearbox set in motion by an engine below. The analogy fails to explain: a powerful engine, unobstructed, will make wheels move faster or longer, but it cannot make them do one thing rather than another. The pattern of the mind must itself be different if it is to perform different things, some of them extraordinary. Alternatively, if creativeness comes from the Unconscious, this hypothetical organ must hold knowledge of life and art in solution for crystallization by the mind; but the theory assigns no such range or subtlety to the biological drives.

Besides, the Unconscious is a piece of equipment that by definition everybody possesses. If, as is said, it contains the archetypal forms of feeling and belief that underlie both common thought and works of art, it follows that something else must exist to diversify this common fund of fantasy and make the visions of the poet differ from the daydreams of the ordinary person.

13

Finally, it is notorious that artists, like most civilized people, suffer from neuroses; indeed, they suffer perhaps more, if we may judge from their misadventures in practical life. This realization contradicts the assumption that their remarkable works betoken ready communication with their Unconscious, particular or collective.

What, if anything, do the creators themselves have to say about conscious and unconscious? I mentioned earlier Poincaré's report of his mode of discovery: he struggles with a problem for many days, then lets it go, and in the end the hint of a solution comes to him as he emerges from sleep. Milton's muse, the poet said, "dictates to him slumbering." Mozart wrote that while composing he felt as if he were under the spell of a strong dream. Helmholtz, the German physicist, would take solitary walks for relief from concentration, and the sought-for idea would come unbidden into his mind. Berlioz, in his memoirs, contrasts the unwelcome task of writing prose with that of writing music, which he says happens of itself, as by "an inexplicable mechanism." Wordsworth's often quoted "emotion recollected in tranquillity" refers not to quiet composition but, on the contrary, to the interruption of quiet by a strong welling up of the poetic urge. And there is the suggestive reply of the little girl who was asked what she thought: "How can I tell what I think until I see what I say?" It is hardly necessary to add the commonplace of novelists and playwrights to the effect that their characters, once created, take over the management of the story.

All these observations point to the workings of a nonconscious agency, but is it the Unconscious of theory? The observable agency is put to work by the conscious mind, which demands an object and prepares elaborately to handle the makings of it. Nor is nonconscious incubation reserved for creators. When you cannot remember a name, you try hard at first to bring it back, and fail. Having given up, you find it a while later floating up of its own accord. Professional writers know that the exact word they want but cannot summon will soon present itself if only they keep on writing. Surely the deep Unconscious is not a dictionary, so the word or name that pops up was not among the drives or archetypes but in the subliminal region from which, for example, we draw the ability to play the piano while also talking seriously to a friend. The subliminal is not an originating force, but rather our memories and habits stored away.

It would appear, then, that the mystery of creation defies analysis. It may do so forever, like the workings of mind itself. Yet one student of the mind has offered facts and ideas that seem to me to bring us if not an explanation of genius and creation at least a right conception of their workings. I refer to William James, who took up these questions several times in different connections. He says that geniuses have an enormous capacity for perceiving similarities among disparate things. Their minds dump across the grooves cut by common experience. Theirs are also sensitive minds. Every stimulus starts multiple trains of thought and wildly free associations.

"In such minds," says James, "subjects bud and sprout and grow. . . . Their ideas coruscate, every subject branches infinitely before their fertile minds." This explains why being too good a student can limit creativity—what Berlioz termed "the lack of inexperience"—for learning follows traveled roads. And James, with *his* characteristic genius, draws a comparison which is at once comic and illuminating. He says that the profusion of possible ideas in the creative mind resembles the confusion of the muddle-headed person; hence the *eminently* muddle-headed are in a sense close to genius.

Clearly there is a difference between the two, however, which Harry Wilmer pointed out when he said that the nongenius "lets the awareness slip by." The genius's goal rivets attention and puts order among ideas. In fact, concentration upon the activity required—writing, painting, composing, and (in the sciences) observing, calculating, conceptualizing—becomes an obsession. In this effort, not merely the mind and the will, but the whole organism—muscles, blood, nerves, and glands—are involved.

This mad passion or passionate madness is the reason why psychopathic personalities are often creators and why their productions are perfectly sane. The disturbance makes for the obsession, while the contents of the work are formed by the fertile, subtle, and vigilant intellect. This conception of genius would account for the paradox that it consists of both sudden inspiration and patient, painstaking work, hence also the versatility and often superhuman bulk of its output.

James's description has other corollaries. In essence, one act of creation is as amazing as a dozen, but in practice we reserve our fervent admiration for the artist who creates great works again and again. This custom amounts to a critical principle: magnitude and frequency of success are the proper measure of creativity. Exquisiteness and perfection may occasionally beguile us more, but they are lesser achievements. Again, the error of regarding children as artists is due to overlooking the paucity of their intellectual and emotional resources. Sensitive and uninhibited they may be, but their minds cannot encompass the vast array of thoughts, memories, and associations that the great artist fuses into a single shape. Every good listener has noticed this limitation in the child virtuoso who tries to interpret a masterpiece.

These considerations add force to the suggestion that the term *creativity* should not be loosely applied, squandered upon works and workers that are respectable enough on their own level but that do not stand comparison with genuine creation. Nowadays, originality, the cult of the new, and plain shock power have such a hold on our judgment that we pay humble attention to a great deal of nonsense and charlatanism. This gullibility spreads wide and provides a market for the users of the topsy-turvy as a formula. Present the familiar up side down, and there is originality. Nobody can deny that it is new. It is anybody's guess how much of contemporary art is the outcome of this recipe. One recent example turns up in an unimportant film, but it is typical. The maker of *Without a Clue* tells us: "It was that moment when you think,

15

'There's a good idea.' What if Watson is actually the genius and Holmes is this ridiculous ham in front of Scotland Yard?" Truly a splendid idea for defeating expectations but a far cry from the idea that first created Holmes and Watson out of little or nothing.

It may seem an ultimate paradox to end with an example from a genre that can plead as an excuse that it is not creative but commercial. Yet it is significant for the same reason that led me to distinguish creation from creativity. That reason lies in my conviction that a long period of creation is coming to an end. For some five hundred years, Western civilization has enjoyed a profusion of high art, art "created by genius." Today, the conditions arising from machine industry and the democratic state have persuaded the world that creative power is within the reach of all, by natural right, like political power. That belief has brought out many agreeable things that resemble true creation and are said to be the real thing.

This extensive effort has had unexpected results. It has not only diluted the meaning of creative, but it has also glutted the market with innumerable objects and performances arbitrarily called art, thereby making it even more arduous for true creation to find a public. Still more generally, creative foolery has been distorting, denaturing, destroying the fund of culture amassed since the Renaissance. That is the sense in which the filmmaker quoted above is typical. He found a pair of well-known creations and his creativity prompted him to confound their meaning, blur their appeal. This attempt is in the tradition of Duchamp's putting a mustache on Mona Lisa and many other imitations of that famous decreative act.

The impulse and the clever deeds are part of an irresistible historical sweep. Some of us might prefer to live in a time of construction, which has a different kind of excitement. Let no one repine, however. Rebuilding is bound to come, because true creative power is a phoenix, and the forces of destruction are clearing the space for its new flight, none can tell when or where. Meantime, if we are to recognize the bird when it appears, let us not forget that creation means making something new and making it out of little or nothing.

Discussion

PARTICIPANT: You have used *creator* and *genius* throughout your discussion, and creative genius many times. Is that a double positive? Must one be judged a genius only if one creates? Must one be a genius in order to create?

JACQUES BARZUN: I should say "yes." I started out on purpose with God's creation. I quoted Tasso saying, "God and the poet are the only creators." We have to stick to certain conventions of meaning. Creating implies, to my mind, the extraordinary, the astonishing, the unexpected, the unpredictable. I am perfectly willing to look for another term for inventiveness, ingenuity, and originality of many kinds quite far below true creation.

PARTICIPANT: How important is it for us to be conceptually clear about creation? It is fine to know what the word means and to use it right, but wasn't wonderful and splendid art created by ancient artists who had no conception of artistic creation whatever?

BARZUN: That is true. We don't have to put back our ideas and terms into periods which knew nothing about them. We do recognize in those periods, however, the kind of work which would, if produced today, deserve that term. I may have failed to make sufficiently emphatic a point toward the end, which is that if we misuse *creation* and *creative* in the way we do now, we hamper the work of the creator. We fail to distinguish the creative from the merely talented, the merely inventive, the merely refreshingly new.

It is a sad fact that with all the agencies we have in this country for supporting the arts, the half-dozen persons whom I consider particularly creative in our time got absolutely no encouragement or support from those agencies or even from patrons peculiarly enlightened. I think, for example, of Harry Partch in music, whose name is probably not known to any of you. It would be invidious to name others. I may not be right about their transcendent genius, but I am sure, from talking with other people, that everyone has a little list of people — creators who have been denied creativity because they did not fall into the routine ways we now call creative. It is important from a practical, functional point of view in the arts and sciences to keep things separate. That's why I called it "quality control."

PARTICIPANT: I was concerned about your comment that this was an end of an era of creators. Would you comment more about that?

BARZUN: One great fact behind the necessary elimination of what we may call Renaissance-Romanticism-Modernism is the tremendous amount of art in all styles and all forms which that produced and that weighs on modern artists to such a degree that they cannot do anything except the topsy-turvy, the comical, the pointless, and the meaningless. If you analyze modern art in a generic way, you see that it is a fairly steady, systematic avoidance of everything that was done down to 1914. Those are the signs of the end of a period — something that has happened many times before. It doesn't mean the end of everything, as I tried to say at the end of my talk. Creative genius is potentially everywhere — around the corner. All it needs is an opportunity to start fresh. We cannot go on either doing what has been done or doing the opposite. We need the really new.

PARTICIPANT: The discussion of creative genius and the rise of that discussion goes hand in hand with the concept of the individual as it was developed in the Enlightenment and the post-Enlightenment periods. In the eighteenth century, Diderot insisted that creative genius was based on pre-science. In the nineteenth century, Nietzsche insisted that creative genius was a balancing of impulses. For the former, creative genius was there for something that emerged through society. For the latter, creative geniuses necessarily pitted themselves against society. I'd be interested to know what your ideas are on the relation between creative genius and society in the twentieth century.

BARZUN: The two examples you have given provide an answer. By the time Nietzsche was writing, which is little more than a century after Diderot, artists were embattled against society. They felt misunderstood, neglected, denied the comforts and amenities of modern life. It was a perfectly true description. They set about doing the work of destruction at which I have hinted. In the eighteenth century, the enthusiasm of the period for an ideal society, for the reign of reason and order in the future, enabled Diderot to see that art does come out of society. But it has to be a society that permits art to come out.

Now the further paradox here — we do everything to bring out art and artists, but they have lost their power to create because of this accumulation

18

of masterpieces in the past. We have lost the knack of recognizing the great artists through the same operation of industry, mass production, and advertising, in short, the commercialization of art on a large scale (which, let me add, is in certain ways beneficial). I am not attacking this, that, or the other. I am only trying to set out what I see as the forces in conflict. Some of them are conscious, as when the artist attacks society, and some are absolutely unconscious, as when well-meaning people support second-rate artists as if they were great.

PARTICIPANT: Is it not true that the pedestrian and prosaic individuals end up historically defining who is a genius and who is not? I think the collective intelligence throughout the ages defines who is a genius. I am sure that contemporaries of Beethoven and Mozart were also producing music, but it was a lot of other people unable to create music who ended up defining them as the creators of art.

BARZUN: Yes. We mustn't ask artists, even great artists, to judge one another, because the obsessive drive toward a particular goal frequently prevents a great artist from seeing the merits of something that is going toward another goal, in another direction. It is not sensible to require them to be critics.

As for the general intelligence, I have my doubts. It works very slowly and only fairly well. If you look at the literature on any artist that you care about from the past, you find that the reputation goes up and down. The coming up of one artist often brings down another. There is always a slump after the death of a recognized artist. Then there is a revival. We're always rehabilitating someone. Look at the work of digging up that T. S. Eliot and his friends did, beginning with the metaphysical poets and then going on to other writers, sometimes French or German as against English. It is a continual muddle, and very often those who seem to survive do so merely as names.

We've spoken of Shelley, for example, this evening. Obviously someone here reads Shelley, since he was quoted. I read Shelley, but I haven't a single friend who thinks that Shelley was a good poet. The whole Academy of Arts and Letters would sign a document saying he was not a poet. My good friend W. H. Auden abominated him. He said there was no poet he detested more than Shelley, unless it was Racine. Those are the real opinions, but, of course, in the schools and textbooks and conventional talk, Racine and Shelley are great names. Somehow that doesn't seem to me good enough. I think the only real admiration consists of direct enjoyment. Look at the way Mahler has come out of the ground after an unconscionable time. I continue to dislike Mahler, but I am glad that he is out in the open to be shot at, as well as enjoyed.

PARTICIPANT: Would you say something about the condition of the publishing business in the United States today—perhaps, particularly Scribners and Macmillan and their relationship? With all this merging and submerging of the publishing houses, can we expect that the artistic quality of literature will be enhanced, or are they going to have to pay more attention to what will be popular? Will the artistic books of genius have to be published by the academic publishers?

BARZUN: You are quite right. The situation of publishing in the Western world is appalling. For decades, publishers have refused to pay attention to the means of distributing their product. If they made corn flakes and handled distribution as they have done, every child would starve to death. Publishers turn out books and don't care what happens to them. In one sense, they do care. They want them to sell. They are always looking for something that will sell half a million copies in two weeks. But that is not caring for the distribution of books. The only invention we have had in our time is the book club, and it has its limitations.

The modern conglomerate publisher who is always looking for the widely popular book will, as an act of contrition and repentance, publish a few first novels but do nothing about their dissemination. The shelf life of a newly published book in the United States now is six months. After that, it goes to be pulped because the former remainder business has fallen on evil days. You cannot sell at remainder prices because the remainder houses cannot dispose of what they used to buy since nobody hears about those books. There is no distribution system.

The reviewing system has also collapsed, under the enormous burden of overproduction: too many books published on too many subjects, too many books that are made up of newspaper articles published within the previous half year. If you'll notice, one out of two books and maybe more are about recent events. Someone makes an assassination attempt on X, Y, or Z and immediately there is a book about that. Any disaster, any scandal, any rise to prominence in the popular art world will bring out a biography, a book about the scandal or disaster. Those, in a sense, are nonbooks. They are merely journalism in hard covers.

The only hope for new literature is, as you said, academic publishing. The university presses have gradually taken over a portion of the former trade publishing. They used to publish only scholarship. Now they publish scholarship plus the kind of book that used to be brought out by Harper's and Scribners, which now they won't do. The only other hope is the rise of a great many small firms. Any intending novelist, poet, or essayist here should not waste time submitting a manuscript to any of the big publishers whose name he or she knows. Find some small firm that brings out ten books a year, those ten books being all that they do. They care about each, and they go to work and try to do that extraordinary thing — sell them.

PARTICIPANT: I have a question about the quality of creation. You mentioned in one of your lectures in *The Use and Abuse of Art* the fascination with the interesting as opposed to what was formerly the fascination with the beautiful or the spiritual. I wanted to know what you thought of the role of the publishing and film industries in consciously choosing to disseminate an inferior product. I have traveled a little bit in Europe, and I've noticed that the general quality of French film was, on the whole, in narrative technique and directors and composition, higher than what I see coming out of Hollywood. Yet I don't think we're intellectually inferior to the French, genetically anyway. I feel frustrated as an aspiring writer myself. Who is going to read my product? I would really like to think that I have more impact, and I think that I have more to offer than just to an elite coterie of fellow poets. Yet I feel frustrated with what is being published and disseminated.

BARZUN: I agree with everything you've said. You demonstrate by it to what extent conditions modify not the product necessarily, but rather the emergence of the product. I'm no expert on the film industry, but I imagine that the French films cost less, are aimed at a smaller audience, are not required (as I understand that most American films are required) to be intelligible and interesting to adolescents. Films abroad do not have to be taken up by a huge continent, only a small country. Those things matter. If, however, you were to work in film in France, you would find that the French, too, have their limitations. Certain ideas and traditions, in addition to a kind of provincialism that is notorious in France, would exclude some of the things you might want to do that are very good. As I said in my talk, people who are really hewing to their own lines today and not trying to suit a market have just as difficult a time as if we didn't have any national endowment or state councils for the arts or the many foundations and groups ready to support. It is a tragic situation, with good will and money on the one hand, and the frustrating efforts (to use your words) of young creators on the other.

21

PARTICIPANT: I believe when you started out your discussion you talked about the possibility of understanding creation and the creative genius through the creation of the world. Most people associate it with the philosophy of religion and pause at its qualities inside the creative genius through attributes that they see in the creation. An example would be all powerful, all knowledgeable — whatever. Is this the way we really understand creative genius today in art, or is it possibly some sort of relation (I hate the word *metaphysical* but we'll slide that in there) between the work and what we see going on around us?

BARZUN: If I understood your question, the answer would be something like this. When the word *create* or *creator* began to be applied to the arts, it was a figurative term alluding to the creation of the world, an event which I think was far more present to people's minds than it is today. The bare fact of church attendance, Bible reading, and catechism classes made people aware of the act of creation — an extraordinary thing. Then, by metaphorical application, the notion was applied to extraordinary works of art that nothing seemed to have led up to.

Last, we get in the writings of Virginia Woolf and E. M. Forster and others the idea that the great work of art is "a world in itself." It has no connection with any other work or even with real life. The advanced criticism before the very last wave made that point over and over again. That is why they resisted the cultural or historical analysis of poems and novels. They were to be taken just as they were, complete.

When we speak of a creator, we invoke this figurative idea. That is one reason why — since the figure is based on a religious model — it should be kept fairly pure, making us think only of the remarkableness, the unexpectedness, the massiveness of the particular work. Hence, my implied objection to the use of creativity for someone who puts a suggestion in the box at the office and has it accepted. Here is a person full of initiative and good ideas, but not a creator.

PARTICIPANT: First of all, I came to hear you today because of a book you wrote in 1945, *Teacher in America*. I read that as a high school senior. It brought me to teaching and made me go to the University of Texas for a liberal arts education, rather than for the school of education, because you state there that teaching is an art and it has pedagogies of different things. I had hoped you would speak of creativity in teaching. You have already answered some of those things with your paradoxes. It has been almost fifty years since you wrote this book and since you have taught extensively at Columbia. What would you say to us about the state of the art of teaching in the United States right now, and its future? The evils that you wrote about in 1945 seem even greater and more prevalent today in the eighties.

BARZUN: You're quite right. Things have gone from bad to worse, and I have absolutely no suggestions or ideas as to how this situation could be turned around. When I wrote in 1945, the universities were still centers of the liberal arts. Now the liberal arts have turned into quasi-sciences. They are taught not liberally or humanistically, but taught as specialties. They are taught as if everyone in the class were going to become a professor of English literature or history. That is deadly and all wrong.

That kind of teaching belongs in graduate school, but it has descended into the undergraduate college, so that neither the schools of education nor the good undergraduate colleges now furnish good material for teachers. If some dedicated person manages to get over the first hurdle and crosses the "no man's land" to public or even private education, he or she finds there appalling conditions, misuse of time and materials, love of gimmickry, and innumerable escapes from direct, solid, useful, effective teaching. Paperwork is one of the curses of the profession. And I don't mean correcting papers, which no one does anymore, thanks to multiple-choice tests, which are also destructive of good teaching.

PARTICIPANT: I was interested in the degree to which you feel that democracy and culture are incompatible. You seem to have implied in some of your earlier comments that actual manifestations of democracy as they have shown themselves in the past twenty years seem to be incompatible with the notion of nurturing and developing culture.

BARZUN: I shouldn't say that they are incompatible. I should say that the democratic atmosphere and institutions call forth and produce a different sort of culture. This belief is so true that recently very sober and thoughtful critics have said that the art of today and the future will be popular art, not high art. That distinction is being made. These critics bend their educated gazes upon all sorts of popular works and deal with them as they would have dealt with the high art that we have had for half a millennium. It is a tenable position. It makes for a different kind of culture. Any kind of dissemination among large numbers changes quality. I won't say reduces, but it seems to dilute high quality in a fashion hard to describe. For example, there is just as much painstaking, just as much inspiration and musicianship in the various forms of jazz as there may be in Mozart or Beethoven. The effect is simply more diffuse. It is not as concentrated. It doesn't call for as much emotional and

23

spiritual attention. And such is popular, democratic culture, something like the culture of the Middle Ages which except for the cathedrals was one of popular art, of very low intensity products.

PARTICIPANT: Your earlier remark reminds us of the flap currently going on in higher education about what it should consist of. What should the core be? What should be the place of the classics? Would you have a comment about that conflict?

BARZUN: It is basically a political conflict. It has very little to do with the classics — what they can do or how they can be taught or anything of that sort. There is a kind of anarchism among students who want no core curriculum but free choice, free electives — something that has made Brown University the most popular in the East. On the other side, people who have entered the university faculties, but also some students who represent the so-called ethnic minorities or women who feel they were previously disregarded, are using the materials of the curricula to make points about social and political matters.

In many cases their points are well taken on social and political grounds, but to object to the Western classics because they do not include those of the Far East or India or Africa is simply a form of obscurantism. It neglects the simple fact that those classics cannot possibly be understood, would not be tolerated, by a freshman class. I just want to see a freshman at the University of Nebraska faced with the Baghavad-Gita. He or she would be right to petition the governor.

PARTICIPANT: You talked earlier about "quality control" in the areas of the arts, so that the artists who were doing truly creative work would be supported. Who would determine the standards of quality? And if there were a standard, wouldn't there be people who were doing work merely to meet just the standard?

BARZUN: Yes, go no further. You went way ahead of me. I wasn't thinking of quality control in the production of art. I was thinking of quality control in the use of descriptive terms about the arts. You may know of an artist who has spent a good deal of time wrapping long sheets of cotton and other materials around fences and bridges and so forth, or an English artist who has specialized in making constructions of brick — two or three bricks high and six wide and ten long, and painting them various pastel colors. I would say with reluctance that to call those "creators" would be ill-advised. It doesn't seem to me that the intellectual or even the physical effort warrants that term.

24

So, "quality control" applies to that critical operation either of art critics in newspapers or ordinary citizens faced with what they find in any gallery of art. I had no thought of anybody being on a board to guarantee quality in the art itself. It is quite enough if you call it bad names.

CHAPTER TWO

Isaac Bashevis Singer

A STORYTELLER

Isaac Bashevis Singer is a storyteller, novelist, lecturer, and short-story writer. He was awarded the Nobel Prize in Literature in 1978 and has won two National Book Awards. The son and grandson of rabbis, Singer emigrated from Poland to the United States in 1935. Since then he has made his home in New York City, although recently he has spent the winter months in Miami Beach, Florida.

After an orthodox Jewish education, Singer began writing in Hebrew, but later switched to Yiddish. Saul Bellow's translation of Singer's short story, "Gimpel the Fool," brought Isaac Bashevis Singer to the attention of the English-speaking world. His stories, which unfold with the richness and narrative ease of parables or fables, are filled with wicked imps, demons, and other supernatural beings that tempt and torment man. His poignantly simple tales reveal complicated truths, and Singer's own personality is like his tales. His recent biographer, Paul Kresh, calls Singer an "ascetic sensualist, innocent sophisticate, friendly loner, a boyish old man."

Singer has written thirteen children's books and numerous books for adults, including *Satan in Goray, Gimpel the Fool, The Magician of Lublin, The Spinoza of Market Street, The Family Moscat, A Friend of Kafka, A Love Story, A Crown of Feathers, Collected Stories, The Penitent, The Image, Exile and Love*, and *The Death of Methuselah and Other Stories*. *In My Father's Court* is an autobiographical account of his childhood in Warsaw.

Images and Stories

This story, "The Missing Line," takes place in Warsaw.

Toward evening, the large hall of the Yiddish Writers' Club in Warsaw became almost empty. At a table in a corner, two unemployed proofreaders played chess. They seemed to play and doze simultaneously. Mina, the cat, had forgotten that she's a literary cat written up in the newspapers and went out to the yard to hunt for a mouse or perhaps a bird. I was sitting at a table with the most important member of the club—Joshua Gottlieb—the main feuilletonist of the *Haint*. He was the president of the Journalist Syndicate, a doctor of philosophy, a former student of such famous scholars as Herman Cohen, Professor Bauch, Professor Messer, Kuno Fischer. Dr. Gottlieb was tall, broad shouldered, with a straight red neck and a pot belly. The setting sun threw a purple shine on his huge bald head. He smoked a long cigar and blew the smoke out through his nostrils. He would not have invited a beginner like myself to his table, but there was no one else available at this hour and he liked to talk and tell stories. Our conversation turned to the supernatural and Dr. Gottlieb was saying:

"You young men are in a rush to explain everything according to your theories. For you, it is theory first and facts last. If the facts don't match the theories, it is the fault of the facts. But a man of my age knows that the events have a logic of their own and that above all they are the product of causality. Your mystics feel insulted if things happen in what we call a natural way. But to me the greatest and most wonderful miracle is what Spinoza called the order of things. When I lose my glasses and I find them in a drawer—which I'm sure I haven't opened in two years—I know that I put them there myself, not that they were hidden by your demons or imps. The eyeglasses would have stayed there forever, no matter how many incantations I would have recited to retrieve them. As you know, I am a great admirer of Kant, but to me causality is more than a category of pure reason. It is the very essence of creation. You may even call it the thing in itself."

"Who made causality?" I asked, just to say something.

"No one, and therein is its beauty. Let me tell you—about two years ago something happened to me that had all the earmarks of one of your miracles. I was absolutely convinced that no explanation was possible. Rationalist as I am, I said to myself, if this actually happened and it was not a dream, I will

27

have to reappraise everything I learned from first-class gymnasium to the universities of Bonn and Bern. But then came the explanation, and it was as convincing and as simple as the truth can only be. As a matter of fact, I thought I would write a story about it myself. However, I don't want to compete with our literati. I guess you know that I don't have too high an opinion of fiction. It may sound like a sacrilege to you, but I find more human fallacies, more psychology, and even more entertainment in the daily press than in all your literary magazines. Does my cigar bother you?"

"Not at all."

"You certainly know, I don't need to tell you, that our typesetters in the *Haint* and in the Yiddish press generally make more errors than all the other typesetters in the whole world. Although they consider themselves ardent Yiddishists, they don't have the slightest respect for their language. I don't sleep nights because of these barbarians. Who said it — that 99 percent of all writers don't die from cancer or from consumption but from misprints. Every week I read three proofs of my Friday feuilleton, but when they correct one mistake they immediately make another one, and sometimes two, three, or four.

"About two years ago I happened to write an article about Kant. It was a *jubilieum* of some sort. When it comes to philosophic terms, our typesetters are especially vicious. Besides, the one who does the layout has a tradition of losing at least one line from my feuilleton every week and I always find it in another article, sometimes even in the news. That day I quoted an expression that was a perfect target for misprints: *the transcendental unity of the apperception.* While I wrote it, I knew that our typesetters would make mincemeat out of it, but I could not avoid it. I read the proofs three times as usual, and miraculously the words came out correct the third time. I even uttered a little prayer just in case. . . . That Thursday night, I went to sleep as hopeful as a writer in Yiddish can afford to be.

"The papers are brought to me about eight o'clock in the morning, and Friday is always my crisis day of the week. In the beginning, everything seemed quite smooth and I hoped against hope that this time I would be saved. But no, the line that began with the words, *the transcendental unity of.* . . had been lost. The whole article became senseless.

"Of course I was angry, bitter. I cursed all the Yiddish typesetters with the vilest oaths. After some half an hour of utter resentment and extreme anti-Yiddishism, I began to look for the line in all the other articles and news items of our Friday issue. But this time, it seemed it had been lost altogether. Even this was somehow a disappointment to me. What burns me up more than anything else is that people in the street, even my friends in the Writers' Club, compliment me, and they never seem to miss the missing line. I have promised myself a million times not to read the *Haint* on Friday, but you know, there is an element of masochism in each of us. In my imagination, I took revenge on the typesetters, the editors, the proofreaders — shooting them, hanging them, or making them memorize all my feuilletons from the year 1910 until today.

28

"After a while, I decided that I had suffered enough and I began to read the *Moment,* our rival newspaper, especially to see what their feuilletonist, Mr. Helfman, had written for that Friday. Of course, I knew beforehand that his piece could not be anything but bad. In all the twenty years we competed, I have never read anything good by this scribbler. I don't know how you feel about him, but to me he is sheer abomination.

"That Friday, his concoction seemed worse than ever — as it does every week — so I gave up in the middle and began to read the news. I was reading a news item with the title, 'A Man, A Beast,' the story of a janitor who came home at night from the tavern and raped his daughter. Suddenly, I saw the most impossible, the most unbelievable, the most preposterous thing that could ever happen — my missing line was right there! I knew that it could be nothing but a hallucination. However, hallucinations seldom last longer than a second or a split second. Here the words lingered before my eyes: *the transcendental unity of.* . . . I closed my eyes, sure that when I opened them again the mirage would have vanished, but I opened them and there it still was — the unthinkable, the ridiculous, the absurd.

"I must admit to you that while disbelieving in what you call the supernatural, I somehow toyed with the idea that one day a phenomenon might emerge in my life that would force me to lose faith in logic and reality. But that a metal line would fly from the *Haint* composing room on Chlodna Street No. 8 to the *Moment* composing room on Nelewski 38 — this I certainly did not expect. My son came into the room, and I must have looked as if I had seen a ghost because he said to me, 'Papa, what's the matter?' I don't know why, but I said to him, 'Please, go down and buy me a copy of the *Moment.'*

" 'But you are reading the *Moment* right now,' my boy said.

"And I answered that I must see another copy. The boy looked at me as if to say, the old man is 'meshuga' altogether. Still, he went down and brought me another copy. Sure enough, my line was there on the same page in the same news item: 'He came home from the tavern and saw his daughter in bed and the transcendental unity of the apperception. . . .' I was so baffled and distressed that I began to laugh.

"To be completely on the safe side, I asked my boy to read the whole item out loud. He again gave me that look that meant 'my father is not all there,' and he read the item to me. When he came to the transposed line, he smiled and asked, 'Is this why you asked me to buy another copy?' I didn't answer him, but I knew that no hallucination has ever been shared by two people and certainly not for such a long time. Unless my boy too became part of my hallucination.

" 'There are cases of collective hallucinations,' I said.

"Anyhow, that Friday and Saturday I couldn't sleep, and I could barely eat. I decided to go Sunday morning and speak to our manager of the printing department, my old friend, Mr. Gavza. If there is a man who cannot be fooled by abracadabra and hocus-pocus, it is he. I wanted to see the expression on his face when he saw what I saw.

"On the way to the *Haint* I decided it would be a good thing if I could find the manuscript of my feuilleton, assuming it wasn't thrown out. I asked if the copy of my article was still there, and lo and behold, they found it, and the words were there as I remembered them. I was eager to find a solution to the riddle, but I didn't want the solution to be based on some silly blunder, ludicrous misunderstanding, or lapse of memory.

"With my manuscript in one hand and the Friday *Moment* in the other hand, I went to Mr. Gavza, and he, too, gave me a strange look because I never go there on Sunday. I showed him my manuscript and said, 'Please, read this paragraph.' Before I even finished my sentence he said, 'I know, I know, a line was missing in your feuilleton about Kant. I guess you want to publish a correction. Believe me, no one ever reads them.'

" 'No, I don't want to publish any corrections,' I said.

" 'What else brings you here on Sunday morning?' Gavza asked.

"I showed the Friday *Moment* with the item, 'A Man, A Beast,' and said, 'Now read this.' Gavza shrugged, began to read, and never before have I seen an expression like that on Gavza's quiet face. He gaped at the news item, at my manuscript, at me, again at the paper, again at me, and said, 'Am I seeing things? This is your missing line.'

" 'Yes, my friend,' I said. 'My missing line has jumped from the *Haint* to the *Moment* a dozen streets away, over all the buildings, all the rooftops, and settled down right into their printing room, right into this item. Or possibly the demons did the job. If you can explain this, then. . .'

" 'Really, I cannot believe it,' Gavza said. 'This must be some trick, some kind of practical joke. Maybe someone glued in the line. Let me see it again.'

" 'No trick and no glue,' I said. 'This line fell out from my article and appeared in the *Moment* last Friday. I have another copy of the *Moment* in my pocket.'

" 'My God, how did this happen?' Gavza asked. Again and again he compared my manuscript with the line in the *Moment*. Then I heard him say, 'If this can happen, anything can happen. Maybe the demons really did steal your line from the *Haint* and carry it to the *Moment*.'

" 'This is the only possible explanation,' I said.

"For a long while, we both stood there looking at each other with the painful feeling of two adult men who realize that their world has turned to chaos, all logic gone, and what is called *reality* totally bankrupt. Then Gavza burst out laughing.

" 'No, it wasn't the demons, not even the angels. I know what happened,' he exclaimed.

" 'If you know, say it quickly before I burst,' I said.

"And here is how he explained it to me: The Jewish National Fund often publishes an appeal both in the *Haint* and in the *Moment*. Sometimes they make changes to adjust the appeal for the readers of the respective news-papers. Then they don't make a matrix but the whole metal page is carried over by car from one newspaper to the other for adjustments. By error, my line must have been put into the metal page of the appeal. It was carried over to the *Moment* and there someone noticed the mistake, took out the line from the appeal page and it promptly got stuck into this news item.

" 'The chances that such a thing should happen are not as small as one may think considering our sort of typesetters and proofreaders,' Gavza said. 'They are the worst bunglers. No, let's not put the fault on the poor demons. No demon is as ignorant and as careless as our printers and the printers' devils.'

"We had a great laugh, and in honor of that historical solution, we went and had coffee and cake. We spoke about old times and the countless absurdi-ties published in the Yiddish press, God bless it. Especially strange were the misprints listed in the back of Yiddish books, such as: 'On page 69 it is printed, "She went to see her mother in Bialystok"—it should be written, "He had a long gray beard.' " Or, 'On page 87, it is written, "He had a very strong appetite"—it should have said, "He went to see his former wife in Vilna.' " 'On page 379, "They took the train to Lublin"—it should have been written, "The chicken was not kosher.' " How a typesetter can make mistakes of this kind will always be a riddle to me. Another article was written about

the TEMPERATURE OF THE SUN . . . (THE HEAT IS $\frac{\text{FAHRENHEIT}}{\text{UNBEARABLE}}$)

Or an article written about the bacteria which are so small they can only be seen with the help of a telescope."

Dr. Gottlieb paused, trying to revive his extinguished cigar, sucking at it violently. Then he said: "My young man, I tell you all this just to prove to you that one should not be in a rush to decide that Mother Nature has given up its eternal laws and that the goblins and sprites have taken over. As far as I'm concerned, the laws of nature are still valid whether I like them or not. And when I have to convey a message to my old wife, or to my not-much-younger girlfriend, I still use the telephone, not telepathy."

The Day I Got Lost:
From the Autobiography of
Professor Shlemiel

It is easy to recognize me. See a man in the street wearing a too long coat, too large shoes, a crumpled hat with a wide brim, spectacles with one lens missing, and carrying an umbrella although the sun is shining, and that man will be me, Professor Shlemiel. There are other unmistakable clues to my identity. My pockets are always bulging with newspapers, magazines, and just papers. I

31

carry an overstuffed briefcase, and I'm forever making mistakes. I've been living in New York City for more than forty years, yet whenever I want to go uptown, I find myself walking downtown, and when I want to go east, I go west. I'm always late, and I never recognize anybody.

I'm always misplacing things. A hundred times a day, I ask myself: Where is my pen? Where is my money? Where is my handkerchief? Where is my address book? I am what is known as an absent-minded professor.

For many years, I have been teaching philosophy in the same university, and I still have difficulty locating my classrooms. Elevators play strange tricks on me. I want to go to the top floor and I land in the basement. Hardly a day passes when an elevator door doesn't close on me. Elevator doors are my worst enemies.

In addition to my constant blundering and losing things, I'm forgetful. I enter a coffee shop, hang up my coat, and leave without it. By the time I remember to go back for it, I've forgotten where I've been. I lose hats, books, umbrellas, galoshes and above all manuscripts. Sometimes I even forget my own address. One evening I took a taxi because I was in a hurry to get home. The taxi driver said, "Where to?" And I could not remember where I lived.

"Home," I said.

"Where is home?" he asked in astonishment.

"I don't remember," I replied.

"What is your name?"

"Professor Shlemiel."

"Professor," the driver said, "I'll get you to a telephone booth. Look in the telephone book and you'll find your address."

He drove me to the nearest drugstore with a telephone booth in it, but he refused to wait. I was about to enter the store, when I realized I had left my briefcase behind. I ran after the taxi, shouting, "My briefcase, my briefcase." But the taxi was already out of earshot.

In the drugstore, I found a telephone book, but when I looked under S, I saw to my horror that although there were a number of Shlemiels listed, I was not among them. At that moment I recalled that several months before, Mrs. Shlemiel had decided that we should have an unlisted telephone number. The reason was that my students thought nothing of calling me in the middle of the night and waking me up. It also happened quite frequently that someone wanted to call another Shlemiel and got me by mistake. That was all very well, but how was I going to get home?

I usually had some letters addressed to me in my breast pocket. But just that day, I had decided to clean out my pockets. It was my birthday and my wife had invited friends in for the evening. She had baked a huge cake and decorated it with birthday candles. I could see my friends sitting in our living room, waiting to wish me a happy birthday. And here I stood in some drugstore, for the life of me not able to remember where I lived.

Then I recalled the telephone number of a friend of mine, Dr.

Motherhead, and I decided to call him for help. I dialed and a young girl's voice answered.

"Is Dr. Motherhead at home?"

"No," she replied.

"Is his wife at home?"

"They're both out," the girl said.

"Perhaps you can tell me where they can be reached?" I asked.

"I'm only the baby-sitter, but I think they went to a party at Professor Shlemiel's. Would you like to leave a message?" she said. "Who shall I say called, please?"

"Professor Shlemiel," I said.

"They left for your house about an hour ago," the girl said.

"Can you tell me where they went?" I asked.

"I've just told you," she said. "They went to your house."

"But where do I live?"

"You must be kidding!" the girl said and hung up.

I tried to call a number of friends (those whose telephone numbers I happened to think of), but wherever I called, I got the same reply: "They've gone to a party at Professor Shlemiel's."

As I stood in the street wondering what to do, it began to rain.

"Where's my umbrella?" I said to myself. And I knew the answer at once. I'd left it — somewhere. I got under a nearby canopy. It was now raining cats and dogs. It lightninged and thundered. All day it had been sunny and warm, but now that I was lost and my umbrella was lost, it had to storm. And it looked as if it would go on for the rest of the night.

To distract myself, I began to ponder the ancient philosophical problem. A mother chicken lays an egg, I thought to myself, and when it hatches, there is a chicken. That's how it has always been. Every chicken comes from an egg and every egg comes from a chicken. But was there a chicken first? Or an egg first? No philosopher has ever been able to solve this eternal question. Just the same, there must be an answer. Perhaps I, Schlemiel, am destined to stumble on it.

It continued to pour buckets. My feet were getting wet and I was chilled. I began to sneeze and I wanted to wipe my nose, but my handkerchief, too, was gone.

At that moment, I saw a big black dog. He was standing in the rain getting soaked and looking at me with sad eyes. I knew immediately what the trouble was. The dog was lost. He, too, had forgotten his address. I felt a great love for that innocent animal. I called to him and he came running to me. I talked to him as if he was human.

"Fellow, we're in the same boat," I said. "I'm a man Shlemiel and you're a dog Shlemiel. Perhaps it's also your birthday, and there's a party for you, too. And here you stand shivering and forsaken in the rain, while your loving

33

master is searching for you everywhere. You're probably just as hungry as I am."

I patted the dog on his wet head, and he wagged his tail.

"Whatever happens to me will happen to you," I said. "I'll keep you with me until we both find our homes. If we don't find your master, you'll stay with me. Give me your paw," I said. The dog lifted his right paw. There was no question that he understood.

A taxi drove by and splattered us both. Suddenly it stopped and I heard someone shouting, "Shlemiel! Shlemiel!" I looked up and saw the taxi door open, and the head of a friend of mine appeared.

"Shlemiel," he called. "What are you doing here? Who are you waiting for?"

"Where are you going?" I asked.

"To your house, of course. I'm sorry I'm late, but I was detained. Anyhow, better late than never. But why aren't you at home? And whose dog is that?"

"Only God could have sent you!" I exclaimed. "What a night! I've forgotten my address. I've left my briefcase in a taxi, I've lost my umbrella, and I don't know where my galoshes are."

"Shlemiel," my friend said, "if there was ever an absent-minded professor, you're it."

When I rang the bell of my apartment, my wife opened the door.

"Shlemiel!" she shrieked. "Everybody is waiting for you. Where have you been? Where is your briefcase? Your umbrella? Your galoshes? And who is this dog?"

Our friends surrounded me.

"Where have you been?" they cried. "We were so worried. We thought surely something had happened to you!"

"Who is this dog?" my wife kept repeating.

"I don't know," I said finally, "I found him in the street. Let's just call him 'Bow Wow' for the time being."

"Bow Wow, indeed!" my wife scolded. "You know our cat hates dogs. And what about the parakeets. He'll scare them to death."

"He's a quiet dog," I said. "He'll make friends with the cat. I'm sure he loves parakeets. I could not leave him shivering in the rain. He's a good soul."

The moment I said this, the dog let out a bloodcurdling howl. The cat ran into the room. When she saw the dog, she arched her back and spat at him, ready to scratch out his eyes. The parakeets in their cage began flapping their wings and screeching. Everybody started talking at once. There was pandemonium.

Would you like to know how it all ended?

Bow Wow still lives with us. He and the cat are great friends. The parakeets have learned to ride on his back as if he were a horse. As for my wife, she loves Bow Wow even more than I do. Whenever I take the dog out, she says, "Now don't forget your address, both of you."

I never did find my briefcase, nor my umbrella, nor my galoshes. Like many philosophers before me, I've given up trying to solve the riddle of which came first, the chicken or the egg. Instead I've started writing a book called *The Memoirs of Shlemiel*. If I don't forget the manuscript in a taxi, or a restaurant, or on a bench in the park, you may read them someday. In the meantime, here is a sample chapter.

Discussion

WILMER: I wondered what you thought when you wrote, "Death is the messiah"?

SINGER: I didn't say so myself. I made my hero of the story say it. I ended "The Family Moscat" with the words that a man who is about to fall in the hands of Hitler says to comfort himself: "The truth is that death is the messiah." Since this man, not I, says that, I don't really have to defend his opinion. All I can say is that if I would be, God forbid, in his situation, I would have the same kinds of feelings. Those were the feelings of the people of the Holocaust when they knew that they were finished because they had fallen into the hands of an enemy who has no heart, no soul, no ethics, nothing but one great desire to destroy people, innocent people, often women and children.

PARTICIPANT: Mr. Singer, I am interested in how much you researched. Your stories are so filled with such a vast array of knowledge.

SINGER: Thank you, you are very kind to say so. I would say in some cases I don't need to research because if I describe my Uncle George or my mother or my sister, I don't need any research. I knew them quite well. I knew their lives. But when I wrote about other aspects of Jewish history, I did a lot of research. The people I lived among often spoke about olden times and told old stories. The fact that a story happened five hundred years ago does not make the story less effective. So by doing a little research and by living amongst people who are interested in the same epoch, I somehow got some research done — call it research or any other name.

PARTICIPANT: How many hours a day do you write?

SINGER: I would say not more than three hours. In other words, I am not one of those people who sits down and writes from the morning to the night. I couldn't do it. I know that there are writers who do this. I don't.

WILMER: I know why he only writes for three hours. He said that ever since he got the Nobel Prize, he only writes between telephone calls. Mr. Singer and I were talking this afternoon and he was talking about retiring. He says nobody in the Old Testament ever retired. Moses never retired. As we were sitting there, I said, "We have about an hour before we go down to your lecture." And he said, "Thank God for every hour."

It's a great tribute to you to have that spirit, and a great privilege for us to have you read these lovely, moving stories to us. I think of you when I think of Tennyson's "Ulysses":

I am a part of all that I have met;
Yet all experience is an arch wherethro'
Gleams that untravell'd world, whose margin fades
Forever and forever when I move.
How dull it is to pause, to make an end,
To rust unburnished, not to shine in use!

Though much is taken, much abides, and though
We are not now that strength which in old days
Moved earth and heaven, that which we are, we are;
One equal temper of heroic hearts,
Made weak by time and fate, but strong in will
To strive, to seek, to find, and not to yield.

To a man who shines and finds and seeks and doesn't yield, we offer our gratitude.

CHAPTER THREE

Naomi Shihab Nye

A POET

Naomi Shihab Nye was born in St. Louis of an American mother and a Palestinian father. Her work as a poet, songwriter, and singer has been influenced by the three cultures that form her background: the Middle Eastern world of her father, the Anglo/American world of her mother, and the Hispanic/Indian world that she was drawn into while growing up in Texas. She graduated *summa cum laude* from Trinity University, San Antonio, where she majored in English and world religion.

Naomi Nye has been a writer-in-residence in many schools in Texas as well as in Maine, Vermont, Berkeley, and Chiapas, Mexico. She has made two tours to the Middle East and Asia for the United States Information Agency.

Naomi claims that she enjoyed childhood so much she has never given it up, and she wrote her first poem at age six when she was astonished by the size of Chicago's skyscrapers. Her first book of poetry, *Different Ways to Pray* (1980), won the Voertman Prize for poetry from the Texas Institute of Letters. Her second book of poetry, *Hugging the Jukebox* (1982), also won the Voertman prize; in addition, the American Library Association named it to its notable books list and it was selected to be part of the national poetry series. Her poems appear in many anthologies and textbooks. Her third book of poetry, *Yellow Glove*, was published in 1987.

Her fiction has appeared in *Georgia Review, Stories, Virginia Quarterly Review*, and *Prairie Schooner*. She has produced two albums, *Lullaby Raft* and *Rutbaga-Roo*. Her song, "Just Like a Recurring Dream," was the title song for the Meisburg and Walters album (Casablanca label).

The *San Francisco Chronicle* said, "It is hard to conceive of a young poet with more ability and potential than Naomi Nye."

Discovering Ourselves Through Words: Pajamas in the Wind

At age three, I lay on the grass in our backyard under a clothesline strung with my father's windblown pajamas. The legs and sleeves puffed and rose as I nearly hypnotized myself by repeating the word *pajamas* over and over again, a litany of languid syllables on the tongue. Tasting the word, rolling it around, feeling the strangeness of meaning attached to sound, I consciously discovered the pleasure available to us through the odd and miraculous names we have given to things.

When my mother found me sprawled in my reverie, it was hard to describe what had happened. Later I would wonder, "What did lying on the ground under a clothesline have to do with the power of words?" Such exhilaration didn't happen often enough. As I grew, I would learn how words may become magical for us in many ways, repetition being only one of them.

Three years later, my parents took us to Chicago for the first time. We rode the train from St. Louis, where we lived, and I swirled headlong into the panorama of a vast city, unknown streets and buildings, swarms of mysterious faces on every corner. That night in the hotel room I felt humbled to think that all this Chicago had been happening before I ever heard about it, in a world filled with cities, each one equally real, bustling, and unknown to me. Explosive with discovery, I sat before a large piece of construction paper, the kind on which I still favor writing. (How early children cramp their generous hands onto stiff-lined tablets!) I wrote just four lines, suggesting my awe; a wave of joy washed over me as I did this. Having just learned to write, to shape the fat letters somehow tactile as zoo animals, it seemed particularly wonderful to me that words could do whatever we wanted them to on the page. You could take familiar words and connect them in new ways to make your own story. I think I began discovering just then what writers have felt down through the ages — that sense of possibility coupled with responsibility — now that we have this tool in our hands, what are we going to do with it?

Later, back at school, I asked if I could post my poem in the hallway. Students often displayed photos from birthday parties or gargantuan autumn leaves. Weeks later, a student I didn't know — probably a third grader since she was huge — caught up to me to ask, "Did you make that poem in the hall?" Startled, I said, "Yes!" She said, "Well, I know what you mean," and skipped off. To me that was the most amazing moment of contact, that someone, whose name I didn't know, could know what I *meant*. The world had suddenly grown larger again. I began sending poems out to children's magazines shortly thereafter.

Years later, I was asked to write a poem about the first poem I'd ever written and did so, in nearly as primitive a style.

The First Poem I Ever Wrote

I was not divinely inspired, I was excited,
at six many things were new, fresh, they still are,
then they were even newer, to me.
I'm speaking for myself.

At six
speaking for myself
was new.

I lived in St. Louis,
banks of the Mississippi,
Gateway to the West,
it was my place,
the only place,
even though my father was an Arab
I thought the whole world lived in Missouri,
I thought everybody knew everybody,
I was absolutely positive
everybody knew me.

We took a trip to Chicago, on a train,
my father had business in Chicago,
I had business in Chicago,
I had a poem waiting for me,
it would be there when I got off the train,
watching for me, shyly,
behind the tracks of the Elevated Railway,
inside the starred dome of the planetarium,
at the corner where the streets went up to make channels for the boats.
It would disguise itself as the faces passing,
the odd faces, the twisted faces,
the sad hopeful faces I had never seen before
though they were part of me, all of them.
I was a city, a big city,
a city I would explore forever,
and that was the poem.[1]

For me, starting early and casually like that, publication was never a proof of worth but was simply a trading place for ideas, where people shared whatever had arrived in their minds. I liked to read, savoring sentences. I would close a book, nodding. I believed in that one person in the whole wide world who would do that for any one of my poems, and that was enough.

In second grade, I had a magnificent elderly teacher who believed firmly that poetry was at the center of the universe, and she had us memorizing, reciting, and writing every day. That was all I needed to shoot me full speed ahead into the world of words. She was the one teacher I had in my entire academic career who was openly passionate about writing. She sent her students off believing they could all be authors, if they chose. Many years later, when I had published books and she was in her nineties, I was able to thank her. Her reply?

"I'd just like to ask you a lot of questions."

From the beginning, writing was a way of discovering my own memory, sifting through stores of images inside to find out what was there. With so much around us continually blurring, other idiosyncratically selected memories, lines, and people seem to remain vivid forever. I heard a Texas writer say once that everything important we ever write about occurs to us somehow in seed form before we are seven. I don't know if this is true, but it certainly

---

[1]David Kherdian, ed., *Sing the Song of Myself: An Anthology of Autobiographical Poems* (New York: Greenwillow Books, 1978).

41

seems we are always returning to that home ground from which we first viewed the world, trying to figure things out.

As a child, the memory from which I wrote loomed very recent, whereas adults naturally travel further back, endlessly reexamining, rediscovering, and linking up with the present in unexpected ways. I remember feeling wistful, homesick at ages two and three, for something I could never name. Later when I read Carl Jung, he mentioned that quality of eternity present in childhood, and I wondered if my homesickness leaned toward that eternity. I could write about things, always, that it would have been much harder to speak about aloud, or to say to that elusive appropriate listener. A child can't say, "Excuse me, I'm homesick all the time," and expect to be embraced by the people *at home*. But I could write it. I could speak to the always-listening air and feel it there.

And writing did more — it helped me linger, pay attention. The writer-monk Father William McNamara describes contemplation as "long loving looks at things" and I think writing, for many people, is the vehicle toward such perception. In this world, which swoops into the future faster than we might like it to, writing seems to be one way to steady the ground. You can begin something now and come back to it. The past may become absolutely present again. We are constantly discovering landmarks in our lives that may be much more steadfast than the days.

For years, I felt uncomfortable by the title, "creative writer," which seemed, in itself, redundant. I understand that "creative writer" may be used to distinguish more literary individuals from journalists, but the banner word "creative" was never one I wanted to wave as my flag. Weren't we all potentially, if not actively, creative in one way or another?

In a college communications course taught at Trinity University, Professor Dave Burkett introduced students to the "creative process" as he defined it, although we hoped it was something we had been living all along, in varying degrees. He described the five stages of the creative process:

1) Acquisition — taking things in, acquiring information, experience, images

2) Association — putting things together, making personal connections

3) Expression — even the way a person walked down a hall was expressive of something!

4) Evaluation

5) Perseverance

Once I saw this neat, cyclical process spelled out, the whole concept of "creativity" seemed somehow easier to understand. We may imagine creative people to be those who are all the time producing — making things and sending them out into the world — but the creative person actually is one who is taking *in* as much as possible—a continuously receptive gesture. The creative person associates ideas and experiences in ways that may be foreign to the patterns of one's own family or peers. I liked particularly how the evaluation step was separated from the expression step. Later I would read that American poet William Carlos Williams had described himself as really being two poets—the one he was when he wrote, and the more critical one who returned to his writing later and decided what to change and what to keep. Suddenly it seemed simple and matter-of-fact to think of oneself as a "creative person," concentrating not on output but on ways to enlarge the realm of taking in and putting together.

Much of contemporary poetry roots itself in unabashedly personal material. People who say they don't like or understand poetry often may be remembering the lofty verses studied in school. Contemporary poetry has taken on a much more immediate and colloquial tone. I have visited with writers in Asia and the Middle East who occasionally feel that writers are obliged somehow to "speak for the masses," if such a thing be possible, rather than to tell what happened in their own lives yesterday. We have debated this at length, and I continue to feel the best writing of any tradition accepts and illuminates the personal story. "Speaking for the masses" teeters into rhetoric too easily.

Perhaps the greatest gift here is that the most personal elements of our lives end up being the most universal. If someone writes a successful poem about a brother or sister, you are momentarily introduced to that person but you are also introduced to your own brothers and sisters over again. How wonderful and mysterious that one writer telling his or her own stories can suddenly make a whole group of people feel rich again, filled with their own telling! One wealth triggers another. New York writer David Ignatow has said in an interview, "now I realize the social condition is as strongly in me as it is outside of me. So, when I deal with the social condition today, I think of it in terms of myself, knowing what I reflect, how I've been conditioned, that all of history is in me, especially all of the history of the last fifty years. And when I write, I write of me."[2] William Carlos Williams said, "To be universal you must first be local."

Often a memory that is deeply potent and enduring for one person may have been utterly forgettable for the other people involved. My mother claims no memory of the odd line she offered as solace in the scene that became "Making a Fist."

---

[2]Ralph J. Mills, Jr., ed., *Open Between Us*, Poets on Poetry Series (Ann Arbor, Mich.: The University of Michigan Press, 1980).

43

Naomi Shihab Nye

MAKING A FIST

"We forget that we are all dead men conversing with dead men."

Jorge Luis Borges

For the first time, on the road north of Tampico,
I felt the life sliding out of me,
a drum in the desert, harder and harder to hear.
I was seven, I lay in the car
watching the palm trees swirl a sickening pattern past the glass.
My stomach was a melon split wide inside my skin.

"How do you know if you are going to die?"
I begged my mother.
We had been traveling for days.
With strange confidence she answered,
"When you can no longer make a fist."

Years later I smile to think of that journey,
the borders we must cross separately,
stamped with our unanswerable woes.
I who did not die, who am still living,
still lying in the backseat behind all my questions,
clenching and opening one small hand.

Ignatow talks about keeping "the door open" between ourselves and others, between our unconscious and conscious memories. If the door stands open, we may often be surprised by what steps through. The memory of "Yellow Glove" flooded back upon me one day when I really needed it and had not thought of it in years.

YELLOW GLOVE

What can a yellow glove mean in a world of motorcars and governments?

I was small, like everyone. Life was a string of precautions: Don't kiss the squirrel before you bury him, don't suck candy, pop balloons, drop watermelons, watch TV. When the new gloves appeared one Christmas, tucked in soft tissue, I heard it trailing me: Don't lose the yellow gloves.

I was small, there was too much to remember. One day, waving at a stream — the ice had cracked, winter chipping down, soon we would sail boats and roll into ditches — I let a glove go. Into the stream, sucked under the street. Since when did streets have mouths?
I walked home on a desperate road. Gloves cost money. We didn't have much. I would tell no one. I would wear the yellow glove that was left and keep the other hand in a pocket. I knew my mother's eyes had tears they had not cried yet and I didn't want to be the one to make them flow. It was the prayer I spoke secretly, folding socks, lining up donkeys in windowsills. I would be good, a promise made to the roaches who scouted my closet at night. If you don't get in my bed, I will be good. And they listened. I had a lot to fulfill.

The months rolled down like towels out of a machine. I sang and drew and fattened the cat. Don't scream, don't lie, don't cheat, don't fight — you could hear it anywhere. A pebble could show you how to be smooth, tell the truth. A field could show how to sleep without walls. A stream could remember how to drift and change — the next June I was stirring the stream like a soup, telling my brother dinner would be ready if he'd only hurry up with the bread, when I saw it. The yellow glove draped on a twig. A muddy survivor. A quiet flag.

Where had it been in the three gone months? I could wash it, fold it in my winter drawer with its sister, no one in that world would ever know. There were miracles on Harvey Street. Children walked home in yellow light. Trees were reborn and gloves traveled far, but returned. A thousand miles later, what can a yellow glove mean in a world of bankbooks and stereos?

Part of the difference between floating and going down.

SURE

Today you rain on me from every corner of the sky.
Softly vanishing hair, a tiny tea set from Mexico
perched on a shelf with the life-size cups.

I remember knotting my braid on your bed,
ten months into your silence.
Someone said you were unreachable,
we could chatter and you wouldn't know.
You raised yourself on magnificent dying elbows
to speak one line,
"Don't — be — so — sure."
The room was stunned.
Lying back on your pillow, you smiled at me.
No one else saw it.
Later they even denied they heard.

All your life, never mind.
It hurts, but never mind.
You fed me corn from cans, stirring busily.
I lined up the salt shakers on your table.
We were proud of each other for nothing.
You, because I finished my meal.
Me, because you wore a flowered dress.
Life was a tablet of small reasons.
"That's that," you'd say, pushing back your chair.
"And now let's go see if the bakery has a cake."

Today, as I knelt to spell a word for a little boy,
it was your old floor under me,
cool sections of black and white tile,
I'd lie on my belly tracing their sides.
St. Louis, movies sold popcorn,
baby lions born in zoos,
the newspapers would never find us.

One moth lighting on the sink
in a dark apartment years ago.
You point, should I catch it?
Oh, never mind.
A million motions later, I open my hand,
and it is there.

46

Through the continual application of words to the page, we may also discover our own symbols — the points of gravity in the tangible world to which we keep returning for clarification. The first time I ever kept a dream journal, I wrote quickly, wildly each morning, never rereading preceding days, until we were asked to go back and note recurrent symbols. Was a curtain always blowing in one window? Did we lift a ringing phone repeatedly to find no one on it? I remember how intrigued we all were to discover peculiar recurrences that we had not expected and the private meanings these began to take on for us. Writing poems or stories over a period of time, one senses the same power at work, the same radiant elements surfacing.

I've also been intrigued by the gift that creative interpretation brings to our understanding of one another's work. Once after a reading, a man thanked me for my many considerations of water. Water had figured importantly in his life, too. My first impulse exclaimed, "What? There's no water in my poems!" I realized quickly enough, however, that the water was his own image, which had somehow been triggered by something I had read. To contradict its presence would only have been diminishing. We must be creative readers as well as creative writers.

I had not realized the importance of vegetables as images to me until a woman in Abu Dhabi asked me rather ferociously why I was so fond of the marketplace — couldn't I raise my thoughts to a higher level? I fumbled with a reply, acknowledging, "Well, I do love to cook, and don't fruits and vegetables echo human beings in diversity and growth? We live with them; we think we understand them; maybe we each turn to what's near for comfort." She stalked off, unimpressed, but I had learned something.

THE WORLD IN TRANSLATION

It was a long climb out of the soil. She counted off whole continents
as she lifted each foot,
imagined her dark years falling away like husks.
Soon she could feel objects come to life
in her hand, the peel of banana,
a lightly waxed pepper,
she accepted these into her home,
placed them in bowls where they could be watched.
There was nothing obscure about melons,
nothing involved about yams.
If she were to have anything to do with the world,
these would be her translators,
through these she would learn secrets of dying,
how to do it gracefully as the peach,
softening in silence,
or the mango, finely tuned to its own skin.

47

THE GARDEN OF ABU MAHMOUD

West Bank

He had lived in Spain
so we stood under a glossy loquat tree
telling of madres y milagros
with clumsy tongues.
It seemed strange in the mouth
of this Arab, but no more so
than everything.
Across his valley the military
settlement gleamed white.
He said, That's where the guns live,
as simply as saying, it needs sun,
a plant needs sun.
He stooped to unsheathe an eggplant
from its nest of leaves,
purple shining globe,
and pressed it on me.
I said No, no, I don't want
to take things before they are ripe,
but it was started already,
handfuls of marble-sized peaches,
hard green mish-mish and delicate lilt
of beans. Each pocket swelled
while he breathed mint leaves,
bit the jagged edge.
He said every morning found him here,
before the water boiled on the flame
he came out to this garden,
dug hands into earth saying, I know you
and earth crumbled rich layers
and this result of their knowing—
a hillside in which no inch went unsung.
His enormous onions held light
and the trees so weighted with fruits
he tied the branches up.
And he called it querido, corazon,
all the words of any language
connecting to the deep place
of darkness and seed. He called it
ya habibi in Arabic, my darling tomato,
and it called him governor, king,
and some days he wore no shoes.

48

The motion of travel, its constant change and surprise, has been another crucial element in my work and life; travel generates a heightened observation, all the senses leaping awake. The mind and heart gather images so rapidly sometimes only a pen can piece them out. I think travelers reach a point on any trip when eyes get full, and they don't want to hear or see anything new for awhile—they just want to return to the familiar and begin sorting through what has been gathered. Journal-keeping during a trip, collections of snips and bits of papers, and notes, become invaluable friends at this point. Every writer writes not with a sense of conclusion ("where you want a piece to go") but with a sense of continual unfoldment. "I learn by going where I have to go," wrote Theodore Roethke.

What if we could live at home with the same sense of wakefulness and alertness that travelers have? As if even home were just another stop on the road? What would this do to our creative lives? Once, driving west from Fort Worth, I was startled by a road sign, startled into the same slant of consciousness that first caused me to write all those years ago in Chicago. Startled by how near to and far we are, daily, from those things that might answer a few of the yearnings and mysteries that seem to be our birthrights. The highways toward discovery are many; for those who choose writing, or who feel writing has chosen them, so are the comrades. Occasionally, we pass, recognize a flash in the glass that looks like *friend*, and wave.

Naomi Shihab Nye

NECESSITY IS ONLY 8 MILES AWAY

West of Weatherford, Texas,
west of Palo Pinto and Mineral Wells,
west of the red brick highway
and the deserted Baker Hotel
standing watch on its huge emptiness
is a sign: NECESSITY 8.
It points left.
Left is a small road,
bare branches tangled with snow.
I don't turn.
Something in me swerves, shouts
WHAT IS IT? WHAT DO WE NEED?
but I keep on driving,
past the WATCH FOR ICE bridges
and the lonely highway patrolmen
with no one to chase,
past Breckenridge to Albany,
small towns fastened like buttons to the plains.
And on and on, forever, I can see it,
for thousands of miles
we will thread space
with our irregular journeys
stopping now and then
to rest, to wonder
what we always almost find.

Healed

"Mama! Mama! I had a bad dream . . .
But I'm still happy."

Madison Nye, age 2

Some days a wisp of light delivers
everything I need
blink of earliest morning
sharp blade of air
wherever I look breathes in and in
till the silent root shines

even the moon wafer tied to our door
a kite we couldn't pull back

I ask to be found by
corners pockets stones
when a little boy gifted me with seven stones
he counted them soberly into my palm
making sure no one had been lost
I lined them in this windowsill
months later I will tell
how I have tried to be worthy

each day early the hand opens
toward light so much older and cleaner
than anything we might fill it with
slow pulse of trees inhaling shadows of sleep

on my desk the letters wait
for words to equal them
light waves triangles on the ceiling
so bright the baby asks who's here

Naomi Shihab Nye, 1989

CHAPTER FOUR

Lee Marvin

AN ACTOR

Comments by Mrs. (Pamela) Lee Marvin: Lee and Harry Wilmer met more than twenty-five years ago while filming a segment of Harry's life called *People Need People*. Their working relationship quickly turned into a deep and lasting friendship that Lee cherished. His involvement in Harry's endeavors throughout the years was tremendously stimulating and rewarding. It included, among other things, critiquing the prisoners' plays at San Quentin with Harry, the psychiatric film festivals in San Antonio, and the Institute for the Humanities at Salado. We are all here because of Harry's past accomplishments and his guiding force in our lives.

Lee Marvin (1924–1987) was an actor who reached superstardom. After a decade of supporting roles, he became the screen's archetypal villain, but his colorful career also included sensitive, evocative roles. His tour de force acting in the comedy *Cat Ballou* won him an Oscar in 1966, and his gravelly voiced rendition of "Wanderin' Star" in the musical *Paint Your Wagon* became a record hit in Britain.

Marvin, whose ancestors arrived in America in 1633, referred to himself as a Puritan in his attitude toward life. He grew up in New York City, and all of his life he was a rebel — creative, imaginative, and fiercely independent. He was without sham or hypocrisy and could be shockingly candid. He had high standards for himself as an actor and turned down lucrative roles in such movies as *Jaws* and *Earthquake*, calling them "sick films." He also refused to do a beer commercial because he felt he would be "selling out" since he didn't intend to drink that beer.

The public relished Marvin in his tough-guy roles even before the critics began comparing him favorably to Humphrey Bogart and Clint Eastwood. The public made him a star. Marvin's many movies include: *The Big Heat*, *The Wild One*, *A Life in the Balance*, *Dog Days*, *Death Hunt*, *The Delta Force*, *The Professionals*, *The Killers*, *Point Blank*, *Monte Walsh*, *Bad Day at Black Rock*, *The Dirty Dozen*, *Cat Ballou*, and *Paint Your Wagon*.

Deeply interested in the humanities, Marvin was a member of the Board of Trustees of the Institute for the Humanities at Salado from its inception. He addressed the Institute twice. The symposium "Understanding Evil" (October 23–25, 1987) was dedicated to the memory of Lee Marvin.

People Need People:
Greater Consciousness of
Human Values

Before Lee Marvin's commentary and dialogue with Harry Wilmer and the audience, the members of the Institute were shown *People Need People*, a sixty-minute ABC network Alcoa Premiere film. For his starring role in this film, Marvin was nominated for an Emmy. The dramatic documentary film is based on Harry Wilmer's book *Social Psychiatry in Action*, which describes his Navy experiences during the Korean War. Fred Astaire hosts the film, and Arthur Kennedy portrays Dr. Wilmer. The themes of the film are masculine war and the feminine psyche, the psychological consequences of war, and the struggle of violence and human values. *People Need People* tells the story of a war veteran becoming painfully conscious of the values of life and death. Here, Lee recalls the making of the film.

MARVIN: I remember a funny little thing that happened to me when they brought me in. They put this restraining belt on me—I never had one on before. It was an old, used restraining belt—well worn. On the inside, burned in like a brand, it said "San Pedro Receiving," and all those holes had been pulled. When they put that thing on me, I didn't like it. They put me down on the stretcher and tied me in it. Suddenly panic hit me because I was looking at the ceiling of the studio. If this place caught on fire now, I couldn't get out. And I was really this close to panic. When they finally released me, I told Harry about it. He asked me how I felt, and I said, "I felt awful." And he said, "Good." And I said, "Oh, that's where we are going?"

I don't know what the other actors did at home or how they or their wives or their girlfriends or their mothers survived, but we did take the emotions home. We lived it for the ten-day cycle in the film that showed what the ward was like. We were actually patients even though we hadn't been committed officially. That became very interesting. I was in the Marine Corps, and I did have the kinds of dreams portrayed in the film. The project gave me a chance to break through that wall of acting because although I experienced all that

53

kind of stuff and was scared, I couldn't tell anybody about it. Here was a chance to act out my fright, my cowardice, my very weaknesses – not necessarily the mother theme as in the last scene or in reference to *my* mother, but I could at least finally experience what I had never felt before. After this presentation, I think I became a difficult actor.

These directors or writers say, "Here's what you do." You say, "Well, it's not that simple." So I became a layman, which is worse than being a professional, right? You know they know it all. I think I have been a troublemaker ever since in my performances. I did have a lot of fears doing the film because I thought I might show something in myself that I didn't want to see. I'm not proud of my performance; I'm proud of the guy up there, not of me. I still have that rationale on my mind. It is an interesting thought. I was one of the few guys in the Marine Corps who really had a chance to act out the fears for profit. Since then, I have been free to do anything I want to do because I know I am acting out *me*.

There are a million stories about the production of this film. The director-producer went through a horrible time. He was so frustrated with the front office, he'd actually break into tears. He finally got it to be what he wanted, but he was a wreck. I think he was ready for the ward after we finished the film. We all got out, but I think we put the director in.

And the questions – everybody would come and ask Harry questions. Harry, the authority over there in the corner. "You know he's a psychiatrist." Maybe some of the guys were afraid to act in front of him. They would say, "Who was this guy really?" I'd say, "He is a psychiatrist from Palo Alto." What we had to do was fall back on our own feelings. That is a tough thing to do – not to pretend. When you're acting, you're pretending to be somebody else. In this film, however, you had to pull it from yourself. All these guys felt the same. Any guy could have played any of these roles when this was over; there was as much compassion among the performers as was depicted among the patients in the ward. It's a great thing when you're pulling for the other guys and up they come. That was one of the big uppers of doing this thing.

PARTICIPANT: Were you playing real characters or composites?

MARVIN: They were composites of individuals in Harry Wilmer's history of the original event. But I think the actors ended up playing themselves, not the characters.

WILMER: So the events that you portrayed as Sergeant Hughes happened, but you weren't Sergeant Hughes – you were Lee Marvin.

MARVIN: That's right.

WILMER: That's the point. Lee's script happened to follow one man's story more closely than the other actors' scripts did, but he wasn't playing the man. Similarly, Arthur Kennedy was playing me, but he wouldn't talk to me.
     Lee, what about that call you got from San Quentin about *People Need People*?

MARVIN: Oh, yes—the prison. Some young guy decided he wanted to make a play out of it up there. So this kid wrote the thing into a three-act play. Harry was the psychiatrist at San Quentin and decided it might be a good project for these prisoners. They wanted me to come up to be a technical advisor on acting. And Harry said, "Come on up, you'll enjoy it." Enjoy it? So I went up to San Francisco. Harry took me out to San Quentin and showed me around. These guys started to rehearse. The little guy running it, the director, was tiny, and his cellmate was playing my part. This kid ran it with the iron hand of an inmate. Some of the questions were really stunning. They'd say, "Well, what do you think about that, Lee?" And I'd say, "Well, you tell me." The director would say that's what he was going to do anyway. So my advice in the entire rehearsal period was absolutely nothing. I just kept my mouth shut because they were showing me. They in turn were acting out. That was the amazing thing—to see what they came up with. They were good, but that doesn't have anything to do with it. They got a chance to act out within a disciplined form, which was really exciting. It was an exciting thing to watch these guys work in a structured form—together. Because they are not a true group. They are all individuals in the joint, so to speak.
     Harry drew me inside a circle of sixty-five big prisoners in a therapeutic community he had established on a ranch. They were talking and Harry said, "Well, take over, Lee." There was silence until one guy finally said, "I don't know about you actors. You hide out in the hills in Hollywood. You don't want to talk. You don't want to see the publishers. Boy, if I was in your place, I'd be strutting down Hollywood Boulevard." I said, "You did, didn't you?" He said, "Yeah, yeah." They caught him. It was a tremendous experience.

PARTICIPANT: Did you find in working with the prisoners that they began to help each other as the patients helped each other when you were working with them, Harry? In other words, did the prisoners acting in San Quentin end up helping each other as the patients helped each other in the actual hospital?

MARVIN: They wanted to be good, so they had to make the move. They were going to show this to the A block, their block in the prison, and the B block. Since they didn't want to look bad, they had to cooperate. Looking bad was the most severe punishment they ever had up there besides beating. So they all cooperated to reach a performing level.

WILMER: They all knew Lee when he came there. The first day he walked in through the main gate and down the cellblock, you could hear cries of "M Squad, M Squad."

PARTICIPANT: I have two questions—one for Harry and one for Lee. Harry, it is my impression that the therapeutic communities are still very much the exception. I would love for you to contradict me, but I'd like for you to comment on that. For Lee, a few years ago I had a job doing psychodrama with a group of actors who were going to perform *One Flew Over the Cuckoo's Nest*. My job was to give them a structure for getting in touch with their craziness, their isolation, and also to bring them out of that before it went too far. I'm curious about your personal experience in that. After the shoot, how did you let go of the role once it was past?

MARVIN: You don't let go. You live with it. What happens is that it eventually goes away because other things supersede it. Fortunately, another job comes along. You don't cut off the role; it wears out. This project opened up perspectives in myself that I still haven't figured out because this opening is an ongoing process.

Now, about how far an actor should go—there is a danger point, but then, of course, if they hit that danger point, let them go. Maybe you can get them out if it gets too bad. They must reach in all that way. This is the fateful process of acting. What you do is make sure the actors don't get hurt physically and just hope that you can handle the mental results when the scene is over. It is a dangerous business in that area.

WILMER: I don't remember if I've ever asked you this, but in one scene, you throw yourself against the gridded door with such violence that I always could feel it. It was hardly acting. I just wondered if you really hurt yourself?

MARVIN: What happened there, you remember, was that we tried the scene and the door gave way. We had to get some more stage braces to stick up against the door to keep it from giving way. You can't fake that. It is part of the commitment of acting—there are certain things that you have to do. And so I just did it until I literally couldn't do it any more and that's the scene. That's the obligation of the actor to the scene, and that's how far you must go.

56

WILMER: In reply to the other question, this was the first therapeutic community in the United States. That is why they made a film of it, I think. At the time, the hierarchies and traditions of mental hospitals were rather dictatorial and rows of people were in restraints and seclusion. Since then, a vast number of therapeutic communities have arisen. They have become as rigid and autocratic in a democratic way as the hospitals were repressive before, and they're not much better. But there has been an increasing liberation from that kind of dictatorial power. I had a therapeutic community veterans' hospital for my Vietnam veterans. It was an uphill struggle all the way, because now the climate is not conducive to this as much as it is to dealing with the milieu in drugs.

PARTICIPANT: The sergeant came pretty close to hitting you [Wilmer] with that file cabinet. Did you have any closer encounters?

WILMER: That was the only close encounter of the whole year. Actually it was a board thrown at me, not a filing cabinet. They changed it for the film. My only reaction was that I couldn't believe it was happening. Nobody was hurt. Inside seclusion rooms in other wards, people committed suicide, people were hit, all sorts of violence occurred. That just didn't happen on my ward, and a thousand men went through that admission ward in a year, each staying for ten days. After the incident happened, I felt fear. That was one encounter that frightened me — one of the few. After it happened, the studio wanted me to take one of those nurses to a restaurant in Chinatown and get a call on the telephone and race across the Bay Bridge and all sorts of crazy stuff like that. They wanted Lee to put his fist through a television. But none of that junk happened and we refused to do it. We stuck to the events almost as they had actually happened.

PARTICIPANT: I wondered, since this film was about soldiers, if it could be done today without having an antiwar bias. That leads me to another speculation. My students were talking the other day about the need for young men to go out and prove their courage. The question that came up was, Is there a substitute for war?

MARVIN: Any substitute for war is OK by me, but mostly it occurs on the ball field, doesn't it? Within disciplined forms, such as football, basketball, and track. Courage is a male demon, and I don't know what we're going to do with it. Maybe just the family has to handle that one. As to doing the film with an antiwar bias, war just brought these things to a sudden head. The masses started coming. The mental cases just developed more rapidly within a

57

government-paid situation. In civilian life, it takes a much more sensitive attitude to discover these people and to get them into a situation for which they or the families must pay. I think that's why the war theme is behind all these. They were simply under the auspices of the government, don't you think, Harry?

WILMER: Yes, yes, true.

PARTICIPANT: Have you had the opportunity to follow up on any of these patients twenty or thirty years later to see what has happened to them?

WILMER: No, some of these men have stopped by to see me or written me. It would have been impossible and incorrect to have tried to say that their recovery or failure to recover was due to the ten days they spent on my admission ward. From there they went to all sorts of other wards including repressive wards in the same hospital, if you can believe that. But gradually, over the next year and a half, all the wards in the hospital became sort of therapeutic communities. We simply were unable to follow these people although the question of what happened to them is the scientific and humane one that everyone would want answered. The men I did see and those who wrote to me were all profoundly affected in positive ways by this totally unexpected experience.

MARVIN: I can tell you about a reaction up at the penitentiary. The guy playing my role was a heavyweight champion at San Quentin and all other penitentiaries. He was in on a death sentence, but got an eleventh-hour stay and was pardoned for life. At the time, I was glad, in a sense, because he was a tough boy. About five or six years later, I was in San Francisco. Someone rapped on my hotel room door, and there he was. I said, "Rick?" He said, "Yeah, hi, Lee." "I thought you were over the wall," I said. "I was just wandering," he said. "I thought I'd say hello, and here's an eight-by-ten composite with my credits on the back. If there is anything you can do for me, don't fail to give me a ring." I said, "I won't fail." That's a follow-up?

PARTICIPANT: Harry, what do you think of some of the mechanisms that result in abnormally aggressive behavior?

PARTICIPANT: In most characters who display unacceptable hostility, what are some of the causes that result in that sort of behavior?

WILMER: The most important lesson, I think, in working with violent people, whether they are Vietnam veterans or Korean veterans or veterans from any war or just the ordinary stream of life, is that we all have within us this violent potential. And it is dangerous to deny it or to hint to children or other people that they might be that way—but *I'm* not. Such condescension about anger and its expression would tend to not repress it but rather to cause it to come out in various ways. Most of the men who are pictured in the film were subject to what now would be called post-traumatic stress disorder. Some violent situation in Korea or elsewhere that they could not integrate led to immediate or delayed stress. That needn't be war. It could be fire, an explosion, the downing of an airplane, or similar experiences.

Without being clinical, I would say that the important thing is the compassionate attitude toward that "unacceptable behavior" or toward things that are somewhat deviant from parental attitudes. As a ward psychiatrist in the Navy, I thought it was to be able to tolerate ambiguity, to tolerate the potential for violence and not expect it to happen, because the expectations are often fulfilled in a self-fulfilling prophecy. It happens with parents and children all the time.

PARTICIPANT: What kind of distinctions, if any, would you make between the groups coming out of the Korean War and those coming out of the Vietnam War?

WILMER: I wouldn't make distinctions. It's just a new set of clothes, a new war of weapons—but when it gets down to man-to-man or man alone, it's the same. I think it's an archetypal experience common to all people. During a recent lecture in Switzerland on Vietnam, I was asked this question about the Russians in Afghanistan. I am quite certain that the human being, not the government, that Russians, French, Germans, every other nationality, react on the same level to catastrophic violence, death, and killing. I wouldn't distinguish between the Vietnam and Korean veterans that I saw. Lee, when you were in the Marines, you were wounded, and you spent time in the South Pacific. You know a lot more about this personally than I do. Can you respond to it?

MARVIN: There is only so far that you can go with fear before you are dead. I think that in all wars, there is really no difference at all, because if you're up-to-date with the weaponry, the experience is the same whether it's swords, spears, machine guns, or Agent Orange. The fear is equal and the traumas are equal. There is nothing new in the order of fear within man. I would make no distinction at all. As Harry said, the uniforms and the colors are different, that's all.

PARTICIPANT: Have you noticed any difference in recent years in young men and their experience to, say, extreme frustration or danger that you might attribute to the amount of openness that is available to young men now as opposed to in the past?

WILMER: The question is, does it seem that with the more permissive attitudes of today toward expression of feelings, that there really is a difference in the young man exposed to these kinds of traumas. That is the paradox, because if we take Vietnam (which is the last real model we have of this sort of thing), the problem was that they weren't allowed the permissiveness that was the promise of their growing up. There was no way to talk. There was no receptivity—just the opposite. The promise of openness was seen as broken. Therefore, it generated more violence and more things that sink under the surface, so that fathers and sons didn't talk to each other. The mothers and the sons didn't either. The men who went to Vietnam did not have that openness that was the promise of their childhood, so they felt worse. Enacting violence, now, "forgetting" the war, is compounded by the use of drugs. It is a very complicated question.

PARTICIPANT: Lee, a twofold question. First, you mentioned that you really made a quantum step forward in terms of your career in acting out the war in this film. I wonder if you have any other roles in which you had the same kind of experience that really was a help to your career. Second, I wondered if you would discuss the concept that although in this role you played a sergeant, in effect, the character was really you. Are the roles you consider to be the great roles you have played—you?

MARVIN: I haven't played anything new at all. How new a role appears is just a matter of how it is arranged in today's lifestyle or the prevalent lifestyle whenever people view it. When I say a breakthrough, I'm not sure that necessarily means a positive breakthrough. Breakthroughs can be negative, also. I utilize those breakthroughs. It might be in a minuscule strata, but I create these problems for myself in order to have something to fight so it keeps me alive during the filming. An example of one of those roles that you could say was a stepping-stone—one of the most difficult ones I had to do after *People Need People*—was *Cat Ballou*. It's a comedy about this old drunk gunfighter. I thought it was a tragedy, and I played it as a tragedy, because what do old gunfighters do? They die bloody drunk in the street. I don't want to die that way, but I could. So I was fighting that in the film, and it came out as it should. The point you reach might not be the point you originally sought. Does that answer you?

PARTICIPANT: I think it is significant that you picked out what could be considered to be a great role—that's significant. I wonder whether acting is not acting at all.

MARVIN: I agree with you. The more you get into acting, the less you act. There lies the problem, and that's why a lot of the guys quit. They say acting starts to get too close to the bone.

WILMER: I would like to ask you a question about the response to seeing yourself on film that always struck me as interesting. I know some of your feelings about seeing the films that you've made. The producers invited me to the studio to screen the film when the rushes were back and put together and all the actors were still there. After they turned on the lights, they said, "Well, what do you think, Dr. Wilmer?" I couldn't talk. I literally couldn't talk. I couldn't look at this film for a year. It would bind me up. But now it doesn't bother me. How do you feel, Lee, when you see yourself on the screen?

MARVIN: I agree with you totally. I think when you're in the process of doing something, it is a subjective thing. You might look at the dailies, but the only reason you do this is to see if the costume fits or the hat is right. You can't notice the acting because you're still doing it. I have to lay back a good six or eight months to a year before I even see what I did. I was recently at a showing of a film I did called *Point Blank*—a violent film. They made it for the violence. I was shocked at how violent it was. Of course, that was fifteen, eighteen years ago. I almost literally could not stand up, I was so weak. "I did that? I'm capable of that kind of violence?" Therein is the fright, and this is why I think some actors eventually back off. "No," they say, "I'm not going to put myself to those demons again," the demon being the self.

PARTICIPANT: I'm curious about the staff. In the film and in reality, it seemed as though the doctor who orders the patients into seclusion was really never with it in terms of your methods; whereas the nurses and some of the orderlies were. Is this what you found? Perhaps the more educated staff were less able to go along than some of the orderlies were.

WILMER: Exactly. My psychiatric peer group was threatened and tended to sabotage things. The doctor who put the patient in the seclusion room was an exaggeration of this. The nurses, the corpsman, my senior officers offered me tremendous support. I don't mean to cast shadows on all my peers. But, by and large, when you're introducing a new concept into a hospital, and the

61

people at your level there function in a bureaucracy and do not recognize this concept, you're going to get a hard time from them.

MARVIN: Let me answer that also, Harry. One of the actors playing a corpsman had been on the psycho ward a couple years someplace in California. He just looked at me and said, "That's not the way you do it. You just grab a mattress and slam it up against the wall." That's an actor. So where do they come from? The whole world is within the acting sphere.

WILMER: I learned some interesting things in making that film. When the script said, "Your real security comes from here," I would have pointed here [at the heart]. The director, Alex Siegel said, "No, he should point here." [Kennedy pointed with his thumb into his guts.] And I felt that was a point well taken.

MARVIN: When we rehearsed at my house on weekends before we started filming, we argued about that. "No," I said, "real fear, when it hits you — you're useless. You're useless. You can't do anything. It hits you just between your belly button and your pubic area. It's down there." He said "no" because he'd known fear. He wouldn't admit it, so that was his concession. Now Harry says, "Here" [the heart]. See where a man lies? Wild, isn't it?

WILMER: A lot of people are extraordinarily defensive about what they do. Lee, I think one of your engaging qualities is your openness.

MARVIN: I still have a long way to go, Harry. I only gave you that much. That's what I think I know. I'm sure it goes further back, not due to me but just due to the fact that I am a human being.

PARTICIPANT: Harry, you made this film and started that program several years ago. Have you made any changes in the program over the years? Have you seen that you should drop something you were doing or add something? Or is it essentially the same program?

WILMER: No, this thing changed quite a bit. I pay a great deal more attention to dreams now than I did, because I didn't understand them then. I'm still working on it. There are many more sophisticated things that we know about human behavior. In general, my attitude about drugs remains the same — use in moderation and only when necessary. The basic humanity depends on the individual doing it. I will do it one way, and someone else will do it another. I am more tolerant of differences in which people would try to do the same thing than I would have been then.

PARTICIPANT: One of the things that seems to come through in the film is that what was developed in that group was a very strong sense of community. What kind of care does it take to ensure that in a group you're trying to make as open and unrestrained as possible that you end up with that lack of restraint in an open community and don't end up with a free-for-all?

WILMER: To facilitate the kind of community in which people feel safe to say or do what they want is illustrated in the first scene when Nurse Green is being told to shut up—as if we didn't allow people to say what they want. One thing that helped this work was that we had some authority and structure in the Navy. When I began to introduce this program, my psychoanalytic colleagues said, "Oh, you can't do that in the authoritative military organization!" When it got working well, they said, "Well, of course, you can do it because you've got all the authority there." The use of authority and not trying to make a democracy out of a situation that is not a democracy characterized the therapeutic communities that I have run. People never vote because psychiatric wards aren't democracies in a political sense.

I think there is a limit to what you can tolerate. There is a certain tolerance for craziness, and there is a sense of containment that grows in such a community whereby you don't have to do very much. The staff and the patients will do it for you. Once this culture gets going, people will come in and test it as Lee did: "Throw me into a quiet room." And I answer, "We don't use a quiet room here." Then what happens when something doesn't work right? How you deal with it is what makes the guts of the matter. The sense of freedom involves responsibilities to balance these and not try to worship the freedom or the expression of everything, whether it's anger or whatever. I think the more one does with oneself and with one's sphere, the more one thinks maybe the effect will go beyond you. That's as much as any of us can really do—the best within our contained sphere. Today, there are sophisticated theories, whether in physics or behavior, about what one's place is in affecting the world.

At the conference I attended in Switzerland, the Dalai Lama was asked such a question right at the beginning. He spoke in Tibetan. His translator said, "All of us have the responsibility for one another." And the Dalai Lama said to the translator, "No, I said, each of us." That's a profound difference. If I do what I can in this realm, that is one contribution I make.

PARTICIPANT: A lot of our shows deal with craziness or wretchedness or hostility, and actors make a living at it. Does that say something about our society—the fact that our media is so caught up with craziness, hostility, aggressiveness? Is this different from other places in the world? Do either of you have a reaction to that?

MARVIN: All I can say is that in Europe, American pictures are the most popular, which amazes me. They do love the violent pictures. Of course, they have seen violence. Maybe the acting on the screen alleviates the pressure in them. I know when I was a kid and would see John Wayne punch some guy and knock him through the wall, I'd say, "Boy, I'm glad I wasn't that guy." I didn't want to be involved in that relationship, so maybe there is a positive value to it. In acting, when craziness is shown in a sick manner or in other words, "to no value," I look down on it. Real violence is a thing that must not be tolerated, and to be sure you don't tolerate it, you must learn what it is. Violent films with value do come out.

WILMER: I'm turned off by a great deal of violence I see on television and in film. I just can't watch it and don't. We are in violent times. The structure of society and the threats to it are so great that, while on the one hand we are experiencing enormous personal violence in films and television, on the other hand, we are reaching out from the heavens and the spheres and from outer space into something that is a modern mythology or something to do with a greater wisdom from another world that always emerges through violence. I think somehow or another these are expressions of the mythology of our times. As Lee says, one thing that strikes you in Europe, is that these people actually lived through something that we have never experienced here — that is, the violence from an invader, and that is the thing that might have something to do with acting it out.

MARVIN: The Europeans live under a fear that is greater than ours because it is just across the street or the border. They don't want it, but the threat is actually there. To alleviate it, I guess they get it in their films. They soothe themselves with simple violence, even though it is brutal individually. I turn off television violence, too. I say, "What for? If you have a point, OK." In French films, you can't take a drink or light a cigarette unless you give the audience a reason. Interesting.

PARTICIPANT: What do you feel is the effect on a young person in the United States of seeing you brutally killed or murdered and then the next week, seeing you in another movie where you're well and happy? Will the young person think that violence isn't really that permanent or what?

MARVIN: I would certainly say that. But I have been killed in most of my

64

movies. Those were the early ones when I was the bad guy in Westerns. I was shot out of the saddle and through the wall and everything. I wasn't the hero, though, so that is OK. You can get shot every week, and it doesn't affect the child because you are the black hat. But once you get into a hero status in films, you have to be very careful how you die, because the child may take the fact of death as being something that you cure by looking at a different film next week. I think there is a danger and a consideration there. When the dollar moves in, I think the consideration moves out. It is one of those horrible problems.

PARTICIPANT: The character that Lee plays in the film *People Need People* is pushed to the point where he could have taken his own life; after the crisis subsides, the doctor just gives a sigh of relief. Suppose it had gone the other way. Suppose he had committed suicide. Do you think if you were the doctor, you could pick up the pieces of your experiment? What do you think the effect would have been on the other patients?

WILMER: I have done it, so I know it is possible. Not often. There again, I have a kind of belief that because of what I am doing with that person, nothing terrible will happen to that person. Most always that is true, but you know there are limits to it, and your own humanity can't change some things. I think you learn to accept that in time. It would have made a difference to me. Yes. The ward would have gone on — but it wouldn't have been the same. The question of things continuing after acts of violence is a part of life. In the prison, that was happening all the time, but not in hospitals.

PARTICIPANT: What do you think the effects would have been on the other people?

WILMER: Let me tell you the effect of watching Lee in that linen closet with the shears. I'm sitting on the set watching this happen, and I felt a fear. He sat there between takes with the scissors, shears, hitting them on the shelf. I could feel something was happening within Lee, and it frightened me. "If you don't have human feeling, if you simply think, 'Why am I using the shears?' you get nowhere."

PARTICIPANT: Does that mean you have to psych yourself up for this sort of thing?

MARVIN: Yes, and you can't get out of it. If you get out of it, you might lose it, because it is so difficult to find. Once you find it, you've got to keep it.

65

That relates to an earlier question of yours. "Do you take it home and does it affect your family?" Well, you can imagine now. Actors' families have very difficult times because they're living with whatever the role is.

PARTICIPANT: Something that people who aren't familiar with films may not know is that it may take two hours of constant shooting of that same scene over and over again. You're waiting for that camera maybe an hour before you can go back to that character again. The stress on the actor is just phenomenal.

MARVIN: The stress was on the shelf.

PARTICIPANT: Is there some role that you desire to play in the future — some ultimate goal that you think is meant for you? Or is there some role you truly do not want to play?

MARVIN: The way that works is that somebody has to write a film first because I'm not a writer. And somebody has to produce it. Then they can call me. I won't know what it is until I see it. I don't think you ever reach the ultimate role. Acting is just an ongoing process until you wear out or until the audience wears you out. There is not any one thing that I want to do. What another man thinks of me, who has the power to put me in position for a role, is what I will probably do.

WILMER: A comment about violence in groups. After I finished in the Navy, I was a consultant to naval hospitals. I remember sitting in a large group. A man got up and walked behind the group all the time, which was ominous and frightening to me. I couldn't understand why the therapist tolerated this instead of stopping things. Pretty soon, the man hit somebody in the back of his head, sending him flat in the middle of the group. I would not have tolerated that kind of threatening behavior without intervening before violence. When Lee gets up and leaves the group, I go talk to Lee. There is so much that needs some kind of containment, and people are relieved when it happens.

PARTICIPANT: You indicated that there were times when the stress had become so severe that someone did something to himself. How did that affect the weakest member of your group? There must have been some reaction to it from someone who was on a very thin thread of recovery. Did that destroy the group image?

WILMER: I can answer that in terms of a real event that happened at the time of this experiment. One of the men I transferred from my unit to the officers' unit was put in a seclusion room there and hung himself. The reactions of the people with tenuous holds on reality or control was shattering. They fell apart. That mobilized others in my groups, who brought these people together. One has to learn how to cope with tragedies that occur, whether immediate or related. The fact that it was across the courtyard rather than in my ward made a difference. Still, the people least contained are the people who most suffer.

CHAPTER FIVE

Linus Pauling

A SCIENTIST

In 1954, Linus Pauling was awarded the Nobel Prize in Chemistry for his research on the nature of the chemical bond and in 1964 received the Nobel Prize for Peace for his leadership in work for world peace, especially in connection with nuclear weapons disarmament. He has received honorary doctorates from forty-six universities. President Ford awarded him the National Medal of Science, and President Truman awarded him the Presidential Medal for Merit. He has received the Priestley Medal from the American Chemical Society as well as numerous other medals and prizes from scientific and medical societies. And he has also received the Gandhi Peace Prize, the Grotius Medal for Contributions to International Law, and the International Lenin Peace Prize.

Pauling received a doctor of philosophy from the California Institute of Technology, where he was a professor until 1963. At that time, he became research professor of physical and biological sciences at the Center for the Study of Democratic Institutions in Santa Barbara. In 1968 he became professor of chemistry at Stanford University and is now professor emeritus. Since 1973, Pauling has been research professor at the Linus Pauling Institute of Science and Medicine in Palo Alto.

Pauling's sometimes unorthodox ideas have been widely disseminated through more than six hundred scientific papers and some two hundred articles on social and political questions, particularly peace. His books include *The Nature of the Chemical Bond*; *General Chemistry*; *College Chemistry*; *No More War!*; *Science and World Peace*; *Vitamin C and the Common Cold*; *Vitamin C, the Common Cold, and the Flu*; *Cancer and Vitamin C* (with Ewan Cameron); and *How to Live Longer and Feel Better.*

An Extraordinary Life:
An Autobiographical Ramble

I've been invited to talk about myself, and I'll do my best to stick to the subject. I was born in 1901 in Portland, Oregon. My great-grandparents, grandparents, and parents were pioneers who traversed the Oregon Trail. I went to very good schools in the small town of Condon in eastern Oregon. My father was a druggist. The population of five hundred mainly included cowboys, ranch hands, and saloon keepers. When I was eight years old, we moved back to Portland where I continued my schooling. I went to Oregon Agricultural College. In 1922, after I got my degree in chemical engineering, I went to the California Institute of Technology and got a doctorate in chemistry and mathematical physics in 1925. Usually, I say I am a chemist; sometimes I say I am a physical chemist. Probably I should say I am a physicist with an interest in chemistry.

I am moderately smart. I estimate that twenty thousand people in the United States are smarter than I am, perhaps fifteen thousand are women and five thousand are men. I reached this conclusion a month after my wife and I were married. We participated in some intelligence tests, which showed that my wife was smarter than I. Since we were already married, it was too late for me to do anything about it. Of course, I recognize that many physicists are smarter than I am — most of them theoretical physicists. A lot of smart people have gone into theoretical physics; therefore, the field is extremely competitive. I console myself with the thought that although they may be smarter and may be deeper thinkers than I am, I have broader interests than they have. I don't suppose anybody else in the world has a good background, knowledge of physics, mathematics, theoretical physics, *and* knows a great deal about chemistry — the amount that I know.

When I was eleven years old, with no outside inspiration — just library books — I started collecting insects. Not only did I collect insects, I also read about insects. I was filling my mind with a lot of information about the lepidoptera and diptera and so on. My father, a druggist, died when I was nine. When I needed chemicals, even before I was interested in chemistry itself, I went to another druggist who was a family friend. At eleven, I was interested only in insects.

"A person who collects insects needs to have a killing bottle," I said. And I got a Mason jar from my mother. All I needed now were 10 grams of potassium cyanide and perhaps 50 grams of plaster of Paris. Mr. Ziegler, the druggist, gave me 10 grams of potassium cyanide and 50 grams of plaster of Paris. I took them home, went out on the back porch (because I knew that potassium cyanide was dangerous), and dumped the potassium cyanide into

69

the bottle. I mixed the plaster of Paris with some water, put it in the bottle on top of the potassium cyanide, and let it harden. I had my killing bottle. I collected a lot of insects.

The next year I got interested in minerals. I didn't have very many minerals, at least that I could recognize, only agates. So about all I could do was go around Portland looking for piles of gravel where someone was putting in a house foundation or sidewalk. I'd go through the gravel looking for chunks of agate.

Just think of the differences today. A young person gets interested in chemistry and is given a chemical set. The chemical set doesn't contain potassium cyanide. It doesn't even contain copper sulfate or anything else interesting because all the interesting chemicals are considered poisonous substances. Therefore, these budding young chemists don't have a chance to do anything interesting with their chemical sets. As I look back, I think it is pretty remarkable that Mr. Ziegler, this friend of the family, would have so easily turned over one-third of an ounce of potassium cyanide to me, an eleven-year-old boy.

When I was thirteen, a friend of mine my age (later head of the University of Texas psychology department), who went to the same high school, showed me the first chemistry experiments that I had ever seen. I was really enthralled that you could take a chemical substance and convert it into other substances. Because of that, I became a chemist when I was thirteen years old.

What is the history of chemistry? What stage was it in when I was a boy? There were three stages in the development of chemistry. First, you had alchemy up to about 1780. The person who is called the discoverer of modern chemistry is Antoine Laurent Lavoisier. He was the first man to discuss elements and compounds in the modern way. Before that, ideas about whether a substance was an element or a compound were rather vague. Lavoisier compiled the arguments Scheele and Priestley had recently presented that there was a gas called oxygen—that air consists of 20 percent oxygen and 80 percent something else. Priestley was a Unitarian minister in England. When he sympathized with the French Revolution later, his home and laboratory were burned down by a mob. He then escaped to America and lived the rest of his life in Pennsylvania. At the time Priestley began his work, there were three gases that scientists thought of as different. I'm not sure what the three were, but they were not pure substances. Priestley discovered a dozen different gases by his investigations. Why did he do it? He did it for the greater glory of God. He liked to carry out experiments and show the members of his congregation what a wonderful world God had created. He wasn't especially interested in science for its own sake, but included it in his devotion to his religious beliefs.

Because of the discovery of oxygen, Lavoisier formulated the idea that there are elements (substances that cannot be split into two different substances) and compounds (the result of the union of two or more different elements). Take oxygen. You can't split it into two different substances. But if you electrolyze water, it splits into oxygen and hydrogen. Lavoisier studied all of the empirical information, identified about twenty-five or thirty elements, and found a dozen others of which he was not sure—he thought calcium oxide was an element but it turned out to be a compound of calcium and oxygen. He also discussed acids and bases. He had a mistaken idea that all acids are compounds of oxygen, and he named oxygen. I'm not sure he was the original namer, but I think he was the person who called it oxygen, meaning "acid former," because he thought acids were oxygen compounds. Of course, a few years later his head was cut off. He was guillotined. Who knows what more he would have contributed if he hadn't been guillotined?

Then various chemists introduced refinements. An important one was made by Louis Pasteur, who recognized several tartrates—for example, the potassium hydrogen tartrates. He recognized this partially from the optical activity rotation of polarized light, partially from the shape of crystals. He was looking at crystals that he had made of a tartrate preparation, and he noticed that the individual crystals were either right-handed or left-handed. They weren't mirror images of themselves. You take a cube; it is a mirror image of itself. If you cut off three corners of a cube, then it no longer is a mirror image of itself. In this way, he was able to identify different kinds. About 1870 van't Hoff and Le Bel independently recognized that all Pasteur's observations could be explained. Pasteur was about forty years earlier. All could be explained if you assumed that the carbon atom forms four chemical bonds pointing toward the corners of a regular tetrahedron. That was an important step in the development of what used to be called modern chemistry.

Now we come to present-day chemistry, which perhaps we should call modern chemistry, where a lot of these things are understood. Here I have lived through a period when the field changed from the chemistry of Lavoisier, Pasteur, van't Hoff, and Le Bel to the chemistry of today, which is far more powerful, and which permits chemists to make many more predictions than it used to be possible to make. The organic chemists were pretty good at making predictions after van't Hoff and Le Bel came out with their theory, and Alfred Werner presented a similar theory for inorganic compounds in 1890 in Zurich. They still were not nearly so capable as modern-day chemists and molecular biologists (who are just chemists more specialized in a particular field of chemistry than other chemists).

What happened? I was born in 1901. Five years before that, the electron was discovered. I came close to being born in the time of billions of years before it was known that there are electrons in the world. The nucleus of the atom wasn't discovered until 1911, when I was ten years old. Isn't that remarkable? In this marvelous period in a few years beginning in 1896, modern physics came into existence. J. J. Thomson at Cambridge University discovered the electron. An Englishman named George Stoney had predicted that the electron existed. Michael Faraday had discovered the Faraday Law: if you hydrolyze water with an electric potential, the amount of hydrogen you get is

71

proportional to the strength of the current. Faraday knew there was something interesting in the relationship between electricity, the amount of electricity, and the amounts of chemical substances formed by electrolysis. Stoney said this must mean that there is an atom of electricity. Every time you liberate a hydrogen atom from water, you are adding an atom of electricity to the hydrogen atom. That is right. It was the electron, the atom of electricity.

Radioactivity was discovered quickly, and shortly after that X-rays were discovered by Roentgen. Radium was separated from the ore by Madame Curie and her husband. There were other rapid developments, and the modern electronic age began. I was fortunate when I became a graduate student. We knew about the electrons and also knew about quantum mechanics — the theory. We also had X-ray diffraction, electron diffraction, and other techniques for studying atoms and molecules, spectroscopic techniques that provided a great deal of empirical information and gave us the penetrating understanding of the structure of atoms and molecules and crystals that we have now. Of course, it led ultimately by a long series of events, to my interest in vitamin C, nutrition, and health.

I have been fortunate in having seen what has happened with respect to our understanding of the nature of the world in which we live during the past eighty years. A tremendous amount of progress has been made. When I was a boy learning chemistry, quite a lot was known. We had the periodic table and knew the numbers of electrons in atoms — discovered in 1914 by Henry Moseley, a young fellow working at Cambridge with X-ray diffraction, who later enlisted in the British army and was killed at Gallipoli, Turkey. Hydrogen is the first element, helium the second, and lithium the third. Before Moseley, nobody knew how many electrons were around the nucleus of an element's atom. By 1915, however, we knew how many electrons were around the nucleus of the atom.

I would mull over these tables and wonder why some substances were diamagnetic and some paramagnetic. I didn't have enough knowledge of physics to be able to answer rationally. Other people had good ideas about diamagnetism and paramagnetism, but I didn't know about them because I hadn't studied any physics at Oregon Agricultural College.

When I was studying chemical engineering at Oregon Agricultural College, I took all the mathematics they offered my first year. For four years, I had no mathematics courses, and I didn't know enough to know that you could learn just studying by yourself. I thought the only way to learn something was to have some teacher teach you in class. So for four years I didn't study mathematics. In 1922, I became a graduate student at the California Institute of Technology in Pasadena, where I began to learn mathematics and theoretical physics and did a pretty good job. By 1925, when I got my doctorate degree, my subject was physical chemistry and mathematical physics.

I was fortunate when I came to the California Institute of Technology. A new experimental technique had been discovered only eight years before — the determination of the structure of crystals by the X-ray diffraction method. Roscoe Dickinson, the first Ph.D. recipient at the institute, had been using this technique for three or four years there. He was a few years older than I and taught me the technique. I was very excited about it, and it only took him a couple of months to teach me how to determine the structure of a rather simple crystal by taking X-ray diffraction photographs of it and analyzing those photographs.

Perhaps the greatest thing he taught me was how to assess the reliability of my own conclusions. He taught me to ask every time I reached some conclusion: "Have I made some assumption in reaching this conclusion? And what is the assumption? And what are the chances that this assumption is wrong? How reliable is the conclusion?" I have remembered this ever since and have continued to feel grateful to him. If you have an original idea, it is possible to delude yourself into thinking that there are observations that support this idea. Or it is possible that although you think your idea has been developed on the basis of rational argument, somewhere in that argument you have made an unjustified assumption. This idea was important in my development.

I often hear people describing me as a biochemist or as an organic chemist or something else. In fact, I never did like organic chemistry. I liked biochemistry even less. I didn't have any courses to speak of in organic chemistry and no course at all in biochemistry — no course in any aspect of biology or medicine. But I have made contributions in the nutritional and biochemical fields. If I were to go through my eight hundred or so scientific papers to see where I have made contributions in science, I could say I am a X-ray crystallographer. The American Mineralogist Society gave me their Roebling Medal, which they give every year to an outstanding mineralogist, so that makes me a mineralogist. I am a physical chemist because that is what I originally called myself, and that is the title on my Ph.D. diploma.

A degree and five years of practical experience made me a chemical engineer. When I was nineteen years old, I didn't have enough money to return for my junior year at Oregon Agricultural College. As a sophomore I had taken the course in quantitative chemical analysis, and the school offered me a full-time job teaching the sophomore course in quantitative chemical analysis. So I am also an analytical chemist. Since I laid the theoretical foundation for the tetrahedral carbon atom and developed the resonance hybrid concept, I am an organic chemist. I explained a lot of things in organic chemistry. I am a biochemist. I am a molecular biologist, and in a sense originated this field. I am a geneticist and have made contributions.

I am an evolutionary scientist. My student Emile Zuckerkandl and I originated the field of molecular evolution twenty-six years ago. Emile, who had a doctoral degree, was in Vienna up to age fifteen, but then was brought up in France. He worked with me as a post-doctoral student on some problem about metabolism in marine invertebrates. I wasn't very interested in that.

73

"Well," I said, "I'll get apparatus for you, if you will work for three months for me on a problem. I want you to go down to the zoo in San Diego and get some blood out of the gorilla and the orangutan and the chimpanzee and the rhesus monkey. Then pick up blood from a cow and a horse and a cat and a dog and some red-blooded fish that have hemoglobin in their blood. I want you to determine something about the amino acid composition of these hemoglobins."

He had to accept that because he wanted to do his marine invertebrate work and wanted the apparatus. So he went to San Diego. I said, "You should get some blood, too, from a gorilla fetus."

Well, he never succeeded in getting blood from a gorilla fetus, but he did get blood from the gorilla and these other various organisms, and we checked their compositions.

I have known for a long time that the hemoglobin protein — the red protein in the red cells of the blood, differs for different animal species. This was known. But just why were they different? Immunologically they were different and crystallographically they were different, but nothing definite was known about their compositions. In hemoglobin there are four polypeptide chains. With these samples of blood, we found that in both the alpha and the beta chains, between horses and humans (or other similarly distant animals) the differences in the amino acids numbered about 20 out of 140 or 146. We also found that there were about six differences out of 140 or 146 amino acids between humans and rhesus monkey, and we found there were zero or one or two differences between humans' alpha or beta chains and those in gorillas, chimpanzees, and orangutans. We set up the molecular clock. I think it was my idea, but I'm not sure. We were just collaborating on these studies. Perhaps it was Emile's idea. He is, by the way, president of our institute in Palo Alto now, and has been for about ten years.

In 1962, we wrote that horses and human beings, as we know from the geological record, separated from one another — the precursors of human beings and of horses — about eighty million years ago. There are twenty differences in the amino acids of the alpha chain and also of the beta chain. That means that every four million years you get an evolutionarily effective mutation. This is a simple idea, and it is, of course, a gross simplification. Here you have about one or two differences between humans and gorillas, orangutans, chimpanzees — fewest for chimpanzees. That would mean that four to eight million years ago the evolutionary lines leading to human beings on the one hand and these anthropoids on the other hand diverged. Forty thousand years ago, Homo sapiens, modern man, developed. Apparently that hasn't changed much for forty thousand years. So Emile and I developed this evolutionary clock.

Chemistry is, in some ways, a far more interesting subject than physics because it deals with the real world in what seems to me a good "real" way. A physicist may be interested in the properties of metals. A chemist is interested in the properties of lithium, sodium, magnesium, potassium, calcium, titanium, and so on for all seventy-four different metals. Very early on, I became interested in intermetallic compounds. You can make intermetallic compounds if you put mercury in a beaker, warm it up and put some potassium in it. When I did that, it dissolved. Then I put it in a crystallizing dish. After a day or two, it crystallized into beautiful big crystals. This was about 1923, my second year as a graduate student. Why in the dickens should potassium and mercury form a compound with composition KHg_{13}? I still work on that problem. In fact, I am now writing a book on metals and intermetallic compounds.

There was an idea about the chemical bond that chemists had developed (not physicists) that atoms can interact with one another to form a chemical bond. It was a simple idea. I used to tell students that the chemical bond could be thought of as a hook and eye. The alkali atoms (sodium and potassium) have an eye, and the halogen elements (chlorine and fluorine, for example) a hook. The chemical bond consisted of the hook hooking into the eye. Why did I say that it was the halogens that had the hook? Because chlorine gas is Cl_2 and fluorine gas is F_2. At that time, it was thought that sodium vapor was just Na (a single sodium atom, no Na_2's). And the two hooks I said, could also form a bond. So you got F_2 and Cl_2. It really was a primitive picture of chemical bonding, but that was the state of the art. That was the understanding we had of chemical bonds.

In 1937, I was invited to give the prestigious George Fisher Baker Lecture at Cornell University. I went there for one semester. Famous chemists had held this appointment. One requirement was that you write a book. My lectures were on the nature of the chemical bond, and the book came out in 1949, *The Nature of the Chemical Bond*. It was a best-seller, published by Cornell University Press. After a year, the editor of Cornell University Press wrote to me and said, "Your edition of 10,000 copies is just about sold out. Would you prepare a second edition?" And I said, "Well, it hasn't been a year yet. Nothing much has happened, but there have been *some* changes in this field. Why should I prepare a second edition of the book?" He said, "Well, you don't get any royalties from the book. It was a condition of your appointment as George Fisher Baker lecturer in chemistry that you should write the book and present the manuscript. There has never been a George Fisher Baker book that has gone into a second edition, but if you write a second edition, Cornell University Press will give you royalties on it." That was a really good incentive. I got busy and added perhaps ten pages. It came out as the second edition in 1940, and I have collected royalties ever since.

Thinking back about this man, the editor of Cornell University Press, I realize he is really remarkable in that he should think it would be unjust to deny me royalties on a book that had become a scientific best-seller. He was Amish from Pennsylvania, which may have had something to do with his ethical standards. It is a good thing that people have ethical standards.

People keep saying to me, "How does it come about that you shifted

Linus Pauling

your field every five or ten years in a remarkable way?" In fact, all I did was to
expand my field of interest. My first job was to determine the structure of
minerals, and the second job I did was to determine the structure of an intermetallic compound – the first intermetallic compound to have its structure
determined. For about ten years, I worked on the structure of silicate minerals
and of various other inorganic compounds. That was one period.

Then I got interested in the structure of organic molecules and in another
technique. We built the first apparatus in the United States to determine the
structure of gas molecules by electron diffraction. A friend of mine, Hermann
Mark, in Germany was the man who built the first apparatus of this sort. I
began determining interatomic distances and applying quantum mechanics,
which I learned as one of the first people in the field in 1926 when I was in
Germany on a Guggenheim fellowship. All of this related to the question of
the nature of the chemical bond.

In the 1930s, I formulated several new ideas about chemical bonds. In
1935, the Rockefeller Foundation had been supporting my work on the crystal
structure of the sulfide minerals. They said to me, "You know, we're not really
interested in the sulfide minerals. We're interested in biological substances."
They had been giving me five thousand dollars a year. I thought, "What do I
know about biological materials? Not very much. Hemoglobin, red cells in the
blood, molecular weight about 68,000, that has four iron atoms in it. Iron
compounds often are paramagnetic. Why don't I apply to the Rockefeller
Foundation and suggest that I measure the magnetic susceptibility of hemoglobin and hemoglobin derivatives?" I did, and they gave me fifty thousand
dollars. This shows that these fellows in the big foundations can influence
activities of scientists.

We measured the magnetic susceptibility of blood. Venous blood turned
out to be paramagnetic, and arterial blood was diamagnetic, meaning repelled
by a magnet. Careful measurements of this sort gave astonishing information
about the structure of the hemoglobin molecule. Then I thought, "Well, what
about the rest of the hemoglobin molecule? There are four iron atoms and
9,996 other atoms. What are they doing? I had better work on the structure of
proteins." In 1936, I gave a talk at the Rockefeller Institute for Medical
Research about the magnetic properties of hemoglobin. A man named Karl
Landsteiner sent word to me, asking me to come to his laboratory to talk to
him. I did. He said he was making immunological studies – antibodies, anti-
toxins. He wanted to know if I could explain some of his observations. I
thought about them for four years and finally wrote a paper, and when the
second edition of his book came out there was a chapter by me on the molecular structure of antibodies.

I hadn't changed my course. I'd just gone on roads that diverged a little
from the ones I'd been going on.

Discussion

PARTICIPANT: Throughout your life, your independence of mind has been in strong evidence, and I wonder if you would talk to us about your ideas about how your early childhood may have influenced that characteristic?

LINUS PAULING: My father died when I was nine. There was some evidence that he was pretty interested in me. I don't remember much about it, but I have some evidence to that effect. I don't think my mother understood me very well. At any rate, she just didn't know anything about science or academic careers. I studied chemical engineering. It may be that this early period developed in me a sort of independence of thought and decision. I was never pugnacious. I was pretty retiring. It wasn't long, especially when I was in college, that I began to develop self-confidence, confidence in my own ideas. It showed up especially when I was a graduate student. The result was that when the first announcement was made that Guggenheim fellowships were available for people to go to Europe, I applied, and I was one of the first Guggenheim fellows.

PARTICIPANT: It is hard to imagine what it is like to get one Nobel prize. It is impossible for me to imagine what it is like to get two Nobel prizes. Would you tell us a little about what it is like? And not to have gotten the third one, which you should have gotten?

PAULING: I was pretty pleased when I received the Nobel Prize in Chemistry in 1954. I felt that I probably wasn't going to get the Nobel prize although people had suggested that I would. Back in 1931, the *New York Times* said that I would get the Nobel prize for my work on the nature of the chemical bond. I did not think I would get it. The statement by the Nobel Foundation is that the prize is given for the most important discovery made during the past year in the field of chemistry. I couldn't think of any discovery that I had made in one year that deserved the Nobel prize. They also went on to say that the Nobel prize is not given for the lifetime work of a scientist, no matter how important this lifetime work is. So I thought, "That leaves me out." But I had a high old time learning more about the chemical bond and felt myself to be a lucky fellow whether I got the prize or not.

I got it. I think they stretched these regulations somewhat, because the prize said "for his research on the nature of the chemical bond and its application to the elucidation of the structure of complex substances." I published perhaps 250 papers between 1927 and 1953 on the nature of the chemical bond and its application to the structure of complex substances. I thought, "I'm really pleased to have received this."

In 1963, I was notified that I had received the Nobel Peace Prize for 1962. Several reporters then asked, "Of these two Nobel prizes, which one do you value the more?" I said, "Well, I was happy to receive the Nobel Prize for Chemistry, but I had just been having a good time carrying out studies in the field of chemistry and trying to make discoveries. The Nobel Peace Prize is the one I value more because it means there is a feeling that I have been doing my duty to my fellow human beings. And perhaps it means that working for peace has become respectable. They won't take away my passport anymore or call me up before a congressional committee and threaten me with jail anymore. So it is the Nobel Peace Prize about which I feel happier."

The third Nobel prize for which I was nominated was for discovering molecular diseases, through discovering that sickle cell anemia is a disease of the hemoglobin molecule. That led to the development of the lively field of medicine dealing with molecular diseases of different kinds. It also led to my decision to tell Emile Zuckerkandl to get some blood from those anthropoids and other animals and check the amino acid composition of the hemoglobins. It also led to a lot of other results. People have said to me that if I hadn't received the Nobel Prize in Chemistry probably I would have received the Nobel Prize in Medicine for the discovery of molecular diseases. Perhaps so. But it doesn't bother me. Why should I discover everything? I'm satisfied.

PARTICIPANT: Nearly everyone is interested in cholesterol. What is the effect of vitamin C on cholesterol?

PAULING: Cholesterol is an orthomolecular substance, a term that I invented. It means "the right molecules." I said, the right molecules are those normally present in the human body—not drugs such as aspirin, but substances such as the vitamins and cholesterol that are normally present in the human body. Cholesterol is required for life. It is an important lipid in the human body, so important that an average person in his or her liver synthesizes four thousand milligrams every day. People who have high cholesterol have a high probability of developing cardiovascular disease. Everyone seems to agree that there is a good correlation between cholesterol level in the blood and cardiovascular disease. Most people follow the recommendation that if they have high cholesterol, they should stop eating eggs and meat. Eggs and meat are good food. There is a feedback mechanism that seems to operate more effectively in some people than others. If you have dietary cholesterol eating eggs and meat, the liver doesn't work so hard to produce cholesterol so that for some people the cholesterol level doesn't change, and for others it does go up somewhat. Cutting out these good foods — eggs and meat — is not the best way to control cholesterol.

I use another very effective method. My cholesterol level is 170 milligrams per deciliter. For people over sixty, that is considered the bottom end of the distribution curve. Dr. Emil Ginter in Czechoslovakia has reported on several studies he made on people with fairly high cholesterol levels (300 to 350) who are taking a gram of vitamin C per day. Ginter has written a book about this and published several papers reporting that, in his various studies, the cholesterol level drops by 50 milligrams per deciliter or even more when a gram of vitamin C is taken per day. Why? How does it come about? Well, vitamin C is not a coenzyme for any known enzyme system. All the other vitamins perform extremely important functions by combining with apoenzymes to form active enzymes in various enzyme systems of which we may have fifty thousand different ones in the human body.

Vitamin C has not been found to be a coenzyme for any enzyme system, but it takes part in many biochemical reactions. If you didn't have some way of getting rid of cholesterol but kept manufacturing four grams a day, pretty soon you would be nothing but cholesterol. Obviously there is a steady state that results in the cholesterol level in the blood, a steady state between the synthesis, or the obtaining by diet, and the destruction. The destruction is by way of converting cholesterol to bioacids, which are then introduced into the bile and the intestinal contents and finally excreted. Vitamin C speeds up the conversion of cholesterol to bioacids because these are hydroxylation reactions that require vitamin C. The more vitamin C you take, the faster you bleed off the cholesterol. It is like having a barrel. Water comes pouring in through a tap at the top and there is a bunghole. The water comes out of the bunghole and the level reaches a certain steady state level. If you make the bunghole twice as large, the steady state level drops, and that is what happens with cholesterol. The more vitamin C you take, the faster you convert cholesterol to bioacids and the lower the steady state level. Nobody has carried out a good study with five or 10 grams or the eighteen grams a day that I take, except this one study where my cholesterol level becomes 170 milligrams per deciliter. A high dose of vitamin C bleeds off the cholesterol and lowers the steady state cholesterol level.

Now what else happens? You push the bioacids into the intestinal contents, and as these intestinal contents go through the lower bowel, the bioacids are reabsorbed into the blood, taken to the liver, and converted back to cholesterol. This is why these health authorities who don't know the whole story say that you should have fiber in your diet. What does fiber do? Fiber is insoluble material. You take it and you excrete it. On the way, however, it increases the bulk of the fecal material and moves it along faster so that there is not so much time for the bioacids to be reabsorbed if you take fiber. Moreover, it increases the bulk in such a way that the ratio of area to volume is such that even with the same time for reabsorption, the amount reabsorbed is not so great. Instead of bothering to go on a high fiber diet, you can take enough vitamin C to have a laxative action and permit you to get rid of this waste material faster. There is no benefit to hauling it around for an extra twenty-four hours. Get rid of it faster and then the bioacids aren't reabsorbed into cholesterol. If you want to protect yourself against heart disease, cut down on your cholesterol by taking high vitamin C.

PARTICIPANT: I've heard about a dozen Nobel laureates in various fields, and read papers and books by many more. One thing that seems to set those of you who have been recipients apart is your wide-ranging curiosity and your willingness to explore ideas, not only within your domain but well beyond. I've only found one exception to that. One person said he had no interest and no willingness to talk about anything but his subject. That set him off as quite exceptional. This particular characteristic is not necessarily found in many distinguished scholars and scientists. I wonder if you would explore the hypothesis that it is a wide-ranging interest that leads individuals to great achievements that are recognized worldwide.

PAULING: Nobel laureates are far from uniform in their nature. I agree that there are a good number who have wide-ranging interests, and a good number of those are willing to talk about their interests. Others are not willing, and a few who are willing to talk say things that I disagree with thoroughly. Many of them have ideas that I agree with. I can give you an example of a rather exceptional Nobel laureate — Dirac, who died a couple of years ago in Florida where he had retired. He never said anything. Some Nobel laureates are very smart people who make discoveries and that is that. Dirac was a remarkable thinker who, while still an undergraduate at Cambridge, developed his ideas about quantum mechanics, and he never said anything. The last time I saw him was in Florida. I told him that he had been at our home in Pasadena in 1933 and had folded some paper in the form of a bird for our children. And he said, "I've never folded a paper bird in my life." I read his biography, which said that when he was in Japan, he learned how to fold paper into a sphere that could be filled with water and turned into a water bottle. Dirac was an extraordinary man.

Many Nobel laureates are extraordinary people. Some just got lucky by happening to make an observation. I had an undergraduate student named Carl Anderson when I was still a graduate student myself. When he and another boy were juniors, they were given the junior travel prize from the California Institute of Technology and spent six months in Europe. When they came back, Anderson was given a job as an assistant and set up a cloud chamber to study cosmic rays. One day he was looking at the photographs taken of his cloud chamber. He saw electron tracks curling because of a magnetic field, and others that looked like electron tracks but curved in the opposite direction. That would be a possible explanation.

The alternative explanation is that the electron has a positive charge instead of a negative one. Dirac had developed a theory of the electron according to which the electron would have negative energy values as well as positive energy values. He surmised that the negative levels were all filled with electrons, but you might have a hole and that the hole then would appear to have a positive charge. He said that this is the proton. Two or three years later, Carl Anderson was observing something that looked like an electron with the same mass as the negative electron but with a positive charge. He finally convinced himself that it was possible that this really was perhaps Dirac's hole, and that there wasn't any special interaction that would change its mass — that it was the positive electron.

He discovered the positron and received the Nobel prize for this discovery. This was an accidental discovery. He hadn't been looking for the positive electron. Many discoveries are made when someone says, "Why don't I just go ahead and work with perhaps a new technique and see what turns up?" That is one way to learn about nature. In 1935, a student of mine asked me, "Dr. Pauling, how does one go about having good ideas?" I said, "You have a lot of ideas and throw away the bad ones."

PARTICIPANT: What are your comments on vitamin C in relationship to the common cold, cancer, and even AIDS?

PAULING: There is much evidence that a high dose of vitamin C has significant value in preventing cancer and in the treatment of cancer. Much of it has been obtained by Dr. Ewan Cameron when he was chief surgeon of Vale of Leven Hospital in Loch Lomonside, Scotland, out from Glasgow. He and I have collaborated for many years and have published several papers on why vitamin C should be effective to some extent against cancer and what the evidence is. We've written a book, *Cancer and Vitamin C.* I have a chapter in my book, *How to Live Longer and Feel Better*, about this evidence. There is strong evidence that patients with untreatable cancer who take high-dose vitamin C live far better lives and live longer. A few of them live on and on for years — untreatable, terminal cancer patients, about 10 percent taking 10 grams of vitamin C a day. With large doses taken orally, they survive longer. But we don't have good quantitative information about it. Dr. Morishige in Japan repeated the work and got the same results. The Mayo Clinic announced that it had repeated the work and found no value in vitamin C.

Dr. Cameron's patients first received 10 grams of vitamin C by intravenous infusion, and then 10 grams a day orally for the rest of their lives. With 10 grams by mouth, only about 5 grams get into the bloodstream, which is why intravenous infusion with the same amount is more valuable. The Mayo Clinic doctors didn't give the intravenous infusions. They studied patients with colorectal cancer. Although researchers said they gave the patients 10 grams a day, Dr. Cameron is a little skeptical because of the way in which the vitamin C was administered — twenty tablets. He thinks people wouldn't take twenty tablets. Cameron's patients took four tablespoons a day of a syrup he made up.

None of the Mayo Clinic patients died while getting the vitamin C. They got it for only two-and-a-half months. They began to die after it was stopped. The Mayo Clinic concluded that high-dose vitamin C has no value against advanced cancer. One might say that in the clinic's study, high-dose vitamin C apparently was found not to have value for patients with advanced colorectal cancer when it was given for only two-and-a-half months. There just isn't any evidence that what Dr. Cameron observed was wrong.

We strongly recommend that every patient with cancer take as much vitamin C by mouth as possible up to the bowel tolerance level, which for cancer patients usually is 30, 40, or 50 grams a day. But it takes pretty large amounts for a sick person to reach this bowel tolerance level. And we urge that it be taken as an adjunct to appropriate conventional therapy. Do not take it instead of surgery, if it's possible to extricate the cancer, or high-energy radiation, or chemotherapy, if it is a sort of cancer that has been shown definitely to respond to high-energy radiation or chemotherapy. Perhaps 10 percent of cancer patients are in this category. All of them ought to take high-dose vitamin C along with appropriate conventional therapy.

PARTICIPANT: You have dealt with physical matters and made many discoveries. I seem to remember that often scientific discoveries are born of some kind of intuition or even spiritual inspiration. Have you developed any personal hypothesis about how physical matters may or may not relate to intuition or spiritual matters?

PAULING: This is sort of a question about the origin of ideas. I know more about me having ideas than about anybody else having ideas. I sometimes say that I made more discoveries than the average theoretical physicist or chemist or other scientist because I think more about matters. I've also said that several times I've thought about a problem for many years, and then finally found the answer. When I started thinking about the problem, I trained my subconscious mind to keep this problem in view, and from then on, when a new idea entered my mind, my subconscious mind would ask, Does that relate to this problem or not? If it did, it would be brought into my consciousness.

In 1938, I met a physical chemist at Cornell University who had published a paper on hunches. He said he asked a hundred chemists if they had sudden inspirational ideas — hunches. Out of this total, he said a half dozen did not know what he was talking about. I think people differ from one another in this respect. I do not know how many scientists there are who attack problems the way I do.

I remember in 1952 when my son was a medical student at Harvard Medical School and I was a member of the Scientific Advisory Board of Massachusetts General Hospital, the board members were treated to a lecture by Professor Henry K. Beecher at the annual meeting. Beecher, a professor of anesthesiology, talked about new developments in anesthesiology. In the course of the talk, he said that xenon is a good anesthetic agent. Two operations had been carried out with success on humans with xenon as the anesthetic agent. That night I asked my son, "How can xenon be an anesthetic agent? It doesn't form any chemical compounds. If you put it in the human body, there won't be any chemical compounds formed by xenon. So how is it possible?" My son answered that he didn't know. Well, I didn't know either. For a week or two, before I would go to sleep I would ask myself, "How can xenon be an anesthetic agent?"

Seven years later, I was looking through the mail at my office and found a manuscript sent by a fellow at the University of Pittsburgh named Jeffrey, an X-ray crystallographer. The topic was the crystal structure of a hydrate of aminal ammonium chloride. While I was reading this paper (I like crystal structure papers), I suddenly sat up and said, "I understand anesthesia." After seven years, I finally understood why xenon is an anesthetic.

I knew because I had worked on hydrates. I knew that xenon formed hydrates. There is water in the brain. There are molecules with electrically charged side chains and ions such as chloride ions. There is a hydrate of methane, which forms at a certain temperature if you add xenon that stabilizes the hydrate so it forms a still higher temperature. What happens then is that consciousness and ephemeral memory consist of electric oscillations in the brain that are supported by the movement of the positively charged chains and the chloride ions here. When you add the anesthetic agent, the water molecules stabilize microcrystals of hydrates that entrap these electrically charged side chains and ions in such a way as to interfere with the electric oscillations that constitute consciousness in memory. So I worked hard on collecting information on anesthesia and then published my paper on "The Hydrate Microcrystal Theory of General Anesthesia."

PARTICIPANT: You have spent a great deal of your life being interested in the subject of peace. Can you recommend to our country or other countries a strategy that would help to eradicate the violence and war that seems to pervade our world?

PAULING: Yes, I can. A couple of years ago, the mayor of Hiroshima invited me to speak there on August 6th, Hiroshima Day. My wife and I went, and I gave a speech. I said, "It has been forty-one years since the end of the Second World War. The third world war has not taken place. If it ever happens, one hundred million people would be killed if it did not involve nuclear weapons and a billion if it did. The next war has not taken place because everyone recognizes it would be just insane to have a war between the United States and the Soviet Union. We can be glad that this great step has been taken toward the goal of a world without war. We can be happy about that.

"The United States and the Soviet Union cannot go to war. Why don't our leaders in these two countries recognize that? Circumstances demand that they get along with one another. What are they doing? They continue to waste increasing amounts of money on militarism — hundreds of billions of dollars, trillions over the years, wasted on militarism that is pretty meaningless. They ought to have the good sense to recognize what the situation is."

In my Nobel Peace Prize address, I said essentially that the nuclear stockpiles ought to be reduced from their present completely insane levels to somewhat more rational levels. Fifty-five thousand nuclear warheads exist in the world. The Second World War was a six-megaton war. Today, a war would be a twenty-thousand-megaton one. To what does that correspond? It means that if these weapons were to be used, it would equal three thousand Second

World Wars. Just insanity. More and more people and scientists have been saying that there is a good chance that the human race would be wiped out. Civilization would be destroyed. Why aren't they sensible enough to recognize that? Why waste more and more money on a sort of bluff by each of these two sides?

Something else worries me. The United States and the Soviet Union follow an immoral course by spending hundreds of millions of dollars to get young people in underdeveloped countries (such as Afghanistan and Nicaragua) to sacrifice their lives in war. The policies of these large nations foster wars in smaller countries; this is completely immoral. We make a lot of money by selling munitions to underdeveloped countries.

Twenty-five years ago, I read a speech by a member of the war department who was given a medal for his contributions. They consisted of selling fifteen billion dollars worth of munitions to other countries. In his speech, he said that with the proper amount of patriotism and devotion to duty it should be possible in ten years to be selling 150 billion dollars worth of munitions to these underdeveloped countries. What should be done? Make treaties. The Soviet Union has a good record, even better than the United States, in adhering to treaties. The Soviets are sticklers to the word. Treaties should be made. A change of attitude is needed to recognize that the United States and the Soviet Union should be cooperating to solve problems in the world. The problems of malnutrition, starvation, increased birth rate, and world population. Problems such as the destruction of the ozone layer need to be attacked.

I think the time will come. It may be that our country will take the lead in this move. It seems to me that Gorbachev has taken the lead during the past year. Of course, I would like to see our country taking the lead. I would like to see people speaking up in Congress saying that we must pass this bill because it is the moral thing to do.

Part II: Reflections

CHAPTER SIX

Joseph L. Henderson

A JUNGIAN PSYCHOLOGIST ON RELIGION

Joseph Henderson was born in 1903 in Elko, Nevada, where he grew up. After graduating from Princeton University with a degree in French literature, he began a writing career in the San Francisco Bay area. In 1928, he began a Jungian analysis. One of C. G. Jung's assistants, who was visiting in Carmel, California, urged Henderson to go to Switzerland to work with Jung himself. Henderson moved to Kusnacht in 1929 and worked with Jung intermittently for nine years. During this interval, Henderson moved to London to become a physician, graduating from St. Bartholomew's Medical School in 1938. While in England, he married Helena Cornford, whose mother was a distinguished poet and whose father was a famous professor of Greek philosophy and mythology at Cambridge University. Her great-grandfather was Charles Darwin.

The Hendersons moved to New York where he set up practice as a Jungian analyst. In New York, Jackson Pollock sought Henderson as an analyst. Because Pollock was so withdrawn, Henderson had Pollock paint his ideas and feelings, and the artist submitted sixty-eight drawings to Henderson.

In 1940, the Hendersons moved to San Francisco where he was a founder of the C. G. Jung Institute. A personal friendship grew between Henderson and Jung in Jung's later years, and in 1959, when Jung began writing *Man and His Symbols*, he invited Henderson to contribute a chapter on "Ancient Myths and Modern Man."

Henderson has published numerous articles on Jungian psychology, drama, mythology, American Indians, art, poetry, movies, and symbolism. His books include *The Wisdom of the Serpent: Myths of Death, Rebirth and Resurrection*; *Cultural Attitude in Psychological Perspective*; and *Shadow and Self: Selected Papers in Analytical Psychology*.

He is emeritus professor at Stanford University. In 1978, on his seventy-fifth birthday, he was honored by a book, *The Shaman from Elko* (Festshrift).

Symbolic Contents of
the Inner World of Imagery

I hope to demonstrate, even in this abridged form, the way in which the Jungian analyst may use mythology, religious history, and philosophy to amplify, by filling in the open spaces or lacunae of the patient's account of his or her dreams with meaningful content, which allows us to interpret the material more effectively.

As a psychologist, I do not ask what religion is or what it means in general, but rather why it is important to so many people and how it functions for them. William James first formulated, for me, what a psychologist can say about religion, as he did so well in *The Varieties of Religious Experience*.[1] This helped prepare the way for Carl Jung to arrive at a deeper formulation of religion as arising from an archetypal center he called the Self. Thanks to James, Jung was able to claim for his study the same spirit of pragmatic inquiry. He once said to me, "James really meant what he said," which told me something that has gradually unfolded over the years — that there is, or should be, a moral quality to this inquiry that transcends pure science.

What James and Jung had in common in this aspect of their work was a religious attitude, which never doubts that there is a spiritual world within the world of appearances. They had no use for blind faith, however, and felt that the experiences of this spiritual world should be tested, compared with discrimination, and evaluated affirmatively. The content of their investigations, however, diverged widely. Jung's main focus of interest lay in exposing symbolic contents of the inner world of imagery as a microcosm of religion. James had a more extroverted approach in revealing the significance of religious beliefs and behavior patterns as a sort of macrocosm. An example of James's method may be seen in his descriptions of a typical American pattern he called "the religion of healthy mindedness." We see this still today, not only in Christian Science but also in everyday life.

When my patients come for their appointments with me, I sometimes ask

---

[1]William James, *The Varieties of Religious Experience* (New York: Longman's Green, 1902).

them how they are. Nine times out of ten they say "fine," and then proceed to tell me how awful they feel. From a Jungian perspective this illustrates how we Americans tend to avoid looking at the shadow aspect of our ego ideals. In general, however, I think there is today a much better recognition of the shadow side of life than there was in James's day, or even in Jung's.

Harry Wilmer's symposium, "Understanding Evil," held here in Salado last fall, is a good example. He could not find room for all the people wishing to attend, and letters of appreciation came in afterward from many who did attend or who had read the account of it or seen the television coverage. This interest is a far cry from the religion of healthy mindedness because it affirms a need for recognition of the archetypal shadow as a kind of evil that is always potentially with us and is not just an absence of good. For Wilmer, as for those people brought together, a false cheerfulness or optimism that ignores the shadow side of life — whether personal or collective — is not healthy, but a balanced acceptance of evil along with good is healthy. It has taken a long time for this need to be met in our society. It has also become clearer that this balance can only be furthered by a different, more realistic religious attitude.

Such a religious attitude would seek to reconcile the opposites of euphoria and depression. In his essay "Confrontations of East and West in Religion," Joseph Campbell writes:

[T]o enjoy the world requires something more than mere good health and good spirits; for this world as we all now surely know is horrendous. "All life," said the Buddha, "is sorrowful . . . life consuming life: that is the essence of its being, which is forever a becoming . . ." and that is what one has to affirm in a knowing solemn stately dance of mystic bliss beyond pain of the god Shiva and his glorious world-goddess, Parvati. . . .

Hence Campbell concludes:

Those who think . . . that they know how the universe could have been better than it is, how it would have been if they had created it, without pain, without sorrow, without time, without life, are unfit for illumination. Or, those who think . . . "Let me first correct society, then get around to myself" are barred from even the outer gate of the mansion of God's peace. . . . So, if you really want to help this world, what you will have to teach is how to live in it. And that no one can do who has not learned how to live in it in the joyful sorrow or sorrowful joy of the knowledge of life as it is. . . .[2]

This is poetry, and we bow before its healing message, but psychology has to find more specific answers to these ultimate questions. I rely on dreams in my practice, and there is very little poetry in these unconscious products of the imagination. The very crudeness of the dream imagery, however, takes us to the basic problems we face in order to find more specific solutions. The psyche thinks in biological, earthy terms, not just in symbolism of a spiritual nature. So I am going to interpret a few dreams, using mythology merely as amplification.

The dreamer was a young doctor who had become successful in his career but with the sacrifice of much that could have made his life richer and happier. In one dream, he thought he had cut up a younger man and eaten the parts. In another dream, the same young man of his earlier dream became a woman, and a woman doctor told him that this woman who had been a man was a virgin. Then he dreamed that he saw a circular object in the sky three inches thick and a foot wide. It was opaque in the center while the periphery was of many colors merging together as the object spun.

In filling out the first dreams with personal associations, I found nothing particularly relevant beyond what this man already knew and had discussed with me. The imagery outlines a mythological pattern, however. I had found a version of this myth in a Hindu story told by Heinrich Zimmer and retold by Joseph Campbell that helped me to discover its inner meaning. This story is called "The Face of Glory." Zimmer tells us that a tyrant king, Jalandhara, sent a messenger demon, Rahu, to challenge and humble Shiva, the god of creation and destruction:

> At that time Shiva was on the point of abandoning his aloof and self-contemplative ascetic life to marry Parvati, the beautiful, moonlike daughter of the mountain king Himalya, the Lady of the Universe (Shakti). She had assumed this human birth in order to be reunited with the person of the God, her eternal Lord. . . .
>
> The challenge brought by the messenger, Rahu, was that Shiva should give up his shining jewel of a bride . . . and turn her over to the new master of existence, the tyrant, Jalandhara.[3]

[2]Joseph Campbell, *Myths to Live By* (New York: Viking, 1972) pp. 102–104.
[3]Heinrich Zimmer, *Myths and Symbols in Indian Art and Civilization*, Bollingen Series VI (New York: Pantheon, 1946), pp. 175–180.

Joseph Campbell continues this narrative by saying:

> [W]hat Shiva did in reply was simply to open that mystic third eye in the middle of his forehead and from it a lightning bolt hit the earth, and there suddenly was a second demon, even larger than the first. He was a great lean thing with a lionlike head . . . and his nature was sheer hunger. . . . Shiva had now to guard and protect the first demon from the second. Which left the second, however, without meat to quell his hunger and in anguish he asked Shiva, "Whom, then, do I eat?" To which the god replied, "Well, let's see: why not eat yourself?"
>
> Commencing with his feet, teeth chomping away, that grim phenomenon came right on up through his own belly, on up through his chest and neck, until all that remained was a face. And the god, thereupon, was enchanted. For here at last was a perfect image of the monstrous thing that is life, which lives on itself. And to that sunlike mask, which was now all that was left of that lionlike vision of hunger, Shiva said, exulting, "I shall call you 'Face of Glory,' Krittimuka, and you shall shine above the doors of all my temples. No one who refuses to honor and worship you will ever come to knowledge of me."[4]

In the patient's dream, he is like Krittimuka who eats a young man, who in the identity of subject and object so common in dreams, is both his own innocent ego and its monstrous shadow aspect. The young doctor's ambition drives him with Jalandhara-like power to disregard everything else, neglects his feeling for life, and becomes, as it were, inhuman. The cure for this hubris is to be found in Shiva's injunction to consume himself as an ego-figure and enter into an as yet undefined state of selflessness. The myth fills out this empty space in the dream by indicating that some kind of evolutionary development is required as the demon eats himself from below upward until only head and face, representing higher consciousness (the Face of Glory), is left.

Now the body of the man who was cut up becomes, in the irrational dream imagery, a woman. Just as in the story of Jalandhara, Shiva, and the demons, the drama so far has been only a masculine affair. The dreamer then awakens to the idea of a feminine version or addition to the story. His masculine curiosity is kindled to explore the anima, as Jung has described the feminine aspect of a man's psyche. Men, especially young men, tend to project this image onto real women, where it finds its worldly home in mothers, lovers, or wives. There may be an awakening, though, to the knowledge that the feminine may be the vessel of spiritual life, like Parvati, the Moon Goddess whom

[4]Campbell, *Myths to Live By*, pp. 103–104.

Shiva loves as equal to himself, a bearer of the archetypal feminine. Our dreamer is told this woman is a virgin, which in the dream means she is symbolically intact and cannot be exploited by power-loving or desirous young men, or anyone else. It evidently takes a woman doctor (as the feminine aspect of his professional identity) to convince the masculine mind of my patient that this is so.

What symbolic meaning can we find in the succeeding dream image of the airborne disc? For a full amplification of this image I would single out Jung's monograph written in the late 1950s, called *Flying Saucers*.[5] In this study, he arrived at the conclusion that the UFO phenomenon was a collective representation, projected outward from an inner image of the Self. Such a projection occurs at times of stress and confusion when a compensatory image of wholeness seems necessary to recreate confidence. It may also have a religious significance as the vehicle for an experience of transcendence. The dimensions of this disc tell us something about this wholeness and its transcendent nature. Three is a number suggesting onward movement, whereas four is a number of stability. If we put movement and stability together, we get twelve, which is three fours representing a form of transcendent stability.

The circular shape of the disc is similar to what we noticed in the story of Shiva, where the third eye is his organ of spiritual power and wisdom (Isvara). In the tradition of the Kundalini Yoga, the spinning disc of all colors anticipates the chakra, *samsara*, or thousand-petaled lotus of supreme conscious enlightenment, as the bliss, but also the danger of unlimited ecstasy. The dreamer had also an association to the disc from a film he had seen called *The Serpent and the Rainbow*. The introduction of the serpent symbol further suggests the Kundalini serpent. The serpent is sinuous and frequently multicolored, but out of the earth. The rainbow is the spectrum of sunlight seen through moist air in sunlight, and we feel that it is a heavenly portent when seen, as it usually is, unexpectedly. The serpent as Kundalini is thought to reside in the body in the perineum and symbolically is the center of the root chakra. With suitable yogic exercises, it awakens and arises to the higher centers, as a guide for elevation to a transcendent experience. It remains a serpent that must return to its earthly place of origin. Hence the return journey to the source of self-awareness is just as important as the departure for a journey to the heights.

From this short dream series, we may now summarize our findings. The power of ego-consciousness is compensated for by self-discoveries of which the dreamer had no previous knowledge. At first, he is a destroyer, cutting up and eating a human body, and a willing bringer of death — but a death that

---

[5]C. W. Jung, *Flying Saucers*, Bollingen Series XX (Princeton, N.J.: Princeton University Press, 1964).

brings new life from a very primitive level. His dream acquaints him with the shadow aspect of life, as in the story of "The Face of Glory," which feeds on itself. A sudden transformation of values leads him to a revaluation of the feminine just as Parvati in the Indian myth comes to heal the severe self-sacrifice of the destroyer and offers herself to complement the masculine god with her own goddess power. Finally this points to a transcendent symbol beyond the opposites that promises some kind of spiritual initiation. As an analyst, I can vouch for the psychological reality of this process, but I cannot know the end result. The spiritual goal cannot be controlled or programmed, and I am the last to know whether it can be realized in later life. Yet experience has taught me to value the reality of the psychic process, whether the ideal goal is reached or not.

The question remains about the relation of religion and psychotherapy. Our amplification has been so fully represented by symbolism of the East that we might forget the equivalent symbolism in the West, especially the Christian tradition. The man whose dreams I have discussed started out with a very strong Christian orientation, so his moving into the East is compensatory to his cultural conditioning. He had many positive dreams with a Christian flavor that made me feel I had to learn a lot I did not know about early Christian origins.

Two books helped me that I can recommend for a good picture of where Jungian psychology stands today in understanding the Christian tradition. One of them is a book by Murray Stein called *Jung's Treatment of Christianity: The Psychotherapy of a Religious Tradition.*[6] He imagines that Jung took on Christianity as a suffering patient who needed his treatment. He describes the diagnosis, then the cure, and, in the end, sums it up by indicating where the patient is now, many years after Jung's death. In general, Jung felt that Christianity today lacked an adequate relation to the archetype of the feminine, and also an adequate representation of the shadow, or dark side of God, which used to be called the Devil. The image of the Trinity lacked a fourth person, and the inclusion of this hypothetical person would be made of the earth as feminine, replacing and redeeming what had been exiled from heaven as a fallen angel called Lucifer.

Murray Stein feels that the original form of Christianity's sickness has improved, and the prognosis is much better now with the inclusion of the feminine. Another thing that has improved the prognosis is recognition by the Catholic Church of science as an expression of a whole-earth principle to balance the principle of transcendence. Teilhard de Chardin and his followers have done a great deal in acquainting religious people with the contributions of

---

[6]Murray Stein, *Jung's Treatment of Christianity: The Psychotherapy of a Religious Tradition* (Wilmette, Ill.: Chiron Publications, 1985).

science that have forced upon us a new and different story of creation. So, many religious people who still profess belief in the Christian mystery can include the earth principle as a metaphor that fits in with our understanding of the Self as an all-embracing archetype of wholeness.

Another book I can recommend in the connection is Jacob Needleman's *Lost Christianity: A Journey of Discovery*.[7] Needleman is a professor of religious history at San Francisco State University. He went around asking a lot of church fathers if there had been some earlier Christian tradition of contemplative practices, similar to yoga practices in the East, that did not survive into modern times. He found a number of them who felt this was true. These particular men seemed to say, in different ways, much the same thing—that there was in the Christian tradition a form of meditation that kept its practitioners grounded at an intermediate center of psychic awareness so that they could avoid the extremes of mystical excitement above or the depression associated with fear of hellfire below.

Next, I would like to present a dream from another patient. His dreams also showed a symbolism of the feminine and of the Self. He was in his late thirties and had been in analysis a considerable time. He was one of those people who normally live close to the unconscious. One might think this state is pathological because it made him uncommunicative. This kind of introvert does not speak unless he or she has something terribly important to say. It is not that they cannot speak, but they cannot say anything they do not really feel, and I have learned to respect their reticence. When one accepts that they are basically sound, they will come out and express a great deal that is meaningful in an original form. They come up with most interesting images and thoughts.

From this type of patient and these types of dreams, I always feel as if I am learning a foreign language. This man said of his dream:

It is dusk and I am walking with an unknown woman along a trail. She wishes to show me something. As we proceed to the place she has in mind, I notice an occasional flower that emits a soft light. We begin to go underground somehow and the flowers become more numerous—each flower emitting the light of its color. Finally we reach what she wants to show me: many flower beds containing flowers of light of many colors. The underground chamber is lit by a marvelous light. Then saucer-shaped swirls of multicolored light appear. They are ten inches in diameter and hover in the air before me. An unknown woman standing near a window remarks, "They are appearing all over the world and will finally convince people of the existence of paranormal reality." I reach out and

---

[7]Jacob Needleman, *Lost Christianity* (San Francisco: Harper and Row, 1985).

touch one—it seems to be made of a fine substance. Then I notice a
wonderful fragrance and realize it comes from those light beams.

The experience reflected in this dream is immediate, calling upon all the
senses to receive it: sight, touch, smell. It is corporeal, yet spiritual in its
symbolism. Here we also have the circular discs, but what a difference between
them and the disc in the previous dream. Here the discs are no flying saucers.
They are products of nature. And who shows them to him? A woman,
unknown. The anima, as we have learned from Jung, is the image of an inner
feminine awareness that may mediate between a man and the unconscious,
where she may guide him to an awareness of the Self. This guidance is true
here, where she shows him an occasional flower that emits a soft light, and the
flowers become more numerous, each flower emitting the light of its color.
This distinction clearly indicates that each one is individual, reflecting the
essential meaning of the Self. It is no abstraction but rather something specific. This Self is something that knows its own ego or something in a person
that knows its relation to the Self. The paradox of Self is something that the
ego can explore and appreciate, but at the same time is so general that no one
can experience it directly, or know its intrinsic nature.

It seems to me that the dream speaks of an experience of individuation
that presents us with the possibility of knowing oneself well in all one's reactions to environment, but it is also deeply concerned with the universal. This
imagery has the quality of an interaction between ego and Self, so that each
has its place in this poetic atmosphere and its special kind of light. There could
not be a better demonstration of what the alchemists, following Paracelsus,
called the light of nature (*lumen naturae*). The saucer-shaped swirls 10 inches
in diameter suggest another ancient conception of wholeness, number 10 being
the Pythagorean *tetractis*. Such wholeness, representing a grounding effect of
the Self, is not found in the mundane world but rather on an introverted level
of awareness. From it, one gets a living sense of the validity of the alchemist's
way of seeing things, so different from the experience of revelation-from-
above in the Christian sense. Yet they speak to each other in the subtle language of individuation. What is above is also what is found below, as the
language of natural philosophy expressed it.

CHAPTER SEVEN

Anthony Stevens

A JUNGIAN PSYCHOLOGIST ON WAR

Anthony Stevens was born in Devon, England. He obtained his master's and medical degrees from Oxford University and was awarded a diploma in psychological medicine by the Royal College of Physicians. Stevens is a Jungian analyst, who is in private practice of psychiatry and analysis in London and Devon. He lectures extensively throughout Europe and America and is a member of the Independent Group of Analytical Psychologists in London.

He is concerned with the causes of war that begin in the minds of men and that are the most powerful challenge to human creativity in our need to understand and promote peace. Stevens maintains that Jungian analytical psychology contributes significantly to unraveling the paradox of the threat of nuclear war, the universality of war, and the ubiquitousness of belligerency. In his lectures and in his writing, he examines the unconscious determinants involved and their biological origins.

He has written many articles on diverse subjects. His first paper was titled "One of the Greatest Institooshuns: Notes on a Psychiatrist's Love Affair with Babies Centre Metera." Other articles range from "Thoughts on the Psychobiology of Religion and the Neurobiological Religious Experiences" to "Attachment and the Art of Staying in One Piece."

He is the author of the book *Archetypes: A Natural History of the Self* as well as *Withymead: A Jungian Community for the Healing Arts*. In 1989, he published *The Roots of War: A Jungian Perspective* and, in 1990, *On Jung*.

War and Creativity*

For those of us who will have lived out most of our life spans in the twentieth century, the history of two world wars (and the prospect of a third) has taught us what a profoundly destructive creature *Homo sapiens* is — great cities destroyed, millions of men, women, and children bombed, blasted, and burned to fulfill the political ambitions of their leaders. To our fin de siècle mentality, war appears a wholly futile, evil activity. Yet it continues to hang over us as a perpetual threat, a horrifying possibility, which we, no less than all the generations that have preceded us, seem powerless to escape.

So strong is our antipathy to war that it comes as a shock to realize that our shared repugnance is of relatively recent origin. In previous centuries, there was no shortage of philosophers, poets, and statesmen willing to extol the virtues of war, arguing that it prevented economic stagnation, promoted innovation, spread the gospel, and carried civilization to backward lands. "Just as the movement of the ocean prevents the corruption which would be the result of perpetual calm," wrote the philosopher G. W. F. Hegel, "so, by war, people escape the corruption which would be occasioned by perpetual peace." And Niccolo Machiavelli advised the Renaissance Prince that he "should have no other aim or target, nor take up any other thing for his study, but war and its organization and discipline."

It is not just the prospect of victory that has always attracted men but the activity itself, which is rich in possibilities for individuation. War brings out both the best and the worst in us. In so doing, it promotes our self-realization: it mobilizes our deepest resources of love, compassion, courage, cooperation, and self-sacrifice. It also releases our capacities for xenophobia, hate, brutality, sadism, destruction, and revenge. It seems that organization for a common goal brings its own deep satisfaction. Cooperation and collaboration, whether for a military operation, a team game, hunting, or clearing the bush, yields a powerful sense of belonging and importance within the group.

---

*This chapter is based on a lecture given by Anthony Stevens at the Institute for the Humanities at Salado on March, 1, 1987. The material presented here is explored in greater depth in his book, *The Roots of War: A Jungian Perspective* (New York: Paragon House Publishers, 1989).

Thus war puts us in a painful double bind. Although we hate it as brutal, cruel, and wantonly destructive, there is something seductive about it which, under certain circumstances, renders it difficult to resist. As a result, armed conflict has repeatedly and remorselessly afflicted every part of our planet where people have come into contact with one another—not only in recent times but also, in all probability, since our species came into existence.

It is one of the bitter paradoxes of human existence that people are never more ingenious than when planning and prosecuting a war. War is the activity *par excellence* in which people pool their creative powers in the service of destruction. This is not so astonishing as it might at first appear. Creativity is, after all, unimaginable without destructiveness. As Jung repeatedly pointed out, there has to be negativity in every situation if the positive is to seem desirable or possess meaning. The utopian prospect of eliminating from life all that is negative (such as war) and replacing it with all that is positive (such as peace) is doomed to failure because the principle of *enantiodromia* (which ensures that any tendency, if persisted in, will eventually go over to its opposite) will not be denied. One opposite can never be used to eliminate another. They will eternally coexist and complement one another—precisely because they *are* opposites. Whatever may be our conscious intentions in the matter, creation and destruction must forever serve one another.

The nineteenth-century French philosopher Pierre Joseph Proudhon believed that human beings have a direct, intuitive knowledge of war, because scarcely a generation passes in any nation without some experience of it. The statistics of history support this assumption: between 1500 B.C. and A.D. 1860 there were in the known world an average of thirteen years of war to every year of peace. In 1971, Dr. Maurice N. Walsh calculated that in the previous 150 years, the major nations of the world had gone to war on average once every twenty years—that is to say, once per generation.

There is little doubt that war, in some form or other, has always been a feature of human existence, and that it has been accompanied by a recurrent longing to live in a world at peace. Each generation has attempted to contain its warlike propensities with concordats, alliances, nonaggression pacts, and peace plans, but all have been equally unsuccessful in eradicating war. Between 1500 B.C. and A.D. 1860, more than eight thousand peace treaties were concluded. Each one of them was meant to remain in force forever. On average, they lasted two years. Far from creating peace, treaties simply indicate that hostilities have, for the time being, subsided. As the old Russian proverb says: "Eternal peace lasts only until next year."

War and peace stand at opposite ends of a continuum: they are both aspects of the same condition—namely, relations between groups of people. War is inconceivable without peace; peace inconceivable without war. As with light and darkness, hot and cold, noise and silence, *les extrèmes se touchent*. Thus history, both ancient and modern, demonstrates a regular alternation between periods of war and periods of peace. The yang of war and the yin of peace appear to represent fundamental forces at work that have proved, up to the present, to be inescapable.

How are we to understand, let alone explain, this profound yet terrible truth? Understand it we must, however. For if we fail to understand it, it seems unlikely that life as we know it on our planet will have anything but a bleak and ghastly future. Has Jungian psychology any insight to offer that may help us to understand war and thus enable us to save our species and our planet?

To many it must seem presumptuous that a Jungian analyst should give his attention to war, for it is a subject normally regarded as the exclusive preserve of military experts — historians and strategists, generals and politicians. However, when one examines what these authorities have to say, one becomes aware of three major shortcomings: they ignore the *unconscious*; they rely too heavily on rational explanations of group conduct; and they attach too little importance to human biology.

Can a Jungian approach do anything to rectify these deficiencies? I believe it can. There is in psychology a principle that should be dignified with the authority of a scientific law. It can be stated as follows: Whenever a phenomenon is found to be characteristic of all human communities — regardless of culture, race, or historical epoch — then it is an expression of an archetype of the collective unconscious. When one compares evidence from such diverse sources as analytical psychology, anthropology, archaeology, biology, endocrinology, ethnography, ethology, history, mythology, neurology, paleontology, and psychoanalysis, the conclusion is as inescapable as an *exocet* missile that our alternating capacity for warlike and peaceful behavior has its roots deep in the collective unconscious of our species.

Space does not permit me to provide more than a minute fraction of this evidence, but here are a few instances:

(1) Practitioners of all schools of depth psychology, who spend their lives working with relatively uncensored material emerging from the unconscious psyches of their patients, agree that aggression forms an essential part of the instinctive endowment of all human beings. Every page of Freud's *Civilization and Its Discontents* is informed with this conviction.[1]

(2) Anthropologists have reported the virtual universality of warlike behavior in human cultures everywhere. Surviving bands of hunter-gatherers who do not display warlike propensities are exceptional because they inhabit remote, inhospitable territories that no one

---

[1]Sigmund Freud, *Civilization and Its Discontents*, James Stracheg, ed. (New York: Norton, 1963).

wishes to take from them. They have consequently allowed their belligerent capacities to atrophy. As the cliché says, timid people tend to live at unfashionable addresses.

(3) Biologists who study the behavior of animals living freely in the wild—the so-called ethologists—have demonstrated that humans possess repertoires of threat, aggression, and appeasement behaviors that bear a close resemblance to similar behaviors in other primates, such as chimpanzees, baboons, and rhesus monkeys, among whom crude forms of warfare have been observed. Although existing monkeys and apes are not our direct ancestors, their social behavior is so rich in parallels to our own that it requires the dedicated blindness of a traditional behaviorist not to see that they share common evolutionary origins with human beings.

(4) Endocrinologists have revealed an association between states of aggression and raised levels of the hormones testosterone and noradrenaline in the blood. Submissive or appeasement behavior, on the other hand, is associated with raised levels of the corticosteroids.

(5) Neuroscientists have shown that centers exist in the limbic system of the brain that are responsible for aggressive states in animals and man, and that other centers exist in the cerebral cortex responsible for the control and inhibition of aggressive behavior.

When one pieces together these threads of evidence, it becomes apparent that our capacity for warfare is much older than history. Homo sapiens has, after all, existed for more than five hundred thousand years, yet history derives its data from only a wafer-thin layer of the recent past. If we are ever to understand what lies at the bottom of all wars, we have no choice but to adopt a perspective that includes our natural history as a species as well as our political history as civilized people. When we examine a phenomenon as universal and phylogenetically ancient as intergroup conflict, we must leave the parochial limitations of history and enter the immensity of biological time. When we do that, it begins to appear that the "causes" historians attribute to past wars are not really causes at all, but merely the triggers that set them off.

Conflict occurs because conflict is, and always has been, endemic in the human condition. Wherever human communities have existed, conflict has been generated both within and between them at all levels of intimacy. Cooperation is found also, to be sure, but conflict is cooperation's shadow. At the group level, conflict has always typified relations between communities, tribes, city-states, nations, and alliances right up to the present time. Wherever one looks, one sees evidence of the powerful human compulsion to polarize things into opposites, to make preferences between them, and to take sides.

When one examines conflict to discover its archetypal components, however, one comes up against a fundamental distinction between two kinds of conflict: within groups and between groups. This is not just peculiar to human beings. All social animals make a distinction, for example, between the sort of controlled aggression they use against their own kind, which rarely results in injury or death, and the more lethal aggression they use against outsiders and members of other species. We, of course, do the same. There is in Brazil a tribe called the Mundurucús, members of which make a distinction between themselves, whom they call "people," and the rest of the world's population, whom they call "pariwat." Pariwat rank as game: they are spoken of in exactly the same way as huntable animals.

Closer to home, there is a story about a little boy who asked a stranger where he came from. His father rebuked him gently, saying: "Never do that, son. If a man's from Texas, he'll tell you. If he's not, why embarrass him by asking?" As George Bernard Shaw observed, "Patriotism is your conviction that this country is superior to all other countries because you were born in it."

The Mundurucús are certainly not alone in their ethnocentric chauvinism. This propensity explains the universal distinction that all human communities make between murder (which is everywhere regarded as bad) and killing in warfare (which is regarded as heroic). Such basic distinctions are an expression of what Erik Erikson called *pseudospeciation*—the tendency for people to regard their own group as special and superior to all others, and to treat the members of other groups as if they belonged to another, "inferior" species. Pseudospeciation reflects a fundamental dichotomy at the heart of the social program that is genetically inscribed in the collective unconscious of our species. It is the "us" and "them" dichotomy.

A capacity to discriminate between friend and foe is clearly a factor of utmost importance for the survival of any social species. It is but an extension into adult life of the attachment to familiars and the wariness of strangers apparent in all human infants, regardless of the culture in which they are reared. Both these forms of behavior have an archetypal core. If the archetype at the core of attachment behavior is the mother, then the archetype at the core of xenophobic behavior is the shadow—the enemy, the evil intruder.

Both these archetypes are crucial to the understanding of war. Just as stranger wariness provides the paradigm for later suspicion and hostility directed toward the enemy, so the powerful attachment of the child to the parents provides the emotional basis for attachment to the group, the nation, and its leaders. We are, in fact, as leader-oriented as any other social primate, and this confers on leaders their extraordinary ability to recruit emotion and channel it collectively in favor of the in-group and in hostility to the enemy. Effective war leaders make skillful use of this mechanism on the principle that those whom you wish to attack you must first pseudospeciate. Hence, we had Hitler's character assassination of the Jews and the Slavs as *untermenschen* (subhumans), which was the necessary prelude to the Holocaust.

When any form of collective possession occurs, an archetype is bound to be at the bottom of it, and this is particularly true of war. Then the group and its leaders become carriers of the superego and, freed of individual guilt, people are able to do collectively what it would appall them to do alone. In the peaceful mode, it is hard to conceive of oneself in the grip of what Konrad Lorenz calls "militant enthusiasm," indulging in slaughter and destruction.[2] Such images become more accessible when the enemy is portrayed as a creature that is not human at all—a rattlesnake for which one feels instinctive fear and loathing. As devil incarnate, such an enemy is to be exterminated without remorse. Destroying the enemy becomes a high duty, a sacrament. War under these circumstances is regarded not only as just, but as holy.

That so many combat veterans suffered guilt and breakdown during and after the war in Vietnam is, I think, because this mechanism failed. Too many withstood possession by the archetypes of war both at home and at the front. Too many persisted in perceiving the North Vietnamese as human beings and not as "gooks" to be "wasted." Too many saw the war as morally unjustified. This view meant that they must bear individual responsibility for what they did, and the remorse and horror were intolerable.

What, then, are the archetypes of war?

The first and most crucial archetypal determinant of warlike behavior is our inherent propensity to make in-group/out-group distinctions so radical as to result in pseudospeciation. This behavior goes along with projection of the shadow onto members of the out-group, which is perceived as menacing. This behavior, in turn, is associated with the experience of xenophobia, paranoid distrust, and violent hostility.

The second, and hardly less important determinant, concerns masculine psychology—the bonding of young males for the purpose of aggressive activity. One anthropologist who has studied this phenomenon is Lionel Tiger of Rutgers University. He concluded that the very existence of any male group is prone to lead to an aggressive relationship between that group and the outside environment. Male bonding, he says, "is both a function and a cause of aggression and violence." The universal tendency of men to band together for the purpose of hunting and warfare is, he says, "an underlying biologically transmitted 'propensity' with roots in human evolutionary history." While Tiger acknowledges that this propensity finds a wide variety of cultural forms, he nevertheless insists that it is what he calls "an irreducible predetermined

---

[2]Konrad Lorenz, *On Aggression* (London: Methuem, 1966).

factor."[3] Now this "irreducible factor" is what Jung would have called an archetype of the collective unconscious.

I am not, of course, saying that these archetypes are perpetually active in us. They exist as latent potential. Most of the time, they lie sleeping in the unconscious waiting to be awakened. To mobilize for war, the archetypal system must be activated and released from moral inhibition. Otherwise the archetypes of war rest cold, blind, and immobile in the dark recesses of the mind, like nuclear warheads waiting in their silos.

Archetypes function as innate biases to learn certain modes of behavior rather than others. Male bonding for aggression is a good example of this, for such behavior is extremely easy to learn and virtually impossible to eradicate once it has been acquired—as penologists know only too well. In modern youth, the propensity to group aggression finds expression in dangerous sports and the violent acts of street gangs, football hooligans, Hell's Angels, and the like. It also can be detected in the kind of films in which the young take pleasure. Like the camera, the box office never lies. The success of Sylvester Stallone and Arnold Schwarzenegger has been founded on their glamorization of savage barbarians such as Rambo and Conan, whose elevating philosophy was summed up in the maxim, "Crush your enemies, see them driven before you and hear the lamentation of their women."

Such excesses are symptomatic of reaction against the antiwar movies of the post-Vietnam period and against the rising influence of feminist thinking. It is instructive that military depots responsible for the training of combat troops do all they can to repress the anima in recruits and strengthen the ego's identification with the masculine archetype in its phallic and aggressive aspects. Throughout military training, poor performance is equated with femininity, which is universally condemned as the antithesis of soldierly conduct. All that is done to recruits is designed to bring out that quintessentially masculine quality, toughness. As one military instructor declared, "Soldiers should be young and fit, rough and nasty, not powderpuffs."[4] This repression of the feminine is associated with the development of powerful feelings of loyalty to the male group. In this manner, a fundamental component of warrior psychology begins to crystallize out of the archetypal matrix provided by the recruits' collective unconscious.

The disagreeable fact is that indulgence in group violence is a means by which young males validate themselves as men. As Robin Fox, another Rutgers anthropologist, has put it, violence is "what men do." He says, "If you take a group of men and oppose them in some way to another group of men, the likelihood of their coming up with a violent way of distinguishing them-

[3] Lionel Tiger, *Men in Groups* (New York: Random House, 1971).
[4] John Hockey, *Squaddies* (Exeter, England: Exeter University Publications, 1986).

selves one from the other, and of organizing themselves internally, is very high.
. . . If a violent solution is not sought, it is usually because of a threat of even greater violence from some other source."[5]

Why should this be? And how have the archetypal inducements to masculine belligerency come into being? That we should be the aggressive, potentially violent creatures we are is not surprising. The ethologists have shown that aggressive behavior occurs throughout the animal kingdom and is as vital to the survival of each species as sex. Aggression is responsible for spreading populations out over the habitat available to them so as to give large numbers access to such valuable resources as territory, water, and food. Aggressive competition within populations ensures the emergence of leaders to maintain group discipline and to make strategic decisions. It is also the aggressive, more dominant males who have the pick of the most desirable females and who sire the next generation, thus passing on genes that are selectively advantageous for the continued survival of the population. Success in the collaborative, aggressive male pursuits of hunting and warfare has thus selected those genes in the human genetic structure that make such behavior so readily available to our species.

The likelihood is that our hominid ancestors learned very early that cooperation within groups is indispensable for defense, hunting, and attack. To begin with, the most dangerous threat came from predators such as lions and leopards, but later on, as our brains grew in size and complexity, as our capacity to seek and cooperate improved, together with our ability to use flint and wooden weapons, the major source of threat came not from predators but increasingly from other hominid groups competing for the same vital resources.

So it seems probable that our capacities to collaborate with members of our own group evolved along with our capacities to hunt and make war. The widespread use of violence between human groups would not have come into being had it not contributed to the survival of the species. Had it been maladaptive, it or the species would have disappeared.

In theory, war could be waged without use of weapons, but in practice it is unlikely that it ever has been. Naked men are poorly equipped for the activities of attack and defense. In comparison with most other predators — the great cats, for example — man's teeth and jaws, his toenails and fingernails, and his capacity for sudden, murderous bursts of energy are not impressive. Lacking the physical structures necessary to wound and kill, man has, as a consequence, had to use his intelligence to compensate for his anatomical deficiencies by developing weapons and the use of collaborative strategies and

---

[5]Robin Fox, "The Violent Imagination," in Peter Marsh and Anne Campbell, eds., *Aggression and Violence* (Oxford, England: Basil Blackwell, 1982).

tactics. To protect himself from carnivores and compete with them for prey, he had to make himself as deadly as they. Human survival and later mastery of the planet has depended upon male cooperation in the development and use of weapons.

One of the great pleasures of life is making things and taking pains to make them as well and as beautifully as one can, whether the object is a garment, a necklace, a pot, a ploughshare, or a weapon. There has probably never been a time when weapons and their manufacture have not been a source of fascination and delight to men. Stone cleavers, knives, and lanceheads of flint, quartz, and serpentine have been collected from Paleolithic sites all over the world, as have knives made from bone and, in northern Europe, from reindeer horn.

The Bronze Age brought marked technological advances. Bronze weapons were stronger, harder, sharper, and longer than their Stone Age equivalents.

Inevitably, the development of offensive weapons was balanced by the development of weapons of defense, the earliest of which (probably made of leather, wood, or fiber) have disappeared. But numerous defensive weapons have survived from the Bronze Age—bronze helmets, cuirasses, arm guards, fingerstalls, and bronze shields. Later use of iron permitted further improvements in the manufacture of all weapons, and warfare began to take on the lethally destructive quality characteristic of modern times.

As offensive weapons have increased their range and destructive power, so defensive weapons have been created to counteract them—and vice versa. These developments have occurred cyclically and in accordance with the principles of homeostasis, operating under the influence of the archetypal systems that govern hostility, defense, and attack. The war historian H. H. Turney-High (1971) refers to this as "the offense-defense inventive cycle."[6]

> Should the aggressor put his sharpened stone on a stick, he has a spear which not only will increase the leverage of his man-piercing tool, but will enable him to stand at a safer distance and poke his foe. This spear may also be hurled. Better yet, it may be hurled with a bow as an arrow, the deadliest weapon man was to know until late in the so-called Renaissance. If the aggressor seeks protection by retiring to a safe distance, the range of the arrow (or cannon or airplane) must be increased, while if he stands in a hole, the spear must then be made stronger to rout him out of his rudimentary engineering work.

[6]H. H. Turney-High, *Primitive War: Its Practice and Concepts* (Columbia, S. C. : University of South Carolina Press, 1971).

In "the offense-defense inventive cycle," we see not only an early version of the contemporary arms race, but also a cultural superimposition on an ancient biological process, which underlies the whole story of evolution. The arms race began very early in the history of this planet. Five-hundred-and-ten million years ago, primitive fish started covering themselves with small bony scales of calcium phosphate to protect themselves from aggressive scorpionlike creatures which preyed on them.

Since man was a hunter before he became a warrior, his original weapons, strategies, and tactics were based on those of his competitors—the lion, tiger, and wolf—who were so much better equipped than he by nature. As a result, his weapons were improvised claws, horns, and tusks, and his tactics were mainly those of surprise from ambush or darkness, followed up by pounce and retreat. Only much later, with the arrival of civilization and professional armies, did complicated tactics involving mass charges and battles of maneuver become feasible and elaborate fortifications get built. Then fighting groups increased in size, discipline improved, engagements were prolonged and more determined, more destruction occurred, and more people were killed.

As society evolved, war thus became better organized and more bloody. The most significant changes arose from the development of agriculture and animal husbandry, which made possible the accumulation of surpluses, the founding of cities, the hierarchical organization of society, the training of large, disciplined armies, the conquest of new territories, the subjugation of whole peoples, the foundation of empires, and the emergence of "superpowers."

In this manner, war has contributed to the evolution of our brains and the development of civilization. One of the most extraordinary events in nature has been the rapid development in size of the hominid brain in the remarkably short time of two million to three million years. The impressive genetic changes necessary to achieve this development could only have occurred in response to powerful and unremitting selective pressures that penalized men with small brains and favored those with larger ones. Evidently what was being selected were those faculties that large cerebral hemispheres impart—intelligence, speech, the capacity for social organization, strategic planning, tool and weapon making, and a more differentiated conscious awareness that enabled men to respond creatively to changes in their circumstances—all of which are invaluable in collaborative hunting and warfare. Those with larger brains could therefore be expected to do better in the competitive struggle for existence than their smaller-brained contemporaries. More favored individuals would be more likely to survive and breed and to pass on selectively advantageous genes to their offspring.

Thus, in the primordial circumstances in which we evolved, our capacity for violent conflict was no threat to the species. On the contrary, it contributed to its success. Our present circumstances are very different. Our contemporary problems are directly due to the fact that through creative use of our ingenuity, we have fabricated a technological culture dangerously incompatible with our archetypal nature. Our instinctive endowment does not properly equip us to live with huge armies and thermonuclear bombs but rather with the intimate personal exchanges, the collaborative hunting, and the brief warlike skirmishes, which characterized what I have called the *archetypal society* of forty or fifty members in which our species has lived out the greater part of its existence.

What constitutes the present threat to our survival is not our ancient capacity for violent conflict but the terrifying weapons that our clever cerebral hemispheres have put into our hands. As Robin Fox points out, our Paleolithic nature continues to prompt us to behave as if great armies were skirmishing bands, as if intercontinental ballistic missiles were flint projectiles, and as if thermonuclear warfare were a raid against a neighboring tribe.[7] Our problem is that while we possess immense technological sophistication, we are still impelled by an unconscious instruction to perpetuate ourselves at the expense of all other species — including our own.

In Paleolithic times, war functioned as a homeostatic regulator. It served to keep the world's population of hunter-gatherers in check — that is to say, spread out over huge areas of the earth's surface, living in a state of balance with the supplies of nourishment provided by nature. There was war in the Garden of Eden, but this was the aeon of stability. It was what Australian aborigines call "the dream time" — the infinitely protracted period during which our species lived in unconscious harmony with "God's laws," being entirely dependent on what the Almighty thought fit to provide.

The serpent tempter changed all that. With what seems to have been a quantum leap in consciousness, we unraveled the mystery of sexual reproduction, not only in ourselves but also in animals and plants. With this knowledge, we turned Eden into a market garden, herding the animals, sowing and harvesting the crops, and using our creative ingenuity to distort in our own interest the delicate homeostatic balances of our environment. This manipulation extended, of course, to war.

Our modern problem with war derives directly from the fact that technology has wrecked the homeostatic system. Archetypes, which predate technology by such vast measures of time, operate homeostatically. Technology, on the other hand, operates through a highly organized abuse of homeostasis. Unless we intervene creatively to rectify this abuse, the probability is that nature will do it for us.

It has, therefore, become a matter of cosmic significance that we should apply our collective ingenuity to the task of bringing to consciousness those

---

[7]Robin Fox, "The Violent Imagination."

archetypal determinants that prompt us from time to time to abandon peace and embrace the state of war.

If Mars is the father of invention, Nature is the mistress of necessity. She has arranged for us the ultimate "Catch-22" that is going to test our inventive genius to a degree never before attempted. What she is saying to us, in effect, is this: "The life of every organism is determined by its archetypal nature. It is part of your archetypal nature to gang up together from time to time to destroy neighboring groups. But now you have thermonuclear weapons, and if you obey your archetypal nature, you will destroy Creation. What are you going to do?"

When one considers the biological precedents to this conundrum, the prospects are grim. The geological deposits of the world are a natural museum filled with the fossils of extinct species, many of which demonstrate the somber truth that selection for success in competition can ultimately prove self-defeating. The very success of the behavior selected can lead to the extinction of the species, for the simple reason that the competitive characteristics selected, while of advantage to certain groups, are not advantageous to the species as a whole. This is the situation in which our species has found itself since the atom bomb was dropped in Hiroshima in 1945. It is the story of Pandora's box, Frankenstein's monster, and the sorcerer's apprentice. What human ingenuity has unleashed, it does not, so far, know how to control.

For other species, the attainment of a similar evolutionary peak has resulted in extinction. Must our species necessarily suffer the same catastrophe? The only difference between us and them is that we are consciously aware of what is happening and possess the capacity to respond creatively to our predicament.

War, which has always been the brutal spur forcing onward the development of human consciousness, now drives us on to the ultimate challenge. The next few decades will determine whether or not we possess the creative wisdom to meet it.

CHAPTER EIGHT

Norman Sherry

A LITERARY BIOGRAPHER

Norman Sherry is the Mitchell Distinguished Professor of Literature at Trinity University, San Antonio, to which he was lured from the University of Lancaster in England where he was head of the department of English. He has been a Fellow at the Humanities Center in North Carolina, and a Research Fellow at the University College of London.

Sherry has served as a foreign correspondent and has lectured throughout the world. He has had an unusual and colorful career as author, traveler, literary sleuth, and scholar and has been the subject of in-depth interviews on BBC Television and in the London *Times*, *The Guardian* and the *Daily Telegraph*. He has been honored as a fellow of the Royal Society of Literature, England, and was a Guggenheim fellow from 1989 to 1990.

His forte is ferreting out information about writers, their lives and travels. For this purpose, he has followed their footsteps to Singapore, Haiti, Paraguay, Argentina, Liberia, Sierra Leone, and Zaire.

He has published articles and reviews in numerous journals and periodicals including *Modern Philology*, *Notes & Queries*, *Review of English Literature*, *Modern Language Review*, the *Guardian*, and *The Academic American Encyclopedia*. He has published books on Jane Austen and Charlotte and Emily Brontë, and is considered an authority on Joseph Conrad. His books about Conrad include *Conrad's Eastern World*, *Conrad's Western World*, *Conrad and His World*, *Conrad: The Critical Heritage*, and *Conrad in Conference*.

Sherry's current research is on Graham Greene. In 1989, he published *The Life of Graham Greene, Volume One: 1904–1939*, and he is currently at work on the second volume of the biography, which will cover the years 1940 to 1990.

Norman Sherry is listed in the 1989 *Debrett's Distinguished People of Today*.

Confessions of a Literary Detective:
Following in the Footsteps of Joseph Conrad
in the Far East and Africa

My career as a literary detective began accidentally and without due deliberation. I simply grew into the part. I had decided after graduating to write the life of Joseph Conrad on no better grounds than that I had admired his work above all others. Alas, I discovered his life had been written very effectively by Jocelyn Baines. It was in that moment of despair, thinking I had lost my subject, that I was struck by a wonderful idea. I would take studies out of the study; I'd refuse to be cabined and confined in a room, but would seek to study the author of my choice on location. I would follow my hero's footsteps and wherever Conrad had traveled eighty years previously, so would I. In this way, I hoped to be more meticulous than other Conrad scholars — and there had been so many. I would go over the ground physically. My investigation would be wider, and I'd see what fish I caught in my nice new net. I had few prospects, no money, and only a passionate concern for Conrad to lead me on. I did not know that the steps I took then would turn me into a kind of wandering Jew, a scholar gypsy.

And so I went to the Far East in the 1960s, because that was where Conrad began his career as a sailor in the 1880s. I landed myself a post as a junior lecturer at the University of Singapore. I had begun to follow the exotic trail of a strange foreign figure of mysterious origin and untold experiences, with a strong foreign accent and a wild Polish temperament obscured by the dress and monocle of an English country gentleman.

Literary detection, the following in the steps of a famous writer, is like a fever — it gets in the blood and rages. You become an intrigued observer, tracing the relationship between fact and fiction, and it exerts a kind of magic on you.

Singapore was the port Conrad had sailed in and out of for some months during the 1880s. I intended to establish in detail his connection with it. The city is one degree from the equator, hot and humid and thriving. Picture me sweating my way through the streets and along the quays, harbors, and docks of Singapore with the works of Conrad in one hand. I became a frequenter of lofty, big, cool, white rooms inhabited by clerks. There were ceiling fans

113

instead of the punkahs of Conrad's day, but the "screened light of day" still "glowed serenely." More importantly, I was given access (with various degrees of willingness) to old records that had withstood the hazards of humidity, silverfish, and the Japanese invasion.

I remember particularly Mr. Kwek of the Straits Times Library. His calm did not allow him to quail at the sight of me, but he would greet me always with sad tidings: "I am sorry for you. The newspaper file for 1889, it cannot be touched. It is crumbling away to dust, man!" or "I am sorry for you. The file for 1878, I cannot find it and you cannot read it." In the end, he took the advice of the Chinese proverb: "Of the thirty-six ways of avoiding your enemy, running away is the best," and disappeared, leaving my persistence to be handled by a lesser man who could appeal to Kwek's absence.

At the same time, I was calling regularly at the Indonesian embassy on Orchard Street, for I wanted permission to travel to the island of Borneo and visit a small inland port that Conrad visited and to which he returned constantly in his fiction. That was a journey I never made, for I could not persuade the Indonesian diplomats that Conrad had been dead for many years. They wanted to know what letters this man Conrad was writing me from Borneo! I did not know then that President Sukarno was preparing, in the area in which I was interested, an invasion of Malaysia. Thus, they found my persistent interest in the area politically disturbing. Ultimately, though, from Australian intelligence, I did get a photograph of that little village upstream.

In spite of difficulties, I persisted and continued my ghostly experience under the blazing tropical sun, walking the midday streets of contemporary Singapore—streets Conrad had known—and visiting buildings he had frequented. Old routes, half-hidden, would stand out in relief, and modern Singapore became a faint background. Much of the city then, in its appearance and spirit, Conrad would still have recognized. He described the "swarm of brown and yellow humanity filling the streets," "the shops of Chinamen yawning like cavernous lairs," "the heaps of nondescript merchandise overflowing from the long range of arcades," "the long sweep of the quay," the ships "like toys with the eternal serenity of the Eastern sky," the Singapore river "where native craft lie moored in clusters . . . the mass of praus, coasting boats, and sampans that, jammed up together, lay covered with mats." Each one, in my day and Conrad's, had a wicked eye painted on the side to ward off the evil spirits of the deep. Today, alas, the colonial world has drifted off. Only the names of streets in Singapore have survived to remind us of that bygone age.

I was looking particularly for the source of one hero, Lord Jim, in Conrad's novel of the same name published in 1900. The hero there, unlike Hamlet, acted first and analyzed his feelings afterward. For me, it was "The Case of the Man Who Jumped Ship," for Jim, if you remember, jumped ship, leaving more than 800 Muslim pilgrims on board to their fate. I had a strong belief that Jim and his story were based upon an actual man and event of which Conrad had known. Conrad himself insisted that he was not a facile inventor—that he could not sustain a telling lie—and confessed in his preface to *Lord Jim* that he had seen the original of Jim: "One sunny morning in the commonplace surroundings of an eastern roadstead, I saw his form pass by—appealing—significant—under a cloud." The details of Jim and his experiences given in the novel have the ring of authenticity: we learn that he is a ship chandler's water clerk, originally came from a parsonage, and was one of five sons. After a course of light holiday reading, his vocation for the sea had declared itself, and he was sent to a "training-ship for officers of the mercantile marine." Later he took a berth as chief mate on a pilgrim ship—the *Patna,* which, "eaten up with rust and worse than a condemned water tank," was engaged in carrying Muslim pilgrims from the "Eastern port" to Mecca. During Jim's first voyage, she was mysteriously crippled and consequently abandoned by her captain and European officers, including Jim, who left the pilgrims on board to their doom, believing that the ship was sinking and knowing there were not enough boats. The captain reported that the ship had been lost, unaware that she had already been towed into port by another ship, crippled but still afloat. So the European officers need not have abandoned their ship. They could have abided by the code of the sea. It was a supreme example, says Conrad, of the "tremendous disdain of the dark powers."

Jim alone of the officers was troubled by the desertion. Looking Marlow, the narrator of Conrad's story, straight in the eye, he asked, dismayed, "I had jumped—hadn't I? That's what I had to live down."

As a sleuth, the questions I wanted answered were, In which eastern roadsteads did Conrad see Lord Jim? Had the original "Jim" served on a pilgrim ship deserted by its European officers? Had one of them returned to some eastern port and become a water clerk for the ship chandler's firm? In the novel, Conrad referred to desertion of the *Patna,* "that scandal of the Eastern seas that would not die out." If this was so, could I find in the 1960s traces of the original scandal, should my surmise that it was based on actuality be true?

If there was indeed a scandal, why would Conrad take the risk of using an actual scandal and pass it off as purely a work of fiction? One obvious reason might be that if the scandal belonged to the Far East, eight thousand miles from England, Conrad could have relied on the fact that it would not be reported in England. In this I was wrong. Another reason might be that the scandal, if actual scandal it was, might have taken place long before Conrad came to write the novel. In this I was right.

So I began to look at old newspapers, actually going back to Singapore's earliest newspapers in 1818, reading them, day in and day out, until I reached the 1880s, the period during which Conrad himself first visited Singapore. Finally, after reading sixty years of newspapers—something like 22,000 of them—my quarry came into view. The story I found was just the kind of story that would have pleased Conrad, because it provided an extreme instance of a highly dramatic situation involving moral responsibilities in which men could be tested. In any case, the scandal I discovered dealt with the desertion by senior officers from a pilgrim ship, called in this instance not the *Patna* but the *Jeddah.*

The first report appeared in the *Singapore Daily Times* of August 1880. It reported the loss of the pilgrim ship *Jeddah*, owned by the Singapore Arab family of Alsagoff and commanded by Captain Clark. The ship had sailed from Singapore on July 17, 1880, for Aden with almost one thousand Muslim pilgrims aboard bound for Mecca and the holy pilgrimage. The report centered around telegrams — two of them — received one after the other. The first, dated Aden, August 10, read:

> To Alsagoff, Singapore
> Aden 10 August 8.20 p.m.
> *Jeddah* foundered. Self, wife, Syed Omar, 16 others saved.
> Signed Clark

The second was dated Aden, August 11, and read:

> To Alsagoff, Singpore. Aden 11 August 9.15 p.m.
> *Antenor* towed down here the *Jeddah* full of water. All
> life saved, now in charge of Government.

Here was the scandal of the eastern seas that would not die out. As Conrad wrote, "that mysterious cable message from Aden that started them all cackling. For a couple of weeks or more . . . the whole waterside talked of nothing else . . . and every . . . loafer in the town came in for a harvest of drinks over this affair; you heard of it in the harbour office, at the ship-broker's, at your agents, from whites, from natives, from half-castes, from the very boatmen squatting half-naked on the stone steps as you went up."

Certainly, the incident set the whole of Singapore talking. On September 13, the *Singapore Straits Times* reported: "Public excitement has risen to fever heat in surveying the conduct of Captain Clark, who is well known here, and his officers and Engineers in deserting the SS *Jeddah*." In another column, I found this leading actor in the drama stepping onto the Singapore stage: "The fame of Captain Clark, who, we believe, is realising his property here with the object of leaving for England, has preceded him." So also had the fame of the chief officer of the *Jeddah,* a man called A. P. Williams, whose arrival in Singapore on the SS *Naples* on September 15, was also reported in the local press.

This scandal was not the property of the East alone, however. There were vivid accounts to be read, I discovered, in the great English dailies of the time, *The Globe*, the *Daily Chronicle*, *The Times,* and the *Daily News.* Indeed, *The Globe* published its first report with the headlines: DREADFUL DISASTER AT SEA —

LOSS OF NEARLY 1000, to be followed the next day by the news that the *Jeddah* had been towed into Aden. It was a scandal of immense proportions. The *Daily Chronicle* began its report with the words,

> That she should thus have been abandoned and her living freight left to their fate is one of the most dastardly circumstances we have ever heard of in connection with the perils of the deep. . . . It is to be feared that pilgrim ships are officered by unprincipled and cowardly men who disgrace the traditions of seamanship."

Something of the hope that Englishmen abroad are honorable comes out in the next sentence: "We sincerely trust that no Englishman was amongst the boatload of cowards who left the *Jeddah* and her thousand passengers to shift for themselves."

The sad fact was, however, that Captain Clark was British and so was the first officer, A. P. Williams. Although both returned to Singapore, only Williams stayed. In the novel, the captain (Conrad makes him an unspeakable German) leaves for America, "departed, disappeared, vanished, absconded" promising, "I vill an Amerigan citizen begome." Clark, I discovered, finished up in New Zealand, after a short time returned as master, served honorably, and saved lives at sea on two occasions. This, I suppose, was his way of dealing with the scandal and the charge of cowardice.

What of A. P. Williams? He fascinated me, for I felt if anyone was the source for Lord Jim, it must be Williams. He returned to Singapore—that I knew—and, like Lord Jim, had been mate on a pilgrim ship, involved in a similar scandal in life like the one described in the novel. But the questions I had to have answered were, Did Williams stay in Singapore, that tiny island where gossip would continue to surround him? If he did, did he get a job as a water clerk, like Lord Jim in the novel? Did he, again like Lord Jim, come originally from a parsonage? Was he one of five sons and had he been trained in a ship for officers of the mercantile marine?

More questions arose and demanded answers. How could I find out about Williams living in Singapore eighty years before my arrival there? How could I carry out such research in that hot little state of Singapore? Did Williams live and die in Singapore or leave soon after Captain Clark to escape the censure of his fellow men? If he returned home, would this scandal perhaps have penetrated even into his father's parsonage, if indeed the original of Lord Jim had even been born in a parsonage? How could I begin? How could I make discoveries?

It seemed, then, that I was looking for the proverbial needle in a haystack, seeking one particular Englishman among an ocean of Asians. This last thought led me on. If he were English, and the English were the colonial masters then, wouldn't Williams have left some record? Should I not treat the novel's data as being based on fact until I found out otherwise? If he lived long in Singapore, he'd need a job. Parson's son or not, he might even have taken — because the scandal would keep him away from the sea at least in the immediate future — a menial job like a ship chandler's water clerk. For this job, as Conrad avers, he would need to have passed no exams, would merely need to have "ability in the abstract."

Thus I went to Raffles library and searched the Straits Directories, blue book after blue book until one day, A. P. Williams's name unexpectedly appeared. My first thought was that if he stayed on like Lord Jim, he could be my man. Williams, the directory told me, began working for the firm of McAlisters, of Battery Road, in 1883 — the year Conrad visited Singapore. McAlisters were and still are ship chandlers, and Williams was employed by them as a water clerk, which was Lord Jim's job exactly. He was almost certainly my man.

The firm of McAlisters stands now, as it did in Conrad's day, within sight of the blue sea-roads and the waterfront of Conrad's eastern port. At McAlisters, they were very willing to help but, alas, their records had been destroyed during the war. I met a Scotsman there who could go back as far as the 1920s (he had been at his post for more than forty years), but that was the limit.

"The only thing the Japanese didn't strip away," he told me, "is that old picture over there." The old photograph was of the firm's employees at one time. They were all lined up, looking like a football team or a school class — pig-tailed Chinese, turbanned Sikhs, dark Tamils, a sprinkling of Malays, and in the center, eight Europeans. Eight Europeans of different ages, but who were they? Was one of them, by any chance, A. P. Williams? Said the old Scotsman, "We would like to know ourselves who they are!"

As I say, McAlisters was very kind and allowed me to take the photograph away — although at that time I couldn't see what use it would be.

It seemed to me, loitering on the steps of the building with the full blast of the tropic sun upon me, that if Williams stayed in Singapore very long, there would likely be some landmark in his life officially recorded, such as a marriage. If Conrad were keeping to fact in his novel when he said Jim came from a parsonage, wouldn't he have married in the cathedral? It was in the shadowed porch of that white cathedral on the padang, the sea-roads only a stone's throw away, that I met a Eurasian woman to whom I explained my search for a family called Williams, the father sea-going once, but then a water clerk in the 1880s.

"I shan't tell you my age," she said, "but I knew a family called Williams. They were a large family, I remember. The father was dead when I knew them, but he had worked for McAlisters. Quite rich."

She became interested in my investigations, promising to help by making inquiries among the Eurasian population of Singapore. She told me that she believed two of Williams's sons were still living in the town, but I later discovered they had died some years previously.

But what of his marriage? I went into the cathedral to check the marriage register and discovered that in 1883, three years after the *Jeddah* scandal, Williams's marriage was recorded—he married at age thirty to a Miss Jane E. Robinson, when she was sixteen. Here also was his full name—Augustine Podmore Williams. Was it a coincidence that Conrad called the cook in *The Nigger of the Narcissus* "Podmore"?

I continued my search among the older citizens of Singapore, making some interesting friends as a result. An old Indian named Sumasamy who had once worked at the Harbour Office—the same Harbour Office visited by Conrad when he was given his first command of the barque *Otago*—was able to go back seventy years when he'd begun work there as a boy. I visited him in a hospital where he had been undergoing treatment for a cataract. He lay in a small, hot room. There was a chair in the room but it was not used by his wife who sat silently on her haunches in a corner, smiling charitably.

He recalled how, when a young man, he called on a friend of his in a Battery Road office of a ship chandler. I asked if it was McAlisters. No, it was Mr. Williams's own firm. Mr. Williams had come in while he was waiting—a big man, with a deep voice. A big man. He repeated this several times.

On another occasion, I met an old man near retirement age, an impeccable chief clerk of an impeccable legal firm. He talked to me about Williams one hot afternoon in his office. He had known him well—everybody did in those days.

"A big man, with a big voice, a kindly man," he said. "He married a very beautiful lady. A very well spoken man. A cultured English accent. He was a manager at McAlisters." The clerk knew nothing of Williams's early life.

Finally, while following up a search for another of Conrad's characters— Captain Lingard, that ubiquitous sea hero—I found an old lady (Miss Brooksbanks, granddaughter of Lingard) who also remembered Williams. She described him as "bluff, handsome, head in the air." She also remembered his home, his wife, and his family.

This emphasis on Williams's height recalled Conrad's description of Jim in the novel: "He was an inch, perhaps two, under six feet [in the original manuscript he is over six feet], powerfully built, and he advanced straight at you with a slight stoop of the shoulders, head forward, and a fixed from-under stare. . . . His voice was deep, loud, and his manner displayed a kind of dogged self-assertion which had nothing aggressive in it." Applying to the registrar of shipping in England, I received a copy of Williams's application for his mate's certificate and learned more about his life. I discovered that he had sailed, when in the Far East, on the *Vidar*, on which Conrad himself later sailed.

My hopes were turning into a fixed belief that Williams was the original character Conrad used to develop his hero Jim. The lives of the two men, Conrad and Williams, almost touched each other. Certainly, seaman stories of Williams and his scandal must have surfaced when Conrad first arrived in Singapore three years after the *Jeddah* scandal.

119

The next big step forward in my investigation came from the Eurasian lady of the cathedral. She had managed to secure for me the address of one of the Williams girls, now living in England! I wrote to her, explaining my mission, asking her to read the first chapter of *Lord Jim* and to compare Jim with her father. It was ironic that I had traveled from England to the Far East to seek out the source of Conrad's characters and the daughter of the source of one of Conrad's most significant heroes was living back in England.

How extraordinary that you should have written to me and how did you find me? I have read *Lord Jim* and it certainly does seem that reference is made to my Father and the description in Chapter 1 seems typical. From my recollection of him as a child, he was powerfully built, very tall and had a deep voice, though gentle at heart. My father was from a parsonage as mentioned in *Lord Jim* and as in *Lord Jim* was one of five sons. He was born at Porthleven, Cornwall, on 22 May 1852. I do not know when my father first came out to the East though it was very early in his life. He was sea-going at first, though no one in the family knows what ships he sailed on. We knew him only as a manager in a Department of McAlisters.

This letter proved that Conrad had known something of Williams's early life, that he was one of five sons and came from a parsonage.

So much for Williams's boyhood, early career as a seaman, short period as chief officer of the *Jeddah,* and life as a ship chandler's water clerk in an Eastern port. In all of these details, his life paralleled Lord Jim's. I have not been able to discover whether Williams, like Jim, was trained at nautical school or on a training ship, but in one of the photographs I obtained of him, he certainly appeared to be wearing a midshipman's uniform that might have been the uniform of an institution.

Yes, I did at last come face to face with my quarry through two photographs sent to me by A. P. Williams's niece who lived in Dunedin, New Zealand. I found her address by seeking out a copy of Williams's will. Not expecting to find Williams's niece alive, I wrote to the town clerk of Dunedin and he contacted her. This letter was only one of many thousands written in carrying out research of this kind, which resurrects the history of long forgotten men and women. With the aid of two photographs of Williams, and the one I had borrowed from the offices of McAlisters, I was able to spot Williams among the eight Europeans pictured there. I could trace the map of his existence from boyhood to past middle age.

In the first photograph, taken in the vicarage garden, he is a young man leaning against a chair, legs crossed casually, hands in pockets, looking firmly and a little suspiciously into the camera. He is certainly "clean-limbed, clean-faced, firm on his feet," and, given a few years more in age, he might well be the Lord Jim who turned away from the other deserters, looking "unconcerned and unapproachable as only the young can look."

The second shows him in his thirties, probably as Conrad knew him, with his wife, who is indeed beautiful. Again one notices his size, powerful build, and direct stare. In the McAlisters group he is older, stouter, worn, no longer upright, yet still facing the camera squarely. The characteristic pose remained in the firmness of his shoulders and the spread of his hands on his knees.

Two other aspects of Jim in the novel also seem characteristic of Williams and make me think Conrad had Williams's problems in mind. The first is the added disgrace brought on Jim because he is a gentleman. The idea of Jim as a gentleman is stressed in the novel. Captain Brierly, who wants Jim to cut the inquiry into the desertion and run, says, "Let him creep twenty feet underground and stay there!" because it's too shocking for a gentleman to face such publicity. Yet Jim insists on sticking it out. In a similar way, Williams, son of a parson, was a gentleman — a gentleman-seaman like Jim. His daughter told me that he carried a seal with his coat of arms on his watch chain.

The determination to stick it out was typical of Williams, returning to a Singapore awash with gossip, to a small, mercantile community in which he could not hope for anonymity and in which he took a humble job as water clerk, gradually establishing himself as prosperous citizen. Lord Jim did have his period of running from his reputation, but he did eventually work out his salvation in the jungles of Borneo. Williams's story is not the same as Conrad's hero at this point — perhaps it was even more heroic of him to stick it out in Singapore than it was for Jim to become a white rajah in a Malay kampong. Williams's house in Newton Road had survived to my day. It had great wooden verandahs around all four sides of the house, although in the 1970s it had become a dreary shop called the CCC Junk Store.

The story of the *Jeddah* stayed with Williams until his dying day. Determined to follow him through to the end, I eventually traced the registration of his death:

Died 1916, April 17 Augustine Podmore Williams.
Aged 64. Master Mariner.
Buried 17 April 1916.
Cause of death: Bulbar Paralysis.

Following this discovery, I was able to find the newspaper obituaries written on the occasion. They revealed that Williams stayed with McAlisters for twenty-seven years and founded his own business three years before he died. One also stated: "The late Mr. Williams was chief officer of the Singapore Steamship Co.'s *Jeddah*, a pilgrim ship which met with an accident in the Red Sea and was abandoned with about 1000 coolies on board." Thus the scandal plagued him even beyond the grave. In his will, Williams stated, "I desire that my funeral should be quiet, cheap and simple and no fuss made about it." After many days searching, I discovered that he was buried in the Bidadari Cemetery. His headstone was engraved with an anchor indicating that he regarded himself as a seaman to the last, in spite of spending the last thirty-four years on land as a result of a scandal he never lived down.

This, then, was the end of my search, for I felt convinced that I had solved the case of the man who jumped ship. His life paralleled that of Conrad's Jim too closely, at too many points, for the parallels to be mere coincidences. Obviously, also, Conrad had done much more than simply see his "form pass by."

During February and April 1899, there appeared in *Blackwood's* magazine a story by a comparatively unknown writer titled, *Heart of Darkness*. It was hailed by many in its day, in particular by Edward Garnett in the *Academy and Literature* as "a most amazing, consummate piece of artistic diablerie—an analysis of the white man's morale when let loose from European restraint and planted down in the tropics as an 'emissary of light' armed to the teeth to make trade profits out of subject races."

Heart of Darkness certainly reveals the corruption of the Belgian exploitation of the Congo during the last century and also records a major traumatic experience in Conrad's life. Conrad himself said, "Before the Congo I was a perfect animal." The experience of human nature was an extremely disturbing one, and physically he was to suffer for the rest of his life from recurring malarial gout. We know that Conrad went out to Africa with high hopes. In 1890 he wrote:

If you only knew the devilish haste I had to make. From London to Brussels and back again to London! And then again I dashed full tilt to Brussels. . . . If you knew in what a universal cataclysm, in what a fantastic atmosphere of mixed shopping, business, and affecting scenes, I passed two whole weeks.

Conrad's desire to leave for the Congo was very great. Although the Belgian company wanted him, and he was to join the company as captain of a trading steamer, there was no vacancy. It looked as if Conrad, who desperately wished to visit the comparatively unknown and mysterious Africa, would not fulfill his boyhood desires. Then, quite suddenly, he obtained his post through the sudden death of the former captain of the river steamer. In his private letter to his cousin he writes jubilantly: "As far as my letters of instruction indicate I am destined to command a steamboat belonging to M. Delcommune's exploring party. I like this prospect very much, but I know nothing for certain as everything is to be kept secret." All this seemed to be true enough, but who was the man Conrad replaced? In *Heart of Darkness* we find this statement:

It appears that the Company had received news that one of their captains had been killed in a scuffle with the natives. This was my chance and it made me more anxious to go. It was only months and months afterwards when I made the attempt to recover what was left of the body, that I heard the original quarrel arose from a misunderstanding about some hens. Yes, two black hens. Fresleven—that was the fellow's name, a Dane—thought himself wronged somehow in the bargain, so he went ashore and started to hammer the chief of the village with a stick . . . he whacked the old nigger mercilessly, while a big crowd of his people watched him, thunderstruck, till some man—I was told the chief's son—in desperation at hearing the old chap yell, made a tentative jab with a spear at the white man and of course it went quite easy between the shoulder blades. Then the whole population cleared into the forest, expecting all kinds of calamities to happen, while, on the other hand, the steamer Fresleven commanded left also in a bad panic, in charge of the engineer, I believe.

I wrote to the trading concern (still surviving in Brussels) that employed Conrad to verify this story. They provided me with the death certificate of the captain. His name was Freiesleben (not Fresleven), and he was assassinated at the age of 29, at Tchumbiri, on January 29, 1890.

Captain Marlow, narrator of the tale in *Heart of Darkness* but fashioned closely upon experiences and sensations of Conrad himself, goes on to say: "Afterwards nobody seemed to trouble much about Fresleven's remains, till I got out and stepped into his shoes. I couldn't let it rest though; but when an opportunity offered at last to meet my predecessor, the grass growing through his ribs was tall enough to hide his bones. They were all there."

Now we have here an incident—an actual event—that demonstrates effectively the casual brutality of the area, the effect of the environment upon human nature that is one of Conrad's themes. The young captain, corrupted by the Congo, is involved in an argument over a trivial issue and is killed. Everyone clears out, and it is left to Marlow to show decency and bury the remains much later.

What, I asked myself, was the truth of the matter? Did Conrad attend to his predecessor in the way Marlow does in the story? It would be a remarkable example of the adage that truth is stranger than fiction if this turned out to be so.

My method was as follows. On the one hand, I began to write to Denmark to seafaring organizations, universities, and Congo specialists. On the other hand, I began to seek out in England and America dedicated men, especially missionaries, who had spent their lives in the Congo. Ultimately I landed up in the Baptist missionary headquarters in London, where for many weeks I pored over the diaries of one George Grenfell and found the following entry from 1890:

> Just as we were leaving [Bangala] the *Florida* came in with the news that on the 29th Captain Friesleden [sic] had been shot by the natives. . . . It is said that he was not dead when the engineer pushed off with full steam — being himself wounded, he would not go back with the crew and bring off the captain's body, or to retaliate.

Quite often it was impossible to read these diaries since the tropics and silverfish had eaten away vital parts, and the ink had faded, but the entry for March 4, 1890, had survived:

> *La Ballay* came in yesterday . . . with Lingenji on board comes in from Churbiri — he tells me that the Lisangi people fired on the *Ballay* two days ago — apparently they are taking up the palaver of the Bankanya people who killed Capt. Freerleban [sic] at the close of Jan. last. Lingenji says the murdered man is still unburied — his hands and feet have been cut off — his clothes taken away and his body covered in a native cloth.

You can see that this is very close to Conrad's experience. But did Conrad bury the dead man as his narrator Marlow does in the story? No, he did not. I discovered that Freiesleben (or what was left of him) had been buried in March, and Conrad didn't obtain his appointment to go to the Congo until May. But I discovered something else — a Captain Duhst. Duhst, a Danish seaman, had been detailed in March 1890 to find and bury Freiesleben's body. In his diary, Duhst records, "grass growing through the bones of the skeleton which lay where it had fallen." Apart from the fact that Conrad's language is more eloquent, it would seem that Duhst's plainer language, the language of a simple sailor, is an account of what he discovered when he first found and then buried Freiesleben.

How then did Conrad learn so much about Freiesleben? Did he know Captain Duhst? He did. Conrad left the Congo, after only six months' service, as a result of fever. In Duhst's journal is the remark: "Met captain Conrad. . . . He is continually sick with dysentery." Obviously, the information Conrad learned about Freiesleben from the man who *did* bury him was stored up in Conrad's mind, in spite of his sickness, and appeared ten years later in *Heart of Darkness.*

When Conrad arrived at Kinchassa, his next task was to travel a thousand miles up one of the longest rivers on earth to Stanley Falls, the place he calls in the story "the Inner Station." He left with the manager of the Kinchassa station, M. Camille Delcommune. They traveled in a steamer that Conrad variously describes as "tin-pot," "like an empty Huntley and Palmer biscuit tin," "a two-penny river steamboat with a penny whistle attached." Its name was the *Roi des Belges*. Conrad describes the journey in the story as follows:

> Going up that river was like travelling back to the earliest beginnings of the world, when vegetation rioted on the earth and the big trees were king. . . . Trees, trees, millions of trees, massive, immense, running up high; and at their foot crept the little begrimed steamboat, like a sluggish beetle crawling on the floor of a lofty portico. . . . The reaches opened before us and closed behind, as if the forest had stepped leisurely across the water to bar the way for our return. We penetrated deeper and deeper into the heart of darkness. It was very quiet there.

Finally they reach the Inner Station, and in the distance, Marlow, looking through binoculars, sees "the slope of a hill interspersed with rare trees and perfectly free from undergrowth. A long decaying building on the summit was half buried in the high grass. There was no enclosure but near the house half a dozen slim posts remained in a row, roughly trimmed, and with the upper ends ornamented with round carved balls."

Later, looking again, he discovered that the carved balls are "black, dried, sunken, with closed eyelids — a head that seemed to sleep at the top of that pole with shrunken dry lips showing a narrow white line of the teeth, was smiling continuously."

In 1924, the year of his death, Conrad wrote an article in which he describes his experiences on arriving at Stanley Falls Station:

> The subdued thundering mutter of the Stanley Falls hung in the heavy night air of the last navigable reach of the Upper Congo, while a great melancholy descended on me . . . there was no shadowy friend to stand by my side in the night of the enormous wilderness, no great haunting memory, but only the unholy recollection of a prosaic newspaper "stunt" and the distasteful knowledge of the vilest scramble for loot that ever disfigured the history of human conscience and geographical exploration.

It is at the Inner Station that Marlow meets the famous (and infamous) Mr. Kurtz who — although initially a man of wide gifts, an emissary of pity and progress, a man of high beliefs and principles — has yet been corrupted by the jungle and his experience of absolute power. Writing a civilized report on the Suppression of Savage Customs, he had suddenly scribbled across his report the words "Exterminate the brutes." The wilderness had found him out and taken a terrible vengeance. When Marlow meets him, he is very sick. He is

Norman Sherry

taken aboard the steamboat and Marlow describes his first view of him: "I could see the cage of his ribs all astir."

Was the original of Kurtz corrupted and were the skulls on poles at the Inner Station based on Conrad's experience of the Stanley Falls Station? I think not, for there came into my hands, finally, photographs of Stanley Falls Station contemporaneous with Conrad's visit there. It looks a tidy civilized station, at least photographically. Yet we know that one district commissioner at that station by the name of Rom had a pathway around his house made up entirely of skulls. All I could discover about the model for Kurtz was that he was reasonably civilized. Thus, Kurtz is not like his source. Many atrocities were committed by Belgians at this time, however, and in that area.

In the novel, the steamboat quickly returns downriver with the sick Mr. Kurtz on board. During the journey Kurtz dies, and Conrad describes his scapegoat hero's death as follows:

> One evening coming in with a candle I was startled to hear him say, "I am lying here in the dark waiting for death." The light was within a foot of his eyes. He cried in a whisper at some image, at some vision, he cried out twice, a cry that was no more than a breath "The Horror! The Horror!". . . I blew the candle out and left the cabin. The pilgrims were dining in the mess room and I took my place. . . . A continuous shower of small flies streamed upon the lamp. Suddenly the manager's boy put his insolent black head in the doorway and said in a tone of contempt, "Mistah Kurtz—he dead" . . . the next day the pilgrims buried something in a muddy hole.

Now, Kurtz was based on Georges Antoine Klein. He was in charge of the station at Stanley Falls; he was sick, and (as in the story) was compelled to leave his station. We know Conrad had Klein in mind since, in the manuscript of the story, Conrad has crossed out Klein and written above, Kurtz. If Kurtz is Klein, was Klein buried in the same way as Kurtz—in a muddy hole? I very much doubted this. No white man would have been buried in this way in the jungle. Much more likely he would have been buried at one of the many missionary stations found up and down the river Congo.

After a truly prodigious search, I contacted a missionary, Angus Macneil, living in the Congo in the 1960s and 1970s. He found for me an old woman—reputed to be then one hundred years old—who recalled the steamboat *Roi des Belges* coming downriver and reaching Chumbiri on September 21, 1890. Macneil, in his letter seventy-eight years after the burial of Klein, writes:

> the old woman remembered seeing Klein's burial and she was able to point out the place where the grave is. Originally the grave was left

unmarked. Around 1940 the Belgian authorities contacted the Mission and promised a small sum of money for its regular upkeep. Since that time and until 1960 (time of independence) the sum of 400 Congolese Francs were provided for the upkeep of the grave. There has been no grant since that date.

Who provided the upkeep for the grave? Could it have been the model for Kurtz's fiancée, to whom Captain Marlow lies about Kurtz's last words?

"The last word he pronounced was — your name." I heard a light sigh and then my heart stood still, stopped dead short by an exulting and terrible cry, but the cry of inconceivable triumph and of unspeakable pain. "I knew it — I was sure!" . . . She knew. She was sure.

I will never now know the source of the money used for the upkeep of Klein's grave, although I tried to discover it in Brussels without success. Yet I would like to think, and am romantic enough to believe, that Klein's fiancée married later on in life, but never forgot her lover buried deep in the Congo jungle — that she had children, that those children or their children's children, kept the torch of love burning, even in the second half of our desperate century.

CHAPTER NINE

Peter Ostwald

A PSYCHIATRIC BIOGRAPHER

Peter F. Ostwald is professor of psychiatry at Langley Porter Neuropsychiatric Institute of the University of California at San Francisco. His research centers on the use of speech, sound, and music in communicating emotions.

Born in Berlin, Ostwald moved to the United States at the age of nine. He has played the violin since childhood, and while a medical student at the University of California, he won two scholarships for advanced study at the Music Academy of the West. He is the leader of a string quartet and has played in several orchestras, including the San Francisco Chamber Orchestra and the Santa Rosa Symphony. He received his M.D. from the University of California at San Francisco and his psychiatric training at the Payne Whitney Clinic of Cornell Medical Center in New York.

Ostwald is the founder and medical director of the Health Program for Performing Artists at the University of California in San Francisco, a diagnostic and treatment center for musicians, dancers, actors, and other performers. In 1987, he appeared on television on ABC's "20/20" program "Performing Arts Medicine." He is the author of four books: *Soundmaking — The Acoustic Communication of Emotion*; *The Semiotics of Human Sound*; *Communication and Social Interaction*; and a biography, *Schumann: The Inner Voices of a Musical Genius*, which won the ASCAP Deems Taylor Award in 1986.

Life and Music of Robert Schumann: On Keeping Music and Musicians Alive and Well

Here we are close to the end of the twentieth century. What happens when people get to the end of a century? They look back to the preceding century. It makes one more aware of the many differences between centuries and the incredible developments that have taken place through the passage of time. We can learn many lessons from the mistakes that were made in the nineteenth century. It was a century during which much beautiful music was composed in Europe while a great many important social and political developments were taking place on the American continent.

Robert Schumann, one of Europe's most important musicians, was born in 1810 when Texas was still a Spanish colony. In 1836, when Schumann was twenty-six years old and composing beautiful music, Texas declared its independence. Schumann never visited the United States, as did some of the other famous musicians of the nineteenth century—notably Tchaikovsky and Dvorak. He did think seriously about immigrating to this country in the 1840s when many Germans moved here. Schumann died in 1856 (in the same year that Woodrow Wilson was born and about a decade after Texas joined the union).

Why Schumann? Why should we talk about him? What makes this man of particular interest to us now at the end of the twentieth century? I've often asked myself that question. The answer is that Schumann has become a symbol. In the history of music, Schumann symbolizes the link between what is called the classical tradition of music—the music of Haydn, Mozart, and Beethoven—and what is called the romantic style, which flourished with composers such as Tchaikovsky, Wagner, Brahms, and Gustav Mahler. Schumann has often been called the father or the creator of romanticism in music, and we will shortly see why. He is yet another sort of symbol. In the history of the humanities, Schumann symbolizes a kind of romantic poet, the self-observing autobiographer, for which the nineteenth century was so famous. He belonged to that tradition of thoughtful people who searched for meaning not only in what they experienced in their social and natural environment, but also by observing within themselves—in their most private fantasies and dreams.

Finally, Schumann symbolizes the archetype of the mad genius—the split personality who lives simultaneously on two levels of consciousness and runs the risk of losing his mind by going to extremes. Thus, he is a very good subject for a biographer, especially someone who is interested in problems of creativity and mental health. Psychiatrists believe very strongly in the evolutionary approach—the study of the different phases of an individual's personality development. We can see when we look at Schumann that already as a child and a teenager, he was experiencing serious difficulties and trying to overcome them in various ways.

His father was a publisher and a bookseller. He had become chronically ill and physically disabled before Schumann was born, which had made it necessary for his wife, Schumann's mother, to help run the family business—publishing and selling books. Mrs. Schumann was six years older than her husband, and she was close to her menopause when Schumann arrived. He was the sixth and last of the children and his mother's favorite. His mother had lost an infant daughter named Laura shortly before Schumann was conceived. She was still in mourning for this dead child while she was pregnant with Robert. Her wish may very well have been to have a healthy daughter, and I say this because her only other daughter, Emily, had recently become mentally ill. Thus, Robert Schumann may have been a disappointment to his mother at first. He quickly made up for that by becoming very submissive to her and by trying always to make her happy. In fact, Schumann may have inherited from his mother his very unusual musical talent because his mother had a beautiful singing voice and a huge collection of songs. She would often sing for him, and he quickly learned how to imitate her. He showed a marked tendency to be very playful and to sing and dance and entertain other members of the family, all of whom seemed to approve of that and enjoy the little boy's showing off.

But tragically for Robert Schumann (and perhaps for civilization, because the tragedy robbed him of what stimulated his creativity), he was separated from his mother and her love when he was two years old. They were apart for nearly three years. This happened when Napoleon was defeated in Russia and returned to Europe with thousands and thousands of sick, starving troops. They straggled through the east part of Germany where Schumann's home town of Zwickau was located. His mother fell victim to a typhus epidemic and had to be quarantined. During her long convalescence, the boy attached himself to another woman, the mayor's wife, who took care of him.

He never forgot his sorrowful weeping, his loneliness, his sleepless nights during that separation. It made him depressed. But it also turned him inward, toward the tunes in his head and the fantasies in his imagination. After his family was reunited, the boy was sent to grammar school where he did quite well. His father invited him along with his older brothers, all of whom later became publishers, to help out in the family business—to work in the bookshop, help read proof, and do other chores. Because of this, at an early age, Robert acquired an intimate knowledge of writing and publishing. Among the musicians of his time, he was really one of the best educated and most literary figures. As a child, he yearned to become a poet and a novelist. He also wanted to study music. He was sent to the church organist in the little town of Zwickau for some piano lessons. Schumann's father, who had become ill, greatly enjoyed Robert's playing and singing. He bought Robert a piano and encouraged him to give little recitals at home. Schumann's recitals became a kind of musical therapy for his father.

By the time Schumann reached adolescence, this scene of domestic happiness was shattered by a series of traumatic events. First, his mentally ill sister committed suicide by drowning herself in a river. That tragedy stimulated terrible fantasies in Schumann's mind about the possibility that he too might one day go mad and drown himself. He tried to put these fears into words by keeping a diary and also by writing gruesome horror stories in the style of the gothic novelists and romantic poets — people like Byron, Sir Walter Scott, and Wolfgang Goethe. Schumann's favorite author was a German writer named Jean Paul Richter. Jean Paul used a kind of free-associative stream of consciousness literary style. It was innovative at the time, and Schumann began to write his diaries and his letters in the same way.

The second terrible event for him occurred when his father died soon after he lost his sister. This was a tormenting loss for the boy. He wrote in his diary, "I railed against fate. Isn't it terrible to be robbed of such a man, such an affectionate father, a loving poet, a keen observer of human nature, and a capable businessman?"

One way that Robert Schumann adjusted to this loss was by making the decision for himself that he would, in fact, become a writer — a literary figure just like his father, thus psychologically taking the old man's place. It was a courageous decision for him but the wrong decision because it led to a dozen unfinished novels and tons of mediocre poetry, which nobody would read and none of his brothers would publish. In fact, it is difficult if not impossible to become a successful writer at so early an age. There have been practically no true child prodigy poets and novelists. It seems that music, mathematics, dancing, gymnastics, and other well-integrated systems can be mastered by the brain of a child, but rarely fine art or literature. These forms of expression demand far greater maturity and much more life experience.

Thus Schumann, who always strove for excellence and wanted to be famous, came to feel frustrated, restless, and dissatisfied with what he was doing. He showed signs of depression: he moped around the house, withdrew from friends, and daydreamed a great deal. One might call it a kind of adolescent identity crisis. Fortunately for him, he was helped through this crisis by a skillful and benevolent psychiatrist who was also a musician. His name was Dr. Ernst August Carus, and he would counsel Schumann. Dr. Carus's wife, a singer, would invite the young man to their house to make music together. It is a good example of how to keep a musician well. In fact, the Carus couple even involved Schumann in some concerts at Dr. Carus's hospital, which was not far from Schumann's hometown. It was an old-fashioned insane asylum where patients in those days received mostly custodial care. Schumann enjoyed playing for the patients as he had for his father. But the huge asylum, located in a forbidding castle, also made him more fearful than before about problems of madness and suicide.

By the time Schumann left home at age seventeen to go to the University at Leipzig, he had started to think about a career in music. In other words, the ambivalence between writing and music expressed itself early, music being his first love and associated with the love of his mother. Rightly or wrongly, however, at that point, his mother was strongly opposed to the idea of Robert going into music. It is a risky profession, full of economic uncertainty with many potentials for disappointment. His mother also objected — correctly — that Robert had no serious training in music except for a few piano lessons when he was a child. At that time, young pianists his age such as Mendelssohn, Chopin, and Liszt were already well known throughout Europe and had been giving concerts regularly. The only concert Schumann had ever given was in his provincial little hometown of Zwickau. So he agreed with his mother and said, "Well, let me try something else." He enrolled at the university as a law student. The university had no music department so he found himself a private teacher, Friedrich Wieck. He began taking music lessons and also gave musical parties in his student lodgings, which he shared with his roommate, Emil Flechsig.

From Wieck and Flechsig and from Schumann's diaries, we know that he was the sort of college student who would be quite well known to the student mental health services nowadays. He rarely attended classes, was excessively shy with other students, and didn't socialize well. He avoided sports, which in those days included a lot of fencing. He drank excessively and seemed like an oddball. He also seemed to be falling in love with boys as well as girls, suggesting a sexual identity problem. After the first year of college, Schumann dropped out of Leipzig University to join one of his friends in the west German town of Heidelberg, at that time considered the center for romanticism in Germany.

Schumann continued to drink heavily and to write compulsively in his diary about the terrible hangovers that often made it impossible to accomplish anything for days on end. He wrote: "Piano out of tune; weather out of tune; no money; no friends; no fun; drank much beer; wandering around at night and the fear of myself; champagne; I lose consciousness; endless hangover; madness in my chest." Several times Schumann was on the verge of throwing himself into the Neckar River. In one letter to his mother, he wrote, "My lodgings face an insane asylum on the right and a Catholic Church on the left. I'm really in doubt whether to go crazy or to become a Catholic." To try to dispel his anxieties, Schumann went to Italy on vacation. He visited museums, attended operas, did a great deal of sightseeing, and once in awhile experimented with prostitutes. Throughout the Italy trip, his emotions cycled from ecstatic highs to miserable lows, and at the end of it, he felt as if he were dead.

What probably saved Schumann from his downward spiral in his life was music. He had been noting inner voices like musical hallucinations ever since leaving home. Back in Heidelberg, these inner voices were giving him a sense of direction. He started to practice the piano again, sometimes all day and even all night — to the point where his right hand would feel numb and painful. We often observe this disorder in pianists who suddenly start to go on a practice schedule for which they are unprepared. We call that an overuse disorder. He was able to perform at only a few parties, but that helped to give him a sense of being accepted. He also wrote a few short piano compositions, which he called "Butterflies."

During the Easter holidays in 1830 when he was nearly twenty years old, Schumann experienced what was almost a religious conversion. He had gone to nearby Frankfurt for a concert by the great Italian violinist, Niccolo Paganini. Not only was Paganini a fantastic virtuoso violinist who could play rings around all other fiddlers, he was also an incredible showman. He was slender and always dressed in black. He would wait until the last minute to go on stage and then appear dramatically. He arranged for one after another of his strings to snap until only the G string remained, and he would play on that string in a most fantastic way. Schumann was completely taken by this man. He started to transcribe Paganini's violin pieces for the piano. He decided to become a virtuoso pianist just as Paganini had been a virtuoso violinist. He was hoping to become a second Paganini. He dropped out of school and went back to Leipzig, to study music more seriously this time.

Here is another example of how to keep musicians alive and well. They must have an opportunity to perform. They need social approval. Outstanding role models are essential. Paganini served that purpose for Schumann. In his performances, Paganini fused the archetypal function of music and magic. And for Schumann, he represented a new father figure. Unlike the earlier father figure — the writer, Jean Paul — Paganini was a great musician. Schumann became almost hypomanic with enthusiasm. He returned to Leipzig and resumed piano lessons with his old teacher Wieck, quite a fantastic character himself. Wieck promised that he would turn Robert Schumann into Europe's greatest piano virtuoso within three years. If Schumann didn't show sufficient promise, Wieck would send him back to law school. Wieck also told Schumann's mother that he was planning to improve her son's character and to make him more manly.

Things went smoothly for awhile. Robert practiced diligently, and he began a love affair with one of Wieck's servants — a woman named Christel. Trouble soon arose again, however. After a particularly exciting weekend with Christel, Schumann, considerably worried, noticed a sore on a part of his body that he had never exercised this much before. He rushed to a doctor who told him not to worry about it and gave him a lotion to soothe the pain. Schumann kept worrying that he might have an incurable venereal disease and started to drink again.

Another source of anxiety lived in his teacher's house along with Schumann and the other students—Wieck's very pretty twelve-year-old daughter. Clara was a child prodigy pianist and had already been playing in public to great acclaim for five years. She was preparing to go on a concert tour. Schumann liked the little girl, and she looked up to him as a kindly, witty older brother. They enjoyed spending time together, playing for each other, talking about music and poetry.

This was the beginning of a long and complicated friendship, tinged with rivalry. Clara, who had a crush on Robert, was upset to see him going out with other girls while Robert, realizing that it was Clara and not he who was Wieck's favorite pupil, stopped taking piano lessons. He moved out of their house and began to practice furiously on his own. In doing so, he reinjured his already painful right hand to the point where he could no longer play the piano—especially in public, which had always made him nervous anyway. He spent a lot of his time in a local beer hall with his cronies—a group of artists and writers who called themselves the "Fraternity of David."

On his twenty-first birthday, when he came of age and had access to his father's inheritance, Schumann decided to give up the virtuoso idea altogether and to become a writer after all. He decided he would fuse music and writing and become a music critic—a wise decision. It enabled him to bring these two talents of his together. It also gave him more time to write music again, to compose. He took some lessons with a local composer named Heinrich Dorn, who taught him the fundamentals of harmony and counterpoint. Other than that, Schumann was essentially a self-taught musician. As before, however, his ambition outstripped his accomplishments. He wrote a symphony, or rather, he tried to write one, which he never actually finished. One movement was performed, and it was not well received.

At age twenty-three, he had his first severe nervous breakdown. He thought he would lose his mind. The anxiety was dreadful. In a panic, he ran from doctor to doctor and finally decided to jump out of a window. Fortunately his friends, including several doctors, intervened and kept him from harming himself. Here again is an example of how to keep musicians alive. After the doctors calmed Schumann down, they treated his underlying depression. It took him about six months to recover. During this time, he lived with another pianist and composer named Ludwig Schunke. We don't know too much about their relationship, but we do know that their landlady complained a lot about what was going on in their apartment—all the carousing and drinking—and asked the boys to move out. We also know that one of Schumann's doctors advised him to get married. And he had no trouble attracting a young woman named Ernestine von Fricken, who was the daughter of a wealthy baron in Bohemia. They became engaged. But soon Schumann realized that he did not love Ernestine. Besides, he discovered that she was the baron's illegitimate child and would be disinherited once they married. He broke the engagement and began going out with his old friend Clara Wieck, who by now was a famous and successful child prodigy—a nubile sixteen-year-old still very much in love with him.

Schumann had begun to make a name for himself as a music critic. He had even acquired control over his own newspaper, which he called "The New Journal for Music." In this journal, he wrote numerous essays, often under assumed names. One of the names he used was "Florestan," and with this name he expressed some of his more daring, self-assertive, rebellious, and masculine self. He used another pen name, "Eusebius," to symbolize his introverted, unhappy, and feminine side. Finally, he used the name "Raro," which combined parts of his name Robert, *ro*, with that of Clara, *ra*. Raro represented wisdom, control, and authority. Along with his success as an editor and critic, Schumann in his twenties made enormous progress as a composer. He was now writing exclusively for the piano, the instrument he himself had failed to conquer while his beloved Clara was playing it superbly.

In fact, Schumann thought of Clara much of the time, and the music he wrote often had autobiographical themes. For example, the composition he called "Carnaval" consisted of short humorous pieces about the various moods associated with his short-lived engagement to Ernestine, and about Clara's jealousy. The "Davidsbundler Dances," another early piano composition by Schumann, consists of miniature portraits of himself in the contrasting roles of Florestan, Eusebius, and Raro. These piano compositions were in a style that departed radically from the older classical traditions of sonata form, with their strict rules. The newer works came closer to the ideal of romanticism— which was to express your emotions freely, to avoid intellectual constraints, and to focus on highly personal ideas often associated with vivid imagery. These pieces of Schumann's are difficult to play. Since he was unable to perform them, he relied on his friend Clara Wieck to play them on the piano. This, of course, brought these two young musicians into more regular contact. As their relationship began to warm up, her father put his foot down.

"I don't want you to have anything to do with this miserable alcoholic who leads such a disorderly life," Wieck told her. "Schumann has already gone mad once, and he'll surely end up insane or in the poor house. Unless you give him up now, you'll go down the drain with him."

This violent opposition only made the lovers more eager to be together. They talked of marriage and secretly got engaged. When Clara's father found out, he flew into a rage and threatened to kill Robert; then he sent his daughter away on a concert tour.

"There's to be no further contact between the two of you *ever*," he fumed. He also spread word throughout Europe that Schumann was an incompetent musician—one who would only be able to compose silly little pieces on the piano, never major works such as symphonies and concertos. His music was of no intrinsic worth, Wieck said. Schumann did not take that lying down, although there were moments when he felt very discouraged and depressed and thought he might go mad or commit suicide.

135

Peter Ostwald

To defend himself against these dangers and also against Wieck's accusations, Schumann began to compose in earnest. He wrote four magnificent piano sonatas—all of them incorporating a theme Schumann had borrowed from one of Clara's piano pieces. She, too, was a composer. The Clara theme in Schumann's sonatas was like a secret message between the lovers. Since they were no longer allowed to be together, or even to write to each other, the music that Schumann composed and Clara performed was the only way that they could communicate. Schumann indeed became an expert in using musical symbols to overcome his loneliness and isolation and to communicate with other people.

To show you what that means, I'd like to discuss in detail some of the musical secrets in one of Schumann's piano sonatas. The first movement of this sonata is called "A Fantasy." The Clara theme comes from her own composition. It is called "Adantino" by Clara Wieck. A theme of five notes—a five-tone scale that contains the notes C and A—refers directly to Clara. It is a descending scale. All of Schumann's piano sonatas and also his piano concerto contain this basic germ of an idea. It was such a compelling idea that Franz Liszt, to whom this composition was dedicated, used the same motif at the beginning of his famous B minor sonata.

Finally, in the "C Major Fantasy," you can hear the theme expressed right at the beginning in this way. That theme is developed in many different ways throughout the piece. The second theme of this movement is something that Schumann wrote about in his letter, saying, "It is the most passionate crying out from my heart to you, Clara." In the middle section of the "Fantasy," you can hear something that he called the "style of a legend," and that is a hidden reference to two other composers—one of whom is Franz Schubert, an earlier composer. Schubert had written a song called "Death and the Maiden" in which he uses this theme. The rhythm of this middle section of the Schumann "Fantasy" also refers to Ludwig von Beethoven's second movement of his seventh symphony, which contains this same rhythm and thematic material. Schumann had actually hoped to dedicate his "Fantasy" to Beethoven's memory. Finally, at the end of the "Fantasy," you can hear again a reference to Beethoven, and this is Beethoven's song, "To the Distant Beloved."

[During the lecture, Ostwald's wife, Lise, played the above movements on the piano for the participants.]

I hope those remarks give you an idea of the many themes crossing through this work and how ingenuously Schumann integrated and combined them.

I wish I could tell you that the story comes to a happy ending, but it has a sort of bittersweet ending. After this period in Schumann's life, he progressed steadily as a composer, became a writer of many songs, symphonies, chamber music, operas, oratorios—a great deal of music. He was able to marry Clara when he was thirty. They had eight children. He continued to have recurrent breakdowns and serious episodes of illness. In those days, no health-care programs existed to give performing artists the proper treatment, although Schumann saw many doctors. This was the nineteenth century, and much of what we can do today for patients with this type of disorder was then not available. When he was forty-three, Schumann went into so severe an episode of psychosis that he attempted to commit suicide and almost succeeded, and that really spelled the end of his career. He was hospitalized. His wife was so perturbed to see him hospitalized that she could never bring herself to see her husband in the hospital — to visit him. He made a good recovery, and he began again to write music and letters. He wanted desperately to come home, but that just wasn't possible. The doctors knew nothing about the methods of family therapy and social therapy that we have today. In the hospital, Schumann again became depressed, and this time succeeded in taking his own life.

Although the ending is sad, we're very fortunate to have the superb music that Schumann left behind and the tradition of romanticism that became so influential in the work of other composers.

Discussion

WILMER: Could you tell us something about Schumann's suicide attempt?

PETER OSTWALD: Yes. He and Clara had moved to Dusseldorf, which is a town on the Rhine River in West Germany. Clara was hoping to concertize in Holland, West Germany, and Great Britain. Schumann had taken a position as conductor of the Dusseldorf Symphony Orchestra. He was not very good as a conductor. He was a very introverted man who had failed previously in a teaching role. It was difficult for him to explain things to the orchestra. He just beat time and never gave instructions, so he was ultimately fired from his position, and he took this as a great personal loss. He again became very agitated and disturbed. He was hearing noises in his head. They had turned into terrible hallucinations, and he told his wife, "I really think I should go to the hospital now." She didn't want that to happen.

She herself then became agitated, and it finally got to the point where a doctor had to be consulted. While this doctor was talking with Clara at the house, Robert Schumann ran out of the house and made his way down to the Rhine River. The Rhine was a magic symbol for many German artists, poets, and composers — "the Father Rhine." He had on a previous occasion actually thrown his wedding ring into the Rhine and told his wife to do the same thing. This later action was ominous because it was in the middle of the early hours in wintertime. He just had a flimsy jacket over his pajamas and he was wearing his slippers. He wandered down to the bridge, crossed over it, and jumped. Fortunately, some fishermen on a boat saw the jump, and they dragged him out of the water. Then he jumped from the boat, but they again succeeded in rescuing him. Only when they took him ashore did they recognize the great Robert Schumann, the conductor of the local symphony orchestra. Arrangements were then made for him to be hospitalized.

PARTICIPANT: Dr. Ostwald, if you had the advantage of a time machine and could use it to transport yourself to the 1830s to treat Robert Schumann for his psychosis, would he have gone on to compose these wonderful, tortured pieces like that sonata, or would he have been a different artist altogether?

OSTWALD: Yes, I think he would have gone on to compose. I would hope that he would have incorporated my initials or some symbol of my name into his work. I hope he would not have had the disruptive recurrence of psychosis that sometimes made it impossible for him to work for as long as a year. He probably would have lived longer, thus composed more music — perhaps another opera, which he had in mind, and more oratorios. Toward the end of his life, he moved away from the piano and was giving vent to the kind of music that Richard Wagner later perfected. That would be my expectation — that with treatment, he would have done even better than he did. I must emphasize that he did receive treatment, but it was not the kind that was truly effective in helping the kind of diseases that he had.

PARTICIPANT: Am I right that in this last century there was a lot of beautiful music, but not very much in the later part of this century?

OSTWALD: We have had, and continue to have, a lot of composers. Probably, like the composers of the nineteenth century, they will only be truly appreciated in the twenty-first century. It takes awhile for artists to find their ways into the hearts of the public. It is my impression that the composers of our time are expressing some of the feelings of our time that are very agitated, anxious, and angry, and that often deal with horrible themes — wars and destruction, which have been so prevalent. Art always gives a certain message about the time of the artist, which is intended for the future.

PARTICIPANT: It would be the same thing as when Brahms wasn't appreciated when he was composing.

OSTWALD: That is correct.

PARTICIPANT: Would you say something about the effect of marriage on his creativity? Also, as I was reading the last chapter in your book, I got so angry with Clara. I could hardly believe that she couldn't bring herself to visit him during that two-and-a-half years because she was a strong woman. I just find it incredible that she couldn't go to visit him when he was in such a distraught state.

OSTWALD: Thank you for those important questions. The first one, the effect of marriage on Schumann, was that it really enhanced his creativity. Up until the time of his marriage, Schumann was writing exclusively as a composer for the piano. He had failed in writing symphonies, and he found successful ways of expressing himself with really one of the most beautiful sonatas. It was only when it appeared that something serious was going to happen with Clara that he began to move into another phase of creativity, which was to merge voice and piano. It was really quite dramatic for that to happen during the time of a court procedure. The future father-in-law was so opposed to the marriage that Schumann had to go to court to get approval to marry Clara.

It was during that very difficult year that he started to write songs — hundreds of them, beautiful songs, some of the greatest songs in the literature. These compositions were very much related to his sense of wanting to join himself and Clara, the voice and the piano. The voice being partly himself, partly his mother; the piano being something they could share.

After the marriage, after they had their first baby, Schumann started to write symphonies. He wrote the "Spring Symphony." Again it was very difficult for him to do it. He had little training as a composer, but he got help and brought it to success. Then he became a wonderful symphonist and wrote great symphonies — four of them altogether. After that, he started to write chamber music, much of it intended for his wife. He wrote the piano "Quintet," for example, which is considered a masterpiece. Without that, we would not have much of the subsequent development in chamber music. He wrote even larger works — opera, choral work.

In respect to the breakdown of the marriage, that was a very complicated business. For one thing, having so many babies is rather incompatible with the life of a traveling concert pianist. We've had two children. Eight children would really be quite overwhelming for this kind of marriage. It seemed the Schumanns were a fertile couple, and they hadn't found a successful way to stop this almost annual pregnancy. I think there was some reason for Clara to fear that if she continued her relationship with Schumann, her own career would be finished. She would then have to devote the rest of her life to taking care of him, supervising the family, and taking care of the children, since he was getting progressively more disabled.

Another factor was that a young composer had come into the Schumanns' life. A great child prodigy named Johannes Brahms went to Dusseldorf to visit them when he was only nineteen years old. This was shortly before Schumann's last breakdown. Both Robert and Clara liked him very much. As soon as Brahms heard that Schumann was hospitalized, he rushed to Dusseldorf and said, "Clara, can I help you?" And she said, "Yes, please stay in our house. Help me take care of the children." As you might surmise, a love relationship developed between Clara and Brahms, and Brahms became a kind of go-between. He would go to the hospital and visit Schumann there and bring Schumann news of Clara and then he would return to Clara, and bring Clara news of her husband.

It was an exceedingly difficult situation. I think Clara was in tremendous turmoil. We have pictures of her. She was really very very disturbed during that whole period of time—not knowing what to do. And she was burdened constantly by this sense of guilt related to her father. She was torn always between her love for her father and her love for her husband. She did finally visit the hospital, when the doctor said, "Look, you had better come and see him before it is too late; he will die." So she saw him a couple of times, very close to the end. By that time, it was much too late to do anything about it. This is a sad aspect of the story, but those are the facts.

PARTICIPANT: I wondered if, out of those eight children, any were musicians.

OSTWALD: Yes, there were four daughters and four sons. Three of the daughters became piano teachers and carried on the tradition that had been established by the mother, Clara Schumann. The sons did not become musicians. One of the sons, who looked very much like his father, did become a poet. Brahms took a great liking to him and set some of this boy's poetry to music.

PARTICIPANT: I wondered if you think there was something in Schumann's illness that gave him a closer contact with his creative unconscious, or did his illness in some way contribute to his creativity?

OSTWALD: Perhaps these marked mood swings did, because whenever he reached the extremes of what we call bipolar affective disorder, he would hear voices that had meaning for him. Later on, when he settled down, and he could collect his thoughts, he would incorporate some of these voices into his compositions. Whether the illness was helpful to his creativity—well, yes and no. It stimulated the creativity as you say. It brought him more in touch with his creative unconscious, but it also hampered him greatly. That, of course, is a great challenge—for the physician to work in such a way to remove the harm the illness produces without removing the benefits of this kind of exceptional insight and inwardness.

PARTICIPANT: Could you technically describe that illness? Was he schizophrenic? I am also curious about this prolonged illness of his father. He

141

must have been seriously ill for a number of years, but you haven't referred to what it was.

OSTWALD: Actually a number of illnesses were involved. I don't think he was schizophrenic. In schizophrenia, what one observes is a progressive diminution of the personality, of the creative capacities, and in Schumann it seemed to be almost the opposite. His creativity grew each time he had a psychotic episode. He either came back to some fresh state of creativeness or even developed a new direction. That is quite unlike what one sees with chronic schizophrenia, where there is a progressive downhill course, although this is a debatable thing, and there is an illness called schizoaffective disorder which might even be applicable to Schumann's case.

There may also have been an organic element, an infection, either syphilis or tuberculosis. Tuberculosis was rampant in Schumann's family, and also syphilis, which he possibly acquired, although I'm a little skeptical about that. One cannot rule it out, however, because there weren't proper tests then. That would have produced certain changes in the brain that would have interfered markedly in his function.

As far as the father is concerned, I wish I knew what was the matter with him. I have tried to find out. There was a tendency toward depressive illness on the mother's side much more than the father's. He seemed to have something more like gout or severe rheumatic conditions, but as a result of his invalidism, he was also quite frequently depressed. We know also the illness of the older sister and her suicide. There was a familial element in this illness that one does tend to observe in the so-called bipolar affective disorders. It is always risky to try to diagnose people from the nineteenth century today because so little is known about the physical parameters, even simple things such as blood pressure and the laboratory tests we would do now to find out what the matter is. Trying to make a diagnosis after the fact is risky business.

Bipolar is a kind of depressive disorder where there are extreme mood fluctuations. One extreme is the so-called mania — the very excited, high mood with enormous energy, overwhelming drive, furious excitement, speech becomes very fast, and behavior becomes very fast and out of control. That kind of maniacal excitement then may go in the other direction to severe depression with a loss of the ability to move, to speak, to think — a sort of stuporous condition. This fluctuation from extreme mania to extreme depressiveness, with suicide a great risk at either extreme, is what we usually call a bipolar form of depressive disorder. We can treat it now with lithium salts, a very effective form of treatment.

There is some evidence to suggest that bipolar depressive disorder and creativity may be linked. A lot of research is going on in that field right now, although I think it is too early to come to a conclusion about it. One treatment for these extreme disruptive mood swings is lithium, which is taken daily. It reduces the amplitude of these swings and allows the creative person to continue to function without having to worry about swinging excessively in one direction or the other with the risk of destroying himself or herself at the extreme of the illness.

PARTICIPANT: Could you tell us what happened to Clara? Also, if a person does have this lithium treatment, does that lower their creativity?

OSTWALD: Clara continued her phenomenal career. She lived to be almost twice Schumann's age. She became a famous teacher as well as a concert pianist. She and Brahms were in love for quite some time, and there was some discussion about possible marriage, but both of them seemed to feel that was not desirable.

The other question about what happens to the quality or the quantity of creativeness often becomes a psychotherapeutic problem. If a creative person believes that these mood swings are necessary for him or her to remain creative, one has to work very carefully with the person to make it possible for him or her to tolerate the sort of mood restriction produced by the lithium. Some people, not only creative people, become rather addicted to the idea of having a very high mood, since there may be a certain joy or pleasure or ecstasy connected with that. Then the downswing mood is terribly painful. One has to work in a psychotherapeutic relationship or in group therapy with individuals who have that condition to help them appreciate the benefits of not having the extreme depressions, and also giving up some of the ecstatic highs that, of course, lead to exactly the kind of disruptive behavior that I described in Schumann's life: the alcoholism, the rushing away from responsibility, compulsive gambling, various other symptoms that can be destructive to the individual and to his or her family.

At this point, we really have insufficient data. It might be even challenging for an institute such as yours to take a look at that, because it is a question that we have to face over and over again when patients come in and say, "What's going to happen? Are you going to take my creativity away?" Of course, you can't take creativity away from someone who is truly creative. What you can do is set up conditions that are conducive for the creativity to flourish. And one of those conditions is better health, both physical and mental health.

PARTICIPANT: My question has to do with the functional capacity of the right hand, which apparently is not too terribly uncommon among pianists. I wonder how strongly that problem might be associated with the fact that there is music written for the left hand alone, but I know of no music written for the right hand alone. I wonder what significance might reside therein. I'd like to know more about this mechanism with the problem of the right hand.

OSTWALD: Your question about the right hand is a very intriguing one. We see over and over again pianists and keyboard players especially, complaining of difficulties with the right hand. Violinists usually have difficulties with the left hand. The reason that Schumann had such extraordinary trouble with the right hand is that he started to treat himself in a very destructive way during one of his phases of maniacal excitement. He made use of a mechanical instrument that stretched the tendons to such a point that there was physical damage in the hand. There have been a number of contemporary pianists who have developed this kind of disability — Leon Fleisher, for example, who no longer performs with both hands. In fact, thanks to Fleisher and his courage in admitting that he had this problem, we now have health programs such as ours. It was necessary for musicians to admit that they had problems before we could openly say, "OK, we are treating them." No musician or athlete wants to admit to a disability.

Why is music written for the left hand and not the right hand? I think this is simply to help these disabled pianists get back to work. It was a tradition that started after the First World War when several pianists lost their hands. A very famous one lost his right hand, and several composers, including Ravel, wrote pieces for him. Lise, as a pianist, do you have any ideas what makes the right hand so much more vulnerable than the left? My wife gives the answer that the violinist cannot give, and this is that the composer writes more complicated things for the right hand. The work that the right hand has to do is much more complicated than the left hand, and although it may not always be so, the right hand usually does most of the work, so it is the one that suffers overuse injuries. On the violin, it is the left hand that does most of the work.

PARTICIPANT: There is a question of Schumann's competency as a pianist, which raises the suspicion that there might have been a hysterical component to that — in the light of what you have just said, maybe even psychosomatic?

Another question: It is often reported that people who are on street drugs and get high as a result think of themselves as being very creative under the influence, but it always turns out that they're not creative at all. I wonder what kind of analogy there may be here. Also, when I look at a painting by Van

Gogh, my impression is that this is a painting by a madman. I wonder if anyone gets an impression of that sort of thing after hearing Schumann's compositions—that they are the compositions of a madman. Or are his compositions, in fact, always typically regarded as the very highest class?

OSTWALD: The first question was about some of the psychological dimensions for the hand paralysis, and there were two. One of them had to do with the fact that Schumann had just come of age for the draft at that time, and he was extremely unwilling to enter the militia. He went to a friend of his who was a physician and said, "Look, I've had trouble with this hand for some time, do you think I would be able to fire a gun?" His friend said, "Let me write an affidavit for you and point out to the military doctors that you're a very nervous person and that you have a paralysis of your index finger and would not be able to carry a weapon." The physician at the draft board insisted that a second examination be made. Another doctor was asked to come in for consultation who wasn't so impressed with the hand problem. He was, however, very impressed with Schumann's emotional problems, and for this reason would not recommend that he serve in the military.

Schumann experimented with what in those days would have been psychedelics—heavy cigars and lots of coffee. He writes about it extensively. As far as I can tell, they did nothing to enhance his creativity, although he wrote some essays where he believed he was writing as well as Goethe or Schiller. I've read them, and he was not writing that well.

Can people hear the madness in the music? This is always a very interesting problem in the assessment of art. If one knows something about an artist such as Van Gogh, then one looks at the painting and says, "Oh yes, of course, I can see this." In Schumann's case, there are people who feel they can detect some kind of nervousness, some kind of disorganization. I've been very skeptical about it. I find his music extremely well organized, even music he wrote close to the time of his death. The German psychiatrist Paul Mobius, who specialized in writing what they called in those days pathographies (the biographies of famous sick people), said whenever he listened to Schumann's music, he could hear his nervousness. I think that may be true of certain compositions. I don't think it is true of the "Fantasy," for example. I find that it is one of the most integrated and successful works. Again with Schumann, his output has a spectrum from his most successful to his least successful works. I dare say in the less successful works, one can hear certain problems. There are also compositions that seem doleful and repetitious and boring somehow. I think one would say he was depressed when he wrote these. Then there are others where he is very healthy.

WILMER: Peter, do you ever think of yourself and Lise as a healthy Robert and Clara?

OSTWALD: The problem is that when you give a talk like this, to bring the facts into focus, some other facts get out of focus. Maybe by emphasizing the clinical dimensions, I've made it sound as though these people were unhealthy. That was not my intention at all. My intention was to show in what ways illness interfered with their health. There is always that polarity in everyone. No human being can avoid that kind of mixture of health and disease, and the disease is in opposition to the health. I don't see Robert and Clara as being basically unhealthy, nor do I see Lise and myself as being always healthy. We have our own problems. It's really interesting when one does psychobiographical work to find the uniqueness — not only in people, but in their families and marriages. My answer to you would be no, I don't make that kind of comparison. I see the Schumanns there; I see the Ostwalds there, the Wilmers there. Each of us has a way of dealing with problems. Sometimes we fail and sometimes we succeed.

PARTICIPANT: I was just wondering if much has not been made about mental illness and artists and composers. I'm glad you mentioned Johannes Brahms, who was a very humble, sedate individual. His caliber of work is about the same as Schumann's.

OSTWALD: The point is that one does not have to be sick to be successful. I would agree with that. It is really an advantage not to have disease, and it is a real advantage to have good treatment if you do.

PARTICIPANT: I was wondering if the creativity, his compositions, had any positive effects on Schumann's times of good health.

OSTWALD: Yes, I think they made him feel stronger and more capable and led to good feedback from other musicians who could appreciate the work. Definitely there is an effect there. The creativity makes the person feel good, and for this reason it is so important to encourage it. Creativeness is a very healthy enterprise.

PARTICIPANT: Did it keep him healthy longer?

OSTWALD: I think I might answer that, unfortunately, negatively. The inability for him to continue to be creative probably led to his final demise. I think the conditions in the hospital were not conducive to creative work, and

146

that is my guess why he started starving himself and ultimately succeeded in destroying himself.

PARTICIPANT: You mentioned the quintet in passing. I find that piece extraordinarily lyrical, and I wonder if you could comment on what role that played in his subsequent development.

OSTWALD: The quintet was composed during those happy years of the marriage. It was really written as a sort of piano concerto that could be played in the household. It was a great success for Clara because she could travel around the world with it. One doesn't always find an orchestra to play something with, and one could play this great work with just four other musicians. The quintet, interestingly enough, contains a funeral march. I think this says not only something about his tendency to go from one extreme to the other, but also something about the romantic spirit and the romantic age that often put gravestones on paintings and tended to dramatize, especially in Germany, the theme of death. In terms of the history of music, the quintet has been very important. Since its composition, many other composers have written piano quintets, including Brahms with his famous F minor quintet.

PARTICIPANT: Would you please elaborate on your work with artists in your clinic in San Francisco?

OSTWALD: The clinic was founded two-and-a-half years ago for two reasons. One of them was that we in San Francisco, I personally and several of my colleagues, had been working very closely with teachers and artists at the San Francisco Conservatory of Music. We wanted to expand that interest to enhance other education programs in the area, and also to bring in consultants in fields other than the behavioral sciences.

The second reason had to do with the practical issues. A program like this one had been started in Boston and was receiving a lot of attention and interest, so that often musicians from San Francisco felt compelled to fly to Boston to get an evaluation. We felt it would be much easier if we had such a program available in San Francisco. The basic rule I have used in seeking consultants to work in the program is that they should be experts on both sides — the performing arts and the medical arts. We have a pianist who is also a neurologist, an ear, nose, throat specialist who is also a singer, and a social worker who is a dancer. That makes it much easier for the patient-healer relationship. There is a sense of rapport not only about health issues but also about professional issues. That has been a guiding principle in our work.

In the meantime, there have been other centers; we were not even the second. A program like this had also developed in Chicago at Northwestern Memorial Hospital. Another one is now in New York at St. Luke's Roosevelt Hospital. One just recently opened in Houston. You will find other programs organized throughout the country because they are very much needed. It is similar to the development of sports medicine, where one tries to find out what the special issues are in the career of the athlete and how one can not only treat problems but also prevent them. Much of our work is preventive medicine — helping students, practicing musicians, and teachers avoid difficulties before they become handicaps.

PARTICIPANT: Would you comment on any work that has been done on the use of music as a therapeutic tool in the treatment of psychosis other than the creative?

OSTWALD: Music has always been associated with the healing arts. The Greeks had the god Apollo, the god of both music and medicine. From time immemorial, one can read about music being used as therapy: David playing the harp for Saul in his depressions, and Bach writing a special set of variations for someone who couldn't sleep at night.

In terms of the modern developments, there are training programs in music therapy, and specialists who work in this direction. I think it is a very important dimension to exploit. I don't know that music is as specific a form of treatment as used to be thought. In early medical writings one finds remarkable stories about music being able to cure plague, reverse strokes, and things like that. I think we have learned to regard music as a more general kind of therapeutic medium as are diet and exercise — things that are needed to help keep people well. Once they become seriously ill, of course, one has to call into play more specific remedies — surgical techniques, antibiotics, and other forms of treatment. Music is also of great help in physical rehabilitation.

[During the discussion, Peter and Lise Ostwald played a violin and piano duet, Fritz Kreisler's "Rondino on a Theme by Beethoven."]

CHAPTER TEN

Douglass Parker

A PARAGEOGRAPHER

Born in 1927, Douglass S. Parker graduated from the University of Michigan and in 1952 was awarded a Ph.D in classics from Princeton University.

He taught at Yale and at the University of California at Riverside where he became a full professor. He was a fellow at the Center for Hellenic Studies and the University of California Institute for the Creative Arts. He spent a year at Cambridge University, England.

In 1968, he accepted the position of professor of classics at the University of Texas, Austin. In 1984, he was awarded a Guggenheim Fellowship. The following year, he received the Graduate Teaching Award at the University of Texas, Austin.

He has been a Shakespearean actor, and, as a jazz musician, plays trombone and trumpet in a group called The Players. He also plays lead trombone in the Austin Community College Jazz Ensemble, a big band.

Parker and his students at the University of Texas create imaginary worlds in a course he originated called "Parageography." In parageography, Parker assigns readings and lectures on the works of Homer, Plato, Virgil, Dante, Sir Thomas More, Rabelais, and Edmund Spenser, as well as L. Frank Baum's stories of Oz, C. S. Lewis's tales of Narnia, and J. R. R. Tolkien's *The Hobbit*. The students then create imaginary worlds of their own. Parker's own world, High Thefarie, has its own language. A large hog is High Thefarie's totem and titular ruler. The principal species that inhabits this world is humanoid but lays eggs, which the males hatch.

Parker, who is a poet, has published five books of verse and a poetic cycle, "Zeus in Therapy."

Places for Anything:
Building Imaginary Worlds

While putting these words together, I found myself in something like an infinite regress; I went back to the beginning, then back before that, then back even further, in the hopes of making everything completely clear. When I had written about three pages, and had not yet reached the beginning of the real beginning, I realized that something might be wrong with my strategy. What I really want to do is to tell you what it is that I do that would account for my being here. Let me put it this way.

I am an authentic academic. (I don't carry a card, but never mind that.) I began teaching in 1952 at the age of twenty-five and have pursued that craft for what is going on thirty-seven years. I reside in the realm of The Classics, which in another time would have meant that I devoted all of my classroom appearances to imparting accurate knowledge, rudimentary and advanced, of two languages — classical Latin and ancient Greek — and the literatures written in those languages, which would be read by the students in those languages. I have done and do my share of this, but it is no more than a share. Throughout my career, as every classicist must in the face of small enrollments in the study of the ancient languages *per se*, I have necessarily taught classical civilization courses or "see-see" courses, as we say in the trade — which means that the subject matter is largely drawn from classical antiquity and that the texts studied are read in English translations.

Over the years in my teaching, I had noted what might be considered a regrettable turn for what we in the classical languages term "a contrary to fact condition." I discovered, in teaching "see-see" courses, that my interests were verging on the different — especially my interests in student performance, in the work submitted to me in papers or on examinations. I didn't want them to regurgitate names, dates, apercus, or interpretations — I didn't want the students to tell me things I already knew. This is not to say that I didn't think that knowing the material was important; I did and do. What I wanted from the students was, increasingly, not for them to tell me what a given author had said, but to do something like what a given author had done. In essence, this was a movement from analysis to synthesis. Don't tell me about something; make me something.

Over the years, curious questions and assignments crept into my courses.

Take this, for example, from a course in Greek tragedy I gave in the early 1960s: "Sophocles wrote a play called *Euryalus* concerning the sad fate of a bastard son of Odysseus, of which only a plot summary has survived. (There followed the paragraph that had come down from Parthenius.) Drawing on your knowledge gained from the study of Sophoclean tragedies in this course, tell me what occurred in the second episode. What was the chorus's reaction in the succeeding choral ode?" An exercise in the hypothetical? Perhaps. But this, and other manifestations, should have told me something: quite simply, that creativity was the important thing to be learned here — how to make something.

In the fall of 1973, I began to teach a course titled Parageography. The title, which for all I know I invented, was meant to imply a link to geography analogous to the link between parapsychology and psychology — which is to say, skewed. The subtitle, however, is really what defines the course: "The Study of Imaginary Worlds." It is a "see-see" course, and as such things go, it is nearly respectable, mainstream, plain vanilla. The initial texts — Homer, Herodotus, Plato, Apollonius, Virgil — are, shall we say, hallowed by time and perfection. The follow-ups — Dante, Sir/Saint Thomas More, Francois Rabelais, Edmund Spenser — are perfectly logical successors in "The Classical Tradition," although the lectures on L. Frank Baum's Oz, C. S. Lewis's Narnia, and J. R. R. Tolkien's Middle-Earth might appear slightly eccentric.

Even the structure of the course possesses what we might call intellectual validity, with its insistence on the way in which poets and others devise or appropriate fantastic landscapes and employ them in their works. Quests, gardens, hells, utopias, fairylands — around all of these a considerable scholarly literature has sprung up. In fact, one of the surprises that teaching this course had in store for me was the discovery that although I had made up the word *parageography*, the thing in fact already existed. There is a field there, although I doubt that I could get any of its practitioners — from literary critics to anthropologists to garden historians — to agree to my term for it. The course had yet another surprise, however. It would not sit quietly and stay still, content to be, shall we say, only a slightly eccentric variation on "The Classical Tradition" and its beneficiaries. Instead, it insisted on veering off into the synthetic rather than the analytic, into the creative rather than the regurgitative. My lectures were (and are) standard and analytic. I dissect Odysseus's voyage when he goes off the map in Book 9 of the *Odyssey*. I trace the allegorization of place when Guyon makes his dangerous way to the Bowre of Bliss in Book 2, Canto 12, of the *Faerie Queene*. I even anatomize the basic centripetal quest that is a necessary part of most of the Oz books.

The purpose of all these items, however, has become entirely different. They are not things to be learned in and for themselves. They are instead studied as models, because the primary goal of the course (which surprised me mightily, some years after I had begun to teach it) has become the creation by the students of their own worlds. After the students have seen and studied some of the best things that have been done in this genre, what I want them to do, first and foremost, is to make me one: a world, or a country, or—and this had happened—a considerable part of one.

This creation does not occur out of the blue, by the way. I am not really interested in the catchphrase of the late 1960s, "Doing One's own Thing," first, because one never does that—there is nothing made in this world that is entirely one's own; second, because it implies a lack of discipline that I insist is not true of this course, or of what I teach and what I do; and third, because the students have been prepared by other sorts of spatial creation.

Let me at this point forestall, or at least anticipate, a possible objection. Why don't I have them write me stories, instead? After all, it's a course in literature, isn't it? What they read is narrative, isn't it? Why not do what really seems logical—call it a course in creative writing and go on from there? The answer to this is that writing is not primarily, or even secondarily, what I'm trying to get them to do. A lot of what they do will be written, since writing is probably our most efficient method of conveying information, but this is really not the point. It is rather that I am trying to get them to use and develop their creative imaginations, which is often quite a different thing.

Let me give an example. Among writers and world-builders, Lyman Frank Baum stands out in this country, largely because of the wide circulation years ago of a television movie based on a book he wrote and published nearly ninety years ago—*The Wizard of Oz*. It, and the Oz books that followed it, represent a considerable achievement. Yet the fact remains that Baum, although he made his living by writing for years, was not really a good writer. He was far from it, in fact. In my youth, you couldn't find books by Baum in public libraries, especially the Oz books, because they were series books and hence "hack" books and therefore not well written and thus Not the Sort of Thing a Library Ought to Have on Its Shelves.

In defense of the librarians, it must be said that at least one of their premises was valid: Baum's Oz books were not well written even by the quite elastic standards of children's books or genre fiction in force at that time or now. But oh, could that man invent! He created color-coded wonderland, a marvelous rectangle in which anything could happen, and usually did. Regardless of his lame sentences, the formulaic (and occasionally pointless) nature of his plots, and the often bewildering sameness of his characters, the place he made, that Land of Oz, and the places inside it, caught and continue to catch readers of a certain age in fascination. They are wonderful inventions. And *invention*, for the creative imagination, is the name of the game.

Which, roundabout, is what I try to elicit in this course. The root skill that this course aims at fostering (said he, in a rather startled tone, as of one who had just discovered an article of belief he didn't know he had) is not writing, but imagining. The writing is subsidiary. The area here in which the imagination operates is the fantastic, although I would prefer to call it the marvelous, not merely because this is what a great deal of the students read out

153

of choice, or because the course deals in fantasy (yes, Virginia, even the *Odyssey* and the *Inferno* are, in our definition of it, fantasy), but because unfettering from quotidian reality is, I think, a necessary easing of the difficulty. It is really much harder to develop a real everyday place than a fantastic place. Also, I find that people respond to my request: Amaze me!

Why (another question may go) a place? The short answer is that's how the course originated, in the study of places. The longer answer begins this way: place is where, unless we are terribly unfortunate, we all have some creative experience, be it only moving a chair to change our environment. Also, at least here, it avoids imposing, almost wholly, at least one sort of constraint — The Way Things Spozed To Be, especially in a place where The Way They Spozed To Be is The Way They Ain't. In being supra- or possibly sub-verbal, it plugs the student almost immediately into the congeries of feelings that we — at least in the sort of learning community of which I am part — pretty much share: shudders at the Dark at the Top of the Stairs (or, come to think of it, at the Bottom); expansiveness toward the West, constriction to the East; ease with flowers (unless too well ordered), rest with trees, all the rest of the topographically induced emotions and thoughts among the paraphernalia we lug about as a matter of course, given where we grew up.

Further, inventing a place is, paradoxically, unfamiliar enough to ensure that the inventor doesn't have painfully acquired defenses, or self-constructed censors, primed to slam into action at the first indication of something personal appearing. People can construct things that are meaningful to them, and in fact fulfill the old saw, "Write about things you know, dear," without knowing much about writing and without having more than the least idea that what is being composed is important to them.

Don't get me wrong on this: I am not a voyeur, or even an auditeur. I don't do this to feed off the inner strife of my students, given that I am the audience for these things. I do, however, appreciate the rightness of that old saw (correctly understood) when it is used to enlist the maker's emotions and expertise and not to forbid any areas that lie outside everyday experience. Making a place, a fantastic place, with few more rules than those you put down yourself, is an excellent way to make a statement about first-order things, even if it is done in a second-order way. It is something that the students can do and in which they can be deeply involved.

There are, however, some rules, some constraints. This is not a blue-sky construct — just go out there and invent. If the course teaches anything, it is that there is nothing new under the sun, that it's all in how you change and group what you take from others. Although size, genre, and absolute originality are not problems, and writing well is not the horrific problem it might be, requirements still must be fulfilled for the world to be a success. It must, first and foremost, have variety. It must not be monochromatic, or indeed mono-anything. Ideally, it should be crammed with places for things — various things, different things — to happen.

154

Although the places themselves may be surprising, they should also possess, for full marks, an inner consistency, which is to say that anything that happens there should never give the feeling of being out of phase. Everything there should have its reason for being, filling in and filling out what is, or will be, a relatively small whole. As to the requirement of amazement, well, this is probably the most difficult part, not because I, their audience, am especially jaded in these matters, or will not replay as though this would be the first time I had ever seen anything like this ("An alternate Europe? Hey, *great!*"), but because they think I am, and therefore push themselves very hard when I adjure them to AMAZE ME. Of course, I wouldn't disabuse them for the world. Certainly not for the world I want them to make. I want it to be hard for them. It's not as though they couldn't do it.

It is, in fact, something for which they have been, in a way, trained. I don't here mean the gamers—those long-time engagers in role-playing games, the D&D-ers, Dungeon Masters—who always constitute some fraction of the course's enrollment. They know the bit, as it were. They've done a lot of "making," and often have worlds on the blocks, just needing that bit of polish for which my course supplies the time, or so they hope. But let it be here said, the worlds they construct are very contentious, what with combats and power ratings, and don't seem to allow much time or space for ordinary living. Gamers *qua* gamers I don't address—nor, on the other hand, do I penalize them for their knowledge. What they're doing is just different, that's all.

But all students in the course have been put through a preparation of sorts to which they can refer when making their worlds. The final project, the World, is the last in a chain of projects.

First in this chain is what I call the "Critical Effusion." This project is the one analytic piece in the course and comes soon after the term's beginning. It is an analysis of the background, or the world, of a work of fiction—any work of fiction the individual student wishes. (This broadness of choice, with the goal of their taking on things that they like, means that I normally get science fiction, which is all right by me. I've read a lot in my time and can always read some more.) This is a very short piece, and it drags, or should drag, their attention away from the story to the background, except insofar as the story necessarily interacts with the background.

Invention, construction, or synthesis starts with the second project, which I call the "Realization." Its object, as stated in the syllabus, is for them "to set forth in considerable detail the physical lineaments of a location which has been noted in much less detail in one of the works studied." The place is not a free choice. I pick it, generally from some classical author (which is what we're doing at that time), give them such other information about it—generally from antiquity—as I can, and turn them loose. That is, "Homer, or Apollonius, or Virgil, mentions this place but doesn't say much about it. What was it really like?"

I've used various locales over the years—the land of the Lotus-eaters

155

(Homer is really shockingly brief); Lemnos, the island of the very, very complaisant women who delay Jason and the Argonauts; and Aeolia, the land of the god of the winds. This year's candidate, due in about a week, is the land of the Hyperboreans, those who live at the back of the North Wind. This assignment is an exercise in, shall we say, bound freedom. The constructor of the new Hyperborea can sneak in anything, of course, but it must fit with the original and subsequent descriptions supplied. What they are doing is fleshing it out, realizing it, as a pianist might realize a figured bass from the symbols before him. They should here be quite full, but full within limits.

The third exercise is rather different, a dry run for the final project. That it is not the Big One is shown by its title, the "Minicreation," and by its minimum size, forty feet by forty feet. It may be a parody or pastiche of one of the worlds studied in class. It should be, in a sense, freestanding, but it is not quite free. It must incorporate within itself three objects, size to be negotiated (which means that it's up to the student), specified on the day the paper is assigned officially.

One year, I recall, the three objects of which I supplied pictures but not identifications, were (1) a Klein bottle—that curious topological manifold, a sort of a three-dimensional Möbius strip, that contains itself; (2) a representation of the never-built Tomb of Lars Porsenna, designed by the French Revolutionary architect Lequeux; and (3) a very strange tree, from a woodcut in a very strange book, the *Hypernerotomachia Poliphili*, which rather looked as if it grew Ping-Pong balls. These items (and others in other years) could be important or not in the finished minicreation, but there, in some way or other, they had to be. It became quite a game, rather, the students interpreting the objects in the farthest-out possible sense, and then challenging me, as it were, to find them. In the end, however, they had built a place, had "done their own their own thing" if you want, but had still done it with some control.

The final project, then, is the result of at least some exercise in acclimatization to the form. They can build something, at any rate, although whether they can proceed to the goal as defined in the assignment is something else again. "The starting point will be the principles and examples exemplified in the reading and expounded in the lectures, but the term project should go far beyond this, using as operative guidelines the words *detail* and *realization*. Your world should be as various and complex, as fully conceived and executed, as is possible, with the object of convincing me of its reality. It is to be bolstered by such items as maps, genealogies, pictures, official documents, letters, travelers' accounts, print-outs, tapes . . . mere examples, but you get the idea."

Even if you were listening closely to the last requirements, you may not have realized that there was a kicker included, and indeed solved, although not directly stated. The final problem is presentation. How are they to tell me all this? ("All" is too much, of course. Within the fifteen-page minimum of the assignment, they can't tell me all about a bungalow, must less a world.) What is the mode of presenting it to be? Narrative, by the way, is excluded — my one act of official tyranny. My objection to narrative is not so much that it masks the background (although it does, and I have to read all the papers in a remarkably short time) as that it tends to take over, to become more important that the background. People, at least the people I get as students in this class, love to tell stories. They will pout when narrative is excluded, and then search for a legal fiction whereby they can tell me a story while, quite legally, not doing just that.

Let us return to the problem of presentation. How is it to be done? One good pattern, if potentially boring, is the encyclopedia article. What this has, of course is a built-in motive for telling anyone anything. That's what people go to encyclopedias for, to be informed, to learn everything they need to know, say, about Belgium, in short compass. It has a logical structure: physical geography, figures, import-export, demographic breakdowns. It does seem rather a shame to let, nay, *force* them to be imaginative in one direction and absolutely forbid it in any other. (Here you see me, as in so many other situations, working against myself.) So I hedge.

"Your world," I say, "is to be bolstered by such items as maps, genealogies, pictures, official documents, letters, travelers' accounts, print-outs, tapes, trivia. . . ." And there, ladies and gentlemen, I have effectively opened the gates to, not Hell, but Chaos — mine, not theirs. I can thus receive as primary documents, in addition to the above, such items as journal entries (I hate these), reports from or to StarFleet Central, purple passages from bad novels (evidence, you see; not embodying narrative), ships' logs, annotated texts, select bits from scholarly wrangles, directions, even menus. It has become, willy-nilly, a playground for the ingenuity, sometimes affording evidence of as much work as the worlds themselves.

I'm not complaining, really — far from it. For the worlds I receive on the last day of class are worth it somehow. I have spent one-on-one time with every student: trying to get them to tell me about their worlds, trying to help them put their specialized knowledge into an unfolding world, sometimes sweating out the stony silence of an experienced gamer who knows quite well what he or she will do and who regards the conference with me as a time-wasting bother, if not actual interference. Certainly it's not the conferences that grab them, or the lectures, or the remarks I write on their preparatory papers. Whatever it is, when those final projects arrive, in whatever media, people appear to have been grabbed. I rarely get lick-and-promise worlds. Rather, what I get in most instances is responsible creation, which, even when I know what's coming in, amazes me.

What type of worlds do I get? There are the inevitable number of Tolkien clones, but with considerable labor to make them different. Then we have the softest of fantastic worlds, although a little lighter on the nymphs and satyrs than the time spent on the pastoral would lead you to expect. I see the hardest of science-fiction worlds, often based on some peculiarity in physical reality.

They have created miniature worlds, alternate Icelands, the world as if settled by Romans, para-Paraguays, relatively young worlds—their physics thoroughly established—where the dominant race has not yet emerged from the sea, medieval quest worlds, infinitely varied metropolises. All kinds, and all showing something about their authors. It's not just the devotion that pleases me. They are genuinely interesting to read. And, given the demands of the course and its reading, quite skilled.

Let me give you an example from the beginning of what appears to be a fairly hard science-fiction world:

Go out on a dark night and find the star Miazr. It is in the forehead of Ursa Major. . . . Near it is another star, very small, very faint, called Alcor. . . . About 811,000 years ago the inhabitants of the Alcorian system began to construct the greatest and last of those grandiose engineering projects that had made them notorious as a race whose energy was matched by their lack of good common sense. . . . [They] decided . . . to melt down the entire contents of their system and a couple of others and build a sphere *around their star*, in order to gain more elbow room for their population of over 690 trillion, and secure energy from Alcor which they had not previously been able to obtain. The Alcorians spent about ten thousand years in the construction of their edifice (some statistics: average radius, 149 billion km; interior surface area, app. 3.8^{17} km^2; star type G2; shell thickness, 4,822 km).

And, of course, since a Dyson sphere of that inconceivable hugeness is inherently unstable, it cracks and disintegrates in a mere 100,000 earth years, and we are treated to an analysis, physical, political, and the like, of one of the fragments.

Or, from a much softer world:

Wallox (pronounced "Wallox") is a lush green country, mostly vineyards and fields (with the entire west coast being used as beachfront). Wallox is the major wine-producing country, and the major vacation spot, of Yggdrasdrill. The eastern half of Wallox is given over to vineyards and groves of lemon and pillyath trees, while western Wallox is mostly beachfront condominiums (rented at mind-numbing rates), convenience stores, hotels, swimming pools, and beach bars. It should be noted that Wallox has the largest GNP of any country in Yggrasdrill as well as the smallest static population.

There are at least some fruits of parageography, which lends itself well to satire, particularly on bigness. There is a flip side to all this, however, one that can be attributed directly to one of my peculiarities. I am a jazz musician, in such spare time as I have, and tend to regard all improvisation as one of the highest practices to which the human faculty can aspire. I find that I have been guided, to a great extent, by two quotes from wildly different sources. The first is from the jazz pianist Thelonious Monk: "The cats I like are the cats who take chances; sometimes I play a tune I never heard before." The second is from the French anthropologist Claude Lévi-Strauss:

> The *bricoleur* [jack-of-all-trades] is adept at performing a large number of diverse tasks; but unlike the engineer, he does not subordinate each of them to the availability of the raw materials and tools conceived and procured for the purpose of the project. His universe of instruments is closed and the rules of his game are always to make do with "whatever is at hand," that is to say, with a set of tools and materials which is always finite and is also heterogeneous, because what it contains bears no relation to the current project, or indeed to any particular project, but is the contingent result of all the occasions there have been to renew and enrich the stock or to maintain it with the remains of previous constructions and destructions. . . .[1]

To be ready, at a given instant, when the pointing finger indicates NOW, to stand up before an audience and create something—that is, for me, the real existential moment, the time when one is really alive. It is perhaps not surprising that something like that has worked its way into this class in speculative fiction, which has somehow become a forcing-bed for creativity.

I suppose the question was, originally, "What should they do on a final examination?" One possible answer was that they could tell me about the texts that we'd been reading all term, but that went against the whole tenor of the course. Obviously, I thought, they should create something, but what? Even I shied away from penning people in a room for three hours with the single command, "Write!" And yet, creating under the gun—improvising creativity, as it were—had an overpowering fascination. How to promote it, so that it could be bound, yet free? Therefore, some years ago, I got into the game myself and discovered a place called High Thefarie. As the White Knight said to Alice, "It's my own invention."

I suppose the Germans would call this a *Lehrweld*, a teaching world, since that is its principal use. Its name is High Thefarie, or, in New High Thefarien, Thuta Thefariei. (Thefarien writing is retrograde, from right to

---

[1] Claude Lévi-Strauss, *The Savage Mind* (*La Pensée Sauvage*) (Chicago: University of Chicago Press, 1966), p. 17.

left.) To anyone experienced in these matters, it is a shamelessly derivative world. It has the north-by-west exposure and the danger in the east to be found in most Tolkien clones. It has a sunken city which has the same name as the Breton legendary sunken city of Ys. Its configuration is clearly derived from part of Italy—Tuscany or, if you prefer, Etruria. Its language bears a distinct resemblance to Etruscan, that fascinating tongue that, in spite of some centuries of work on it, cannot yet be read.

The principal, and humanoid, race that inhabits it is oviparous (a shameless lifting from Edgar Rice Burroughs's Barsoom, or Mars), but the eggs are hatched by the males (not a lifting from Burroughs, shameless or otherwise). Its system of numbering is base five. Its culture, in fact its existence, is cyclic, or rather helical: every 625 years, a violent change occurs, so cataclysmic that it is forced to begin again, not from scratch, but from far down the way it had previously achieved. Its totem, and indeed its titular ruler, is a large hog. Beset on its eastern borders by a variety of natural enemies—wyverns, snollygosters, kobolds—it is technologically somewhat advanced, but has not developed the internal combustion engine, or indeed, much of any engine. Our knowledge of it is spotty in the extreme, yet the account of it presently contains eleven pages of introduction and eighty-three pages of text. The trouble is, the texts are not the systematic presentation desired of every true parageographer, but rather a mishmash of poems, address book entries, inscriptions, folktales, interior monologues, dialogues, descriptions, lecture notes for a history of drama, scores for collective improvisation, and even unanswered questions about the place asked on final examinations in the dim dim past.

Precisely where it is located I have no idea. Its records are only known from information brought back by one Dionysius Simplicissimus Periphrastes (by no coincidence at all, his initials are mine), an American academic of high middle age who was transported there to effect a cyclic change, but the time factor was off. He found himself age eighteen in that strange land with fifty-two years to be lived through until he could fulfill his function and be returned to the American Southwest. Live through the time he did, but with no great distinction. He was ever a loser, trying many professions and succeeding at none. He married the same woman, the estimable Eniaca, six times, once more that What Is Allowed. He sowed disaster in his wake. Further, he was no systematic record keeper. What we know about the place is what he doles out at whim, in dibs and dabs.

You get the idea, I hope. High Thefarie, and DSP's involvement in it, are a fiction, created (a) (the principal reason) to supply raw material for a final examination—or as we call it, a Terminal Praxis; and (b) (a subsidiary reason) to allay the creative gnawings of a professor who can't bear to be out of the act himself. This booklet that I hold in my hand contains all that is known about High Thefarie thus far. It is the base for that Terminal Praxis, on which the students are asked to supply, in three hours max, answers to very searching questions about the place—so searching, in fact, that the answers are not to be found in this booklet, or indeed anywhere. Those answers that the students give must fit, must proceed from what is known about High Thefarie (in this booklet and subsequent handouts), and must not contradict it. Their knowledge of the place must be evident in those answers, which will then, inevitably, be a collaboration by the student with the author, DSP—which is to say, me. The questions, once asked, become part of the data for the next year's account, although they are not always answered.

Let me emphasize here that this is not egomania/self-indulgence run wild, or not merely that. It is a bit off the track, perhaps, but not wild. I do not ask the students to memorize it, for instance. To the Terminal Praxis they bring the booklet, handouts given since it appeared, and any notes and maps they deem necessary. The land is designed to accommodate almost anything, but that argues perhaps too broad a spectrum of potential questions, so I supply them beforehand with a list of six broadly defined areas from which the long questions will be drawn. The short questions, spot identifications of classes of persons, or places, or happenings, of which they have never heard, are perhaps more of a surprise, but then, they are fairly good by this time at making things up. Let me give you a sample of identifications from the year 1985:

Geographical Anomalies

As one might expect of a parageographer's paradise, High Thefarie was absolutely studded with strange places, odd features of landscape, and upsetting geological impossibilities, unnatural markings of a wholly perverse nature. So many, in fact, that they did not find a place on the latest map: Of the ten following items, eight have not been cartographed. But no matter, you know the place. Choose any THREE (3). Write a paragraph on each which will locate it (if necessary), describe it (with particular attention to its strangeness: What does it look like? How does it work?—if that applies), and account for its fame in High Thefarie (What happened there? Who was involved?) Give dates and persons where applicable.

1. The Humongous Geode

2. Lonespire

3. The Mad Mesa

4. Bridgeoak

5. The Flying Island of Tlusc

6. The Damnable Delta

7. Hollowood

8. Vainvale

9. Concertina Pass

10. Downspout

Three out of ten. Not impossible, and I got some very curious, and not all complimentary, replies. Long questions, however, are another matter. I give six options, of which they are to choose one and expatiate on it, spread themselves, demonstrate at length (of less than three hours, of course) their knowledge of High Thefarie and their ability to create. What occurs here is not necessarily geographical, in the narrower sense. I feel free to draw on any aspect of the Thefarien life and thought — history, economics, what have you. In 1986, for example, for the benefit of a pre-med who had grumbled through the term, while doing quite well in the course, that it was biased against life scientists, I included the following item with five others:

VI. Spring, of course, meant much the same to Thefariens as it does to us: freshness, the triumph of light over dark and life over death, rebirth, rejuvenation, fertility on the rise. But there was a darker side to Spring in High Thefarie, especially since Spring$_2$—the Season of Surgery. The butcher's calling had been highly honored in antiquity ["Ytte ysse a poincte compleatly moote," observes a fragment of a chronicle of Snuiaf from mid-XIII, *"whethere ye Yefariens doe abhorre or reveere ye Pigge, but cotte ytte they doe, and with a righte doughtie wille"*], but the sudden taboo on pork which followed the Exaltation of the Swine at the beginning of XIV, and the consequent freeing of hordes of Master Slicers for other work, led to the slow but relentless rise of what we will call Cosmetic Surgery. It certainly had little if any pathological function, this snipping away at the bodies physical that comprised the Body Politic; its aim was the objectification of status by subtracting what was sound; the removal of diseased organs was left to journeymen. The principle was conspicuous consumption, rather: The Master Deller who lacked his little fingers could obviously afford a hireling to perform *Hanguide*. Thus it went, till it appeared that quadruple amputism had slaughtered social one-upmanship. But the Opening of the Chest Cavity in XV/555, abetted by a standardized system of scars denoting what had been removed, spread new fields of endeavor before the eager surgeons, who cut withe a righte doughtie wille until Cyclend. *Describe, in agonizing*

162

detail and with charts, the excess of disposable inner organs with which Thefariens were blessed. Note the social cachet attaching to the removal of each, and specify the scar/sign thereto assigned. (NB: this must be answered inventively enough to overcome your Guide's distaste; he is now sorry he brought the matter up) — One further item: Tell, once and for all, the story of DSP's operation.

I apologize for the length, but the antsiness of the rhetoric will illustrate something about the praxis. The basic supposition, relentlessly maintained, is that they, the students, know everything about the place and are just filling me in, rather than making it all up so as to fit, somehow, with the High Thefarie they have learned about from the booklet, handout, and *obiter dicta*. The actual practice is for them to be engaged in bound creation, to make sense, in the circumstances, of the strange, of the unforeseen, like Lévi-Strauss's *bricoleur*. There is a theory that life is improvisational, or improvisatory, to which I probably subscribe.

Just why this whole process — course, papers, project, and praxis — should work, or even if it does work, I am not entirely sure. Still, results and observation have brought me to these tentative, very unscientific conclusions:

1. Initially there exists, somewhere in a corner in everyone, a great fount of creative imagination.

2. If not used, it atrophies, deserting people somewhere down the line when they really need it.

3. It can still be got at, quickened into life, and possibly preserved, in those in their teens and early twenties.

4. It operates best when compelled by necessity, which the course supplies, and channeled constraint, which the course also supplies.

Let me end with three disclaimers. First, I disclaim revolutionary counterculturing. I am not a hangover from the 1960s, when I was uptight and buttoned down — doubtless more of the problem than the solution, as I probably am now. Certainly I tilt with no administrational windmills: The Powers That Be have been quite nice to me, and I don't take all, or indeed any, opportunities to inveigh against them. I have few illusions about my role: it wasn't the reason I got into this; it was not the result of a reasoned plan at all. It just happened. The educational system, as I see it, progressively excludes the creative imagination, and quite necessarily so, but overdoes it, that's all.

Second, I disclaim universality. What I do, good or not, has affected, on balance in a good year at Texas, possibly one-tenth of one percent of the student body at any given time. It has, so far as I know, produced no bright and shining lights of public achievement who would serve as object examples, justifications of the whole rather messy process. I do not advocate it for everybody, or indeed anyone other than my own students. It is simply what I have found myself doing — a small crack in the system.

Third, I disclaim thoroughgoing populism — that populism which, in this case, would mean that everyone can, and therefore should, create something that has, or should have, a wide audience. Love my fellows I do, but I am not that idiotically sanguine. On the other hand — and this will put me at fairly direct odds with at least one of the speakers to follow me — I am enough of a populist to believe that everyone can and should create, and should find some audience, even if only a deaf superannuated relative who is, quite simply, glad of the attention.

Therefore let me conclude, noting that you are not deaf, or superannuated, or my relatives, and that I have been quite thankful for all your attention.

Discussion

PARTICIPANT: I understand that a lot of the creativity in making these imaginary worlds is just moving around elements that students have found in other fiction or in their own lives. Where do you draw the line between creatively moving around these elements and copying Tolkien or L. Frank Baum?

DOUGLASS PARKER: I suppose part of it goes back to the old academic saw: one source plagiarism, many sources research. There undoubtedly is some, although I don't think that I have ever received any flat-out plagiarism. What I get rather is the other thing. Sometimes they say, "I am worried about this. I am worried about a world that I am developing because I can tell where everything in it came from." Now, it may have come from many sources, which is fine. I admit, on the other hand, I have sometimes probably been snowed. But I have found nothing, however, that was so singly and simply derivative on one thing that I wouldn't say, in the case of the world, *creation* has been involved here. Sometimes the training process that they go through helps this—that is, the Klein bottle from the third assignment may crop up as an item in the final project. I couldn't be happier about this. Admittedly, plagiarism could be a problem, but I haven't encountered that problem as yet. The dividing line? I am not sure.

PARTICIPANT: You mentioned Dungeons and Dragons several times. I have known some children who are very involved with this game. They did know some Arthurian legend and they did know some Greek mythology, but aside from the obvious advantage of taking them away from the television, what are the virtues and vices that you have found with your students who have been involved in this game?

PARKER: Aside from getting them away from television and keeping them off the street, it lets them run with some pretty bright kids. It teaches them more than just a smattering, although a lot of it may be made up. The materials for role-playing games—if you haunt science fiction bookstores as I do, to check out the competition as it were—can be remarkable. Is acting out an advantage creatively? I'm not so sure. It seems sometimes to me second-hand, but it is not absolutely passive. In lots of these games, they develop their own characters. I wouldn't worry too much about it, unless someone goes absolutely glassy eyed and disappears into his role, or into the sewers, like the boy at Michigan State some years ago. He went to the dungeon and never came back.

PARTICIPANT: You said at one point that you learned there is nothing new under the sun. Does that mean there is some kind of closed circuit on creativity and, if so, why should that be?

PARKER: No. I grew up in the radio age and there was always, say, Bob Hope. Those of you who come out of that ancient time may recall that on Bob Hope's radio show, there was a determinedly homely female by the name of Vera Vague. She was protesting to Bob Hope about Hedy Lamarr once, saying, "What's she got that I haven't got?" Hope's reply was, "Nothing, but she groups it better." I have a feeling that, in a sense, it is the grouping more than anything else. Just because you can trace every penny in your pouch, or every penny in a given pouch, to its source — can say this comes from here and that comes from there — does not mean that there is not something new in the combination. What I was trying to get at is this: if you consider single elements, it becomes very hard to find anything that has not been done in one way or another.

PARTICIPANT: Do many of your students, given the opportunity to build a new and creative environment, use that opportunity primarily to get across some political, moral, or satirical message?

PARKER: A good share of them do. The student who wrote the paper I read to you about the people who built the sphere and watched it break up did. Essentially what happened to his Argolians was that some of them emigrated here and interbred with Neanderthals, the docile Neanderthals. The desirable qualities of the Neanderthals and the pushiness of the Argolians resulted in what we have today — that is, people who take on projects that are grandiose and inflated. A lot of them take political satire as a given. I am now wondering if the election this year will produce anything. Four years ago I was on leave, so I was spared that. Yes, some students certainly aim for message.

PARTICIPANT: Is that a valid way of using this technique — to promote a particular political or moral attitude?

PARKER: Swift did it. Rabelais did it. Lucian did it. Melville did it.

166

Charles Kingsley did it. I think if you're erring, you're going astray with pretty good company.

PARTICIPANT: Have you noticed any difference in personality types and their ability to cope with this kind of assignment? In other words, are introverts or extroverts particularly different at doing this?

PARKER: I haven't tried to break it down that way. One would feel that some of the most expansive worlds I receive come from the types you might expect — the bright ones who did everything in high school and continue to try to do it in college, and who have read a lot of science fiction, and creativity comes out their fingertips. This is not necessarily the case, however, because all the worlds don't come out in the same fashion. There is one student about whom I wonder. He seemed perfectly nice, but he developed the most horrific punishment world that I have ever seen. It was one in which a malign deity was deliberately encouraging and then frustrating the efforts of everybody. It was a place that made Hell seem like a weekend resort. The author was rather quiet and reserved, and seemed to be doing fairly well a couple of years later, but I still wonder about him.

As to types, it's a little bit difficult to say. Word has gotten around now, and the class is sort of preselective. Oh, I still get the students who say, "Pardon me, sir, but I need a humanities course that satisfies the Area D requirement, has a substantial writing component, and meets Monday, Wednesday, and Friday from 12 p.m. to 1 p.m. Can I get in your course?" They aren't really what I want, but I get a few of those. Sometimes they gather in clutches — the rowdies and the silent ones out there. And sometimes the silent ones will really surprise me.

PARTICIPANT: The Greeks wrote about their gods, and *Gulliver's Travels* says something about the church. C. S. Lewis, of course, said something about his faith and even "E.T." may say something about God. Do you find in this exercise for yourself and for your students a quest to find God?

PARKER: I examine a number of things. One is the historical mutations of, say, the *garden*, as one goes from two wildly different sources, that is, the Greek pastoral, the idylls (what the Romans would call the *locus amoeuus*, the *plesaunce*. Then the *paradise*, which comes from a Persian word for garden, coming up from one hand a different direction — out of Genesis, picked up in interpretations of "Song of Songs," and that coalescing in another sort of garden. By the Middle Ages you have "the garden," which is at once paradise, then the "Earthly Paradise" — what happened to Eden after they shut the place down. Dante puts Eden on the top of Mount Purgatory, which is at the Antipodes on the other side of the Earth. Dante hadn't had much experience with gardens like that, but he knew a lot about pine forests in northern Italy, so his earthly paradise is a pine forest.

Do they find God? Certainly the Lewis books are about this. I am less sanguine that Tolkien's trilogy, or indeed Tolkien's works, are. I don't think Baum's were at all. Baum's were nationalistic, an attempt to write, shall we say, American fairy tales, American fiction, sometimes urban American fiction. In the rest, one can certainly find theological quests to find God, certainly in Dante. In the Greek items, it is less certain. Odysseus is trying to get home. Aeneas is trying to reach Italy and found Rome, so that a thousand years down the pike there will be something glorious. He has the help of the gods, but this does not develop into a search for God. Certainly theological investigation continues to be an important motive for speculative, fantastic, marvelous literature.

PARTICIPANT: What do you think of Ursula Le Guin? What do you think of her book, *The Left Hand of Darkness*? Do you know it?

PARKER: Yes. I think it is marvelous. *The Left Hand of Darkness* is about a world where it is always winter, or just about always winter. It is a world that appears almost incomprehensible to the earthman discovering it. One finally gets some light on it when one realizes that in this winter cycle, the people are in heat certainly only rarely, at specified times during the year. Indeed, it is not determined whether one is male or female. One may be male one time and female the next time. From that basis — the ever-winter world and the way in which sexual roles develop, Le Guin builds a marvelous fiction. It is all the more marvelous because of the way she tells things, not the usual way one expects science fiction to be told although she has been working in science fiction for a number of years now. A movie was made of one of her books, *The Lathe of God*, where the weather is changed in Portland. The beginning of the film was shot in Oregon and the rest in Dallas — same place with a different climate. She is remarkable.

Still, I rarely teach science fiction. I sometimes do Herbert's *Dune*, because it's a lovely problem. It is a desert world with lovely geography. It also follows the historical development of Islam and works it out quite well. I have taught, among moderns, Roger Zelazny's *Worlds of Amber*, Gene Wolfe's *Earth of the New Sun*, and Stephen Donaldson's *The Land*. This is the only modern, six-volume science fiction novel that has a leper as its hero. Donaldson is remarkable in other ways, but he's chiefly remarkable as a writer who thinks in five-hundred-page chunks.

PARTICIPANT: Did you love this kind of thing when you were a young boy? Did you create imaginary worlds and invent ways of people?

PARKER: No, I didn't create any, actually. I suppose it surfaced late. What I remember most is trying to make a map of the Land of Oz; this occupied me for some years. First I had to acquire all the books. (There are now forty Oz books. They started to re-release the later ones recently, but then stopped.) Next I had to gather all the data. Then I had to allow for the fact that Baum unaccountably changed his mind at one point, and I wasn't absolutely sure whether the Munchkin country was in the East or West, or the Winkie country was in the West or East. This type of problem can compromise all your calculations. Well, I worked on that map for three years, off and on.

PARTICIPANT: You said that you feel that all of your students have the ability to be creative. What about those of us who get older? Do you feel everybody has the ability to be creative?

PARKER: I don't really know. That faculty, like other faculties, if not used, atrophies. I'll find myself writing poetry and plastering it on my office door. There is a certain desperation in this — trying to get to something that has to get out. This parageography course aims at eliciting something one wants to make. Another reason for it is that it is an ego trip. I think the two are intimately involved. I do it because it is the sort of thing that I want to do. When one is older, I don't know. I am sixty-one, and I would hope that creativity doesn't stop. It depends on what has been happening in between. I imagine it could be started again. I do wonder, though, like the Peggy Lee song asks, "Is that all there is?" That's what I worry about. This is why promoting creation occupies what little missionary zeal I have in the world. Creativity should be preserved or at least excited before it does die out.

PARTICIPANT: When my children were very young, I told them stories. Now they are getting bigger, and I'm hoping that if I'm a grandmother, I'll do it again. Isabel Allende was on National Public and said that she told her children stories. I hope that it doesn't dry up.

PARKER: I do too. When my children were twelve, eleven, and six, we went to Cambridge, England. This was in the middle sixties. By that time, I had pretty well stopped reading to them. While we were abroad, however,

169

there we were—five people, a nuclear family, thrown together. I found myself reading out loud like crazy. That was when I first made it through, or almost through, the Narnia books. (I got so mad at the last one, I put it down and didn't pick it up for fifteen years.) And then we read the children's books of Susan Cooper and Alan Garner—who, in my opinion, is the best children's writer in the world. I have no grandchildren and no immediate prospects of them, at the moment. You can't go up to a little girl and say, "Pardon me, little girl, can I read to you?" Not really.

PARTICIPANT: Could you tell us a little bit about the follow-ups of your students? What perceptions have they had as a result of doing this assignment?

PARKER: Some people come back and say, "Hey, that was great!" or they drop in to see me, which indicates that at least a few are still working on it. A student started a novel and was pretty well along in it (heavily influenced by Le Guin, as a matter of fact) but then she abandoned it. I saw her the other day and found she had taken it up again. Another girl in the class wrote rather interesting pieces about being an alien in an Oriental land. She had actually grown up and gone to school mostly in India. I hear from her occasionally.

I started the course in 1973 and retired it in 1978 and then suddenly went to Dartmouth to visit in the winter of 1982. They said, "Do you have any unusual course?" I said, "Well, yes, there is this one rather odd one." And they said, "Fine. It will bring in bodies." It did. It scared me green, but it also brought some remarkable bodies—or, rather, minds. One of the most successful worlds I have ever had concerned a section of Route 92 from Hanover, New Hampshire, to Montreal—a road that somehow had been shut off by a time warp for sixty years. It was about the people who lived on that part of the interstate and was very remarkably done.

PARTICIPANT: I think I understood you to say that creativity is suppressed by society to some extent. When do you feel this starts, and why do we suppress it? What do you feel the role of creativity in most of our lives, especially emotionally, should be?

PARKER: The educational system, almost from necessity, suppresses it. You do things in colors in kindergarten. The whole emphasis, though, particularly when you get into the university, is on getting ahead, learning the right and useful things. Of course, we do emphasize the humanities for people who are going into the nonhumanities. I'm not saying that everybody should be put into a creative course. Beyond this, though, we seem to feel that second-hand exposure to creative works is somehow as good as first-hand — as doing it yourself. I think this is wrong. I have room for both approaches, but I would much rather play music than listen to even the best played music. These are two different things, quite different.

I don't know how one makes people do things. I don't know how to restructure an educational system, one that is geared to produce people to occupy, to consume, to produce, to work the country, so that it can say, "You really ought to learn how to do something in your spare time." Also, I like this course because it operates just barely in the institution, and I worry about institutionalizing something, since then it becomes big and turbid and the stink of death is in it. I don't know how one avoids this. It seems to me that everybody has potential.

When I was in college, I used to work summers at Allis-Chalmers, a farm machinery factory. On the assembly line, I used to wonder, "How do people live like this?" I found that they didn't think about work or the union. What they thought about, where life began for them, was what they did in their leisure time, what they did when they went home, whether it was working part-time as a contractor, whether it was sailing a boat, bowling — something. Somehow, that leisure time ought to be the time when people create — unless one is lucky and gets into a favorite area where creation and producing for one's own consumption come together.

There might be some way to foster this widely, but I have no idea how. I'm not the one to grab people by the lapels and say, "Be creative." Sometimes it is just convincing people — "Look, don't worry about this. You're in the class. Roll with this, think." And then there are the ones who say, "I know what I want to do. And don't you say a word. I'm not going to tell you about it until I hand it in. Goodbye, Professor," I have no really effective way to answer that. What do you do? How do you make most people creative? I don't know — but I think they should be, and can be creative.

PARTICIPANT: You said that you didn't have preplanned or preconceived ideas about the course nor have you produced any creative geniuses. Apparently, if you terminated the class in 1978 and then started it again, it is meeting your expectations. Have you had any surprises? What is it that keeps feeding your ego to continue it?

PARKER: I started this in 1973. I had been ill and thought in this way: How could I, without absolutely dynamiting the structure, talk about things that I liked to talk about? When I had broken in as a university teacher at the University of California at Riverside in the fifties, I'd found myself teaching

171

university extension courses. There was not too much market in Riverside for teaching the classics in university extension classes, so I taught other things that I was interested in: American humor, children's literature, and "modern science fiction," which began in 1952.

One of the authors I taught then was Tolkien because *The Lord of the Rings* had begun to appear in the early fifties — 1953 in England, 1954 in the United States. Finally in 1956, I had written a long review article on it for *The Hudson Review*. Down the line in 1973, I wanted to teach these things again, because I realized they were important. Tolkien, in the meantime, had become a growth stock, and so I taught his books and others like them. Surprise really came to me when I arrived at Dartmouth and found that I had to resurrect it all. You can teach literature by teaching anything you know. Suddenly, the students were very good — and not just at Dartmouth, at the University of Texas, too. They could dig down. I could require more and more, and they would do it. Then I, myself, come into the picture, get into the act. It is almost inconceivable that I wouldn't teach it anymore. The surprise? The success of this off-hand approach.

PARTICIPANT: It seems to me that the kids who are willing to go into an inner world and create out of that are more prevalent now than they were in the fifties or sixties. Do you think that is so?

PARKER: I would think so. I was teaching in the fifties and the sixties — except I wasn't teaching anything like this. I don't know what the reaction to this would have been in the sixties, but I have an idea: it would have been something everybody latched onto and said, "That's for me!" — quite probably for the wrong reasons. The danger of going inside yourself is what the Germans call *innere Fuhrung* — that is, you retreat from the unpleasantness outside, and just go in there and say what's outside isn't happening, doesn't matter. This is not what I think one does in creativity, although I do think that one has to go inside the self and take a shudderingly good look, because everything one writes, in some sense, is autobiographical. I do hate, of course, to think that my Zeus poems are of that nature. Some of the poems are clearly autobiographical. In fact, there is one where Zeus is telling his psychiatrist about an awful dream he had: he dreamt that he was a classics professor.

PARTICIPANT: It occurs to me that a lot of what you are doing, we categorize in psychology under the term "autonomous complexes." You're bringing them out and having people look at them, play with them, and create them. I wondered if you get into any psychological problems or issues with the people who do this, and, if so, how do you respond to them?

PARKER: I teach fifty people in the course. I try to confer with them all. Some seem quite upset about things that they have to do, but the only ones who really have psychological discussions with me are the psychology majors. The others do have their worries: I looked at the pages of that student with the punishment world and said, while backing away ever so slightly, "Well, that is very interesting." He replied, with a very feral grin, "Yes, I like this."

Generally, no; I haven't dug down. If one were really digging and went one-on-one for quite a while, it might touch on problems. I recall trying to talk people into it. It seemed to me we were getting close to something, but often students in that situation simply decide that it is something they won't do and can't do and drop it.

PARTICIPANT: It would seem to me that what you are teaching is very appropriate today. The children of this generation have been so structured in their growing up. They haven't had the time to play and create things as we did back in the early twenties or before when we would spend whole days with nothing to do but dig in the sand making a whole city of our own or make stages and have plays and create things. Children don't have this ideal time today. Your course would teach them how to do this.

PARKER: You remind me of something. I grew up in a small town in Indiana with a number of friends, boys and girls, who liked each other. From about the age of nine until thirteen, we would get together at the home of one of the girls in the group. It was a big, old rambling Victorian house that had an attic with costume trunks — every sort of costume. We would go over there regularly and get involved in really baroque improvised dramas. We would start in the attic, get ourselves dressed up wildly, then sort of spill down through the house, wander all around the block, and then to a vacant lot across the way. This was how we spent Saturday mornings. The fact that Mrs. Lewis baked cookies on Saturday mornings didn't hurt, of course. I think it was very important for me.

PARTICIPANT: Don't you think that making up a world would express a person's inner feelings about the world in which he or she lives? We use art therapy during the time of psychiatric workup. I find that I can really look at a picture and have a feeling for what that person is feeling even though I am not trained in this field. Aren't you surprised that the people's thoughts in this dream interpretation, Jung and Freud, aren't expressed in trying to create a world as an assignment? Why isn't there a correlation?

PARKER: On the other hand, there may well be a correlation. Some of the

173

creations are so obvious a child of six could understand them. That is to say, even I could understand them, and I am not the world's most perceptive human in many areas. Some of this may be due to my lack of training in psychology and psychoanalysis. I know things to do when I see a labyrinth, but not everything: I will go back, to a religious interpretation, probably, and work with that. It is not the case that they don't tell me things about this person, but it is the case that in the conferences we discuss things such as, What are you going to do on the paper? What are you going to write about? These questions are focused toward something that they can produce, rather than something about them. If the creation works, it is generally impelled by what they are. Sometimes I can see that I can understand the person, a one-to-one correlation. On the other hand, many of these students are quite complex, and they can play all the games I can play and can throw them back at me, which is part of the fascination in this. Would this be a good technique for therapy or consultation? I rather imagine it would, but I'm certainly not the one to do it.

PARTICIPANT: I teach elementary school. I find it deplorable now that so many children are not read to sufficiently. They get all of their stories visually. It just soaks in like osmosis instead of having the story read to them and in their own mind picturing the Wilder family living on the prairie. Instead, they see it in living color. I read *Little House in the Big Woods* to my third-grade children because I wanted them to know that Pa was a rough character who had to battle the elements to keep his family together and not a handsome Michael Landon. I think television has stifled much creativity in our small children.

PARKER: The sort of students I get are the ones who take this course because it is the sort of course they like to take. Some children can't picture, and it is quite possible that sense might atrophy. This course does go through one sense, or one faculty, to get at another, and that's why I like it.

PARTICIPANT: You said you grew up during the age of radio. Those of us who did listened to "The Inner Sanctum" or "The Twilight Zone" on radio. It was much more vivid than seeing it on television because you pictured what you thought it was.

PARKER: Yes. A group of us once did *Beowulf* for a radio broadcast on KUT at the University of Texas. It worked out well. I think the best one we did was *Sir Gawain and the Green Knight*, which is just lovely when read as a play. It is marvelous to be able to read to people.

PARTICIPANT: Could you elaborate more on the game playing?

PARKER: Do you mean the people I refer to as "gamers?" Such things known as role-playing gamers exist in this world. Anyone who has children who came of age after the middle seventies should probably be familiar with these. I remember I was teaching when somebody brought three badly mimeographed books and said that this was another world, but that was back in 1974. Now slick operations produce slick products, some of them quite wonderful, if you like that sort of thing. In Vancouver, I think, one company puts out series of gazetteers, an encyclopedia Harnica for a place called Harn. The buyer gets a map and all sorts of information and rules. One also gets power ratings. These are for the edification and use of the people who play role-playing games and follow immensely complicated scenarios, sometimes attaining some mythical goal, sometimes refighting the battle of Chickamauga, more often fantastic than not. They do this in one or a variety of personae, either designed for them or by them. There are rules. Some are set down and some are determined by the dungeonmaster. This game is Dungeons and Dragons, which is copyrighted by TSR. But a number of companies make these types of games.

Participants assemble and act in their personae to win the jewel from the head of the idol, or defeat the evil Ores that stand between them and the princess. The games are very sophisticated and with the coming of the computer they have become remarkably complex. They are also, I would say, a big business. I don't worry about them. It's fascinating to see what they come up with. They make very interesting worlds, always involving a combat situation, an adversary situation. There is always something to overcome.

PARTICIPANT: I understand that when you play jazz you can regurgitate jazz or you can create your own jazz phrases, which I believe you said you did. Don't you find this a somewhat creative enterprise?

PARKER: I think jazz improvisation is probably one of the highest sorts of creation in which I have ever been involved. As to the creation, which goes back to nothing new under the sun, there are dissertations in this field. One of the early analyses on Charlie Parker's style isolated his works and broke down his cliches, to determine what he did in a given harmonic environment. With this information, one can then say, "All right, he will do this in a given situation. He will not do that." In essence, you have Parker and all the phrases that Parker uses and all the situations in which he uses them. Of course, knowing all of these doesn't make anyone a Charlie Parker. I don't feel that I regurgitate jazz. I do know that I have a range of responses that gets me out of certain harmonic situations when I'm playing bebop, which is my favorite type. I keep trying to internalize more cliches, other ones, so that I'll do different things in a given situation. But I doubt that, in the flow of improvisations I ever play any small thing that I haven't played before. Creation is in choosing and grouping.

HARRY WILMER: Why did you stop the course in 1978? And aside from your own imaginary world, what is your favorite creative world? Do you have a favorite and why?

PARKER: I don't know exactly why I stopped the course in 1978. The creative bit hadn't started yet, and I rather felt, "Well, I've done this. I will go try to do something else." I think about that time I began teaching a course in "Wit, Humor, and Antiquity," which I still do from time to time.

My favorite world? I have lots of favorites but the reigning one at the moment, mainly because I haven't worked it all out yet, is the world of Ladovico Ariosto—the world of the *Orlando Furioso* which is a sort of para-Europe but with real differences. Imagine a Europe where it is 800 A.D., but the Moors are battling at the very walls of Paris with Charlemagne inside and all the paladins of Christianity. What Ariosto does to it is just magnificent. He even manages to put a man on the moon, where all the lost things go. Then there is a slight dip down into Hell, although nobody goes into Hell much after Dante. But Ariosto fascinates me. He's very funny. At the moment, that would be my favorite parageographical world.

CHAPTER ELEVEN

Edward Albee

A PLAYWRIGHT

Edward Albee was born in Washington, D.C., in 1928. At the age of six, he began writing poetry. For the next twenty years, he wrote poetry and novels with little success. His success began when he became a playwright starting with *The Zoo Story* and continuing through twenty-one plays. *A Delicate Balance* and *Seascape* both won him the Pulitzer Prize. *The American Dream* won the Foreign Press Association Award, and *Who's Afraid of Virginia Woolf?* won the New York Drama Critics Circle Award for Best Play in 1963. Subsequently, it was made into a successful movie starring Elizabeth Taylor and Richard Burton. His other plays include *The Death of Bessie Smith*, *The Sandbox*, *Tiny Alice*, *Box and Quotations from Mao Tse-Tung*, *The Lady from Dubuque*, *All Over*, *The Man Who Had Three Arms*, and his latest, *Marriage Play*.

Among the plays Albee has directed are *The Zoo Story* (1961 and after, off Broadway and tours), *The American Dream* (1962 and after, off Broadway and tours), *Seascape* (1975 Broadway), *Who's Afraid of Virginia Woolf?* (1976 Broadway revival), *Listening and Counting the Ways* (1977 American premiere), *Albee Directs Albee* (all of the one-act plays, tour). He continues to direct many of his plays both in the United States and in Europe.

Albee is a member of the Dramatists Guild Council, P.E.N. American, and the American Academy and Institute of Arts and Letters, and is chairman of the Brandeis University Arts Commission.

A Playwright and Contemporary Society:
A Discussion

Introduction

Edward Albee arrived in the world a born writer. When he was two weeks old, he was adopted by a wealthy theater chain owner, so he was nurtured by the theater. He received an education that was marvelous for experiencing life, for learning honesty, for becoming a writer — but his schooling was problematic. He was expelled from Rye Country Day School and then went to Lawrencefull Boarding School in New Jersey from which he also was expelled. Next he went to Valley Forge Military Academy — expelled again. He finally made it through Choate School, although he moved on to Trinity College in Hartford, Connecticut, where after two and a half years he was asked to leave for refusing to attend mathematics classes and chapel.

There are all sorts of rebellious people in the world. Positive rebels, as our forefathers and such as Albee, first to adapt to their inner selves — what they really are and not to what society is trying to make them conform. Then they adapt to the outer world. The negative rebellious people end up as lifelong delinquents — in prison, in therapy, in unhappy relationships — and the cruel world often breaks them. Extraordinarily gifted people like Albee have no alternative but to follow their muses and their creative drives, which seems to make them misfits because they tell us things we don't want to know in ways that compel us to hear.

Like Robert Oppenheimer, "after Trinity" Albee had a series of jobs, as office boy, book salesman, counter man at Manhattan Towers Hotel, and as a Western Union messenger for several years.

Finally, after twenty years of writing good but not great poetry and two bad novels, Thornton Wilder told Albee to write plays. He did and in no time at all he skyrocketed to international fame as a playwright. It began with *The Zoo Story*, and then *The Death of Bessie Smith*, *The American Dream*, and *Who's Afraid of Virginia Woolf?*, which was to win the New York Drama Critics Award, the Antoinette Perry Award, the Tony Award, the Obie Award, and the Outer Circle Award. He was denied the Pulitzer Prize by so small a majority of the jury for such spurious reasons that two famous men on the Pulitzer Prize Committee, John Mason Brown and John Gassner, resigned in protest.

Albee wrote *Tiny Alice*, which I loved, and then *A Delicate Balance*, which the Pulitzer Prize Committee loved; they belatedly gave him his much deserved first Pulitzer Prize. This play was made into a wonderful movie. Albee wrote *Seascape*, which absolutely bound me as his fan.

179

Edward Albee

The first time I ever heard or saw him in person was at Southwestern University at Georgetown, Texas, in 1983 where he was a resident director and teacher for five weeks. Photographs of him teaching and directing his play *Malcolm* at Southwestern show his totally captivating presence.

Just before he left Georgetown, I wanted him to come to Salado. It took five more years finally to get him here. It only took two days after he left Southwestern University, however, for them to have to shut down the school theater and declare it off limits because of the sudden development of what their engineers called "structural tension." It turned out that a weld holding a floor beam had sprung. The local newspaper reporting the event noted that it followed the tremor Albee had created at Southwestern University.

Harry A. Wilmer

Discussion

PARTICIPANT: When you create a play and it's made into a movie or produced on the stage, do the producers give you much interference, or do they try to change your words or put words in your mouth that you didn't write?

EDWARD ALBEE: When you write a play and have it performed on stage, you have controls that do not permit distortion, as long as you're there to make sure the distortion is not taking place. You do not sell a play for performance. You lease the performance rights and retain absolute copyright control over every word that you have written so that no one may make a change without your permission. When you sell a play to the film industry, however (and I've done this on only two occasions, *Who's Afraid of Virginia Woolf?* and *A Delicate Balance*), you are taking your chances. They buy what you have written and they can do whatever they want with it. In both of the cases in which plays of mine have been made into films, I've been very fortunate that the result was almost word for word what I wrote.

With *Who's Afraid of Virginia Woolf?*, the producer did write a screenplay. Apparently, after Burton, Taylor, and director Mike Nichols read it, and after their laughter died down, all three announced that they would not make the movie if this screenplay was used. The producer's screenplay was thrown out, and with the exception of a couple of sentences, the final screenplay was my work. *A Delicate Balance* also was word-for-word my play. I haven't gone through the horror stories that so many playwrights tell me of Hollywood studios distorting and destroying their work after buying it.

One of the reasons I do not write for films but write for stage instead is that I prefer to be a pauper among other things, but also that I prefer the control that writing for the stage gives me. If you take the trouble to write for people, and try to share your view of the world with people, you want them to have to participate in it the way you did it. You want to take your own blame and your own credit. You don't want to be stuck with anyone else's interference. That is one of the nice things about not writing for film or for television. In these fields, you're not your own boss; you're a fieldhand.

With plays you are much luckier. If you have written reasonably care-fully and precisely so that it is really difficult for a director or an actor to mess up what you have done, then you are pretty safe. I have seen some productions of my plays that made me wish to leave the theater. Even worse, I remember once (I will not name the city, but it was a dying city on a dead lake) I saw a production of *Who's Afraid of Virginia Woolf?* that was so wrongheaded, so completely in opposition to anything that I might have intended ever, I had to sit there and hold on to my seat so I didn't stand up and say, "Hold. Stop. Put the curtain down. Go away. Go home." Sometimes this happens.

At the same time, I have seen university productions of my plays from time to time that have been absolutely extraordinarily wonderful. Then I have seen other university productions of my plays so devoid of acting, so com-pletely devoid of acting, that something rather interesting happened. Nothing was there to stand in the way of the audience hearing the play pure and complete. A little acting is a dangerous thing. You are somewhat better off in the theater because you have a lot more control than you do in film or televi-sion. I'm not trying to suggest that there is any writing for television—I've never noticed any. They try it occasionally in film. I have written four screen-plays, by the way, all of which were greatly admired by the people who hired me to write them, and each of which was turned down by a whole host of film directors. Do you know why?

"Well," they say, "we can't make a film of this. Albee's done everything. He's written it so completely there is nothing for the director to do. There is no creativity left for the director." Obviously I shouldn't be writing for films.

PARTICIPANT: I wonder if you could back up just a little further in your explanation and tell us about the personal process you go through in writing a play.

ALBEE: It is very difficult to do. I discover that I have been thinking about a play. Somewhere along the line, my mind has decided that it is time for Edward to write another play. So my mind starts evolving the play and maybe several months or years later, my unconscious mind informs my conscious mind that I have been thinking about a play, and I become aware of it. I keep thinking about it until it is time to write it down. This can be six months or ten years after I first become aware of the fact that I am thinking about a play.

Then it is time to write it down. The writing period has never taken me longer than three months, sometimes a lot less. When I start to write the play, I have no idea what the first or second sentence is going to be, but I inform myself. I find it so difficult, as most creative artists do, to talk about the

182

creative act. It is almost impossible to do. Maybe we fear that it is sort of like Aesop's fable about the unpleasant animal who was talking to the centipede and asked him, "Amazing—these hundred legs! How do you walk?" The centipede, very proud, started to explain how he put the front left leg forward and then the right front leg forward and by the time he got to explaining the twelfth or thirteenth leg, he was paralyzed.

Writing, I suppose, is a kind of black magic. In a way, it is something that we are afflicted with, we writers. I write because I am a writer. I write plays because I am a playwright. I get ideas for plays because I am a playwright. It really is no more complex than that. I don't try to examine it too carefully. I do try to examine very carefully what I write down on paper—control it, make sure I'm exhibiting both sufficient freedom for my characters and sufficient control over structure so the whole thing makes sense, and wait with extraordinary enthusiasm to find out how it is going to come out. But it is hard to talk about it.

PARTICIPANT: How do you feel about the status of Texas playwrights? Since you've been down here a while, do you have a sense of whether we have some emerging?

ALBEE: I'm a professor of drama at the University of Houston. I have been for a while, and I have a number of young playwrights in my class. I've taught play writing at other universities, too. I certainly don't find any less talent and creativity among my Texas students than I do elsewhere. I'm terrible with names. I don't think in those terms. I understand in Texas you would think "Texas playwright." I don't know what that means, you see. I just look for a good playwright. Tell me a Texas playwright and I'll tell you if he or she is any good. My students are good. My students are enormously talented.

PARTICIPANT: Two possible people were Sam Shephard and Horton Foote. By Texas playwright . . . we have a lot of pride in people who succeed, who came out of this state that is still close to its frontier, where you do still have maybe more raw material than you do in other states.

ALBEE: Horton Foote is an enormously effective and skillful playwright. Sam Shephard with his seven hundred plays certainly is our oldest and most promising young playwright. I admire the best of Sam's work an awful lot, maybe more than I do Foote's work because I find it perhaps attempts to expand the boundaries of the theater a little bit. I didn't realize they were both Texas playwrights. You lost a good playwright when Preston Jones died. He was on his way to being a first-rate talent when he died so young. I'd never think of anyone being a New York playwright. We don't have the state pride that you have in Texas.

Let me generalize this a little bit to get out of my ignorance of Texas playwrights. We have a great number of enormously talented young playwrights in the United States. Serious, tough, young playwrights — more now than we have ever had. When I started in the theater in 1958, there was no off Broadway. There was no experimental theater to speak of, just one or two theaters here and there. Then a whole new generation of young playwrights just sprang into being with the birth of off Broadway: people like Jack Gelber, Jack Richardson, Arthur Kopit, LeRoy Jones, and myself. A few years after that came Lanford Wilson and Sam Shephard.

There are more interesting, adventuresome young playwrights afoot in the United States now than there were twenty-five or thirty years ago — a great many more. They are getting their works produced. They are getting known. They are not, of course, getting their work produced in the commercial theaters because they are tough, serious playwrights. The commercial theater is less and less interested in the work of serious, young playwrights. There are, however, an awful lot of very good young playwrights in this country now. I'm very excited about what is happening.

PARTICIPANT: Which of the creative artists do you think can help us get back on the right path? Or do you think because the audience does not want to accept the responsibility of seeing the harsh truth that perhaps tough, serious plays will just be for the elite with the theater staying in its current state?

ALBEE: I suppose it would be far too naive and utopian to expect that sometime we would be a society where far more people were listening to the Beethoven string quartets than were listening to Mantovani. I suppose it would be irrational to expect a time when Neil Simon would be less popular than Samuel Beckett. I suppose it would be improper to expect a time when James Merrill's poetry would be more popular than Rod McKuen's. These are foolishnesses. I would imagine that that which is less demanding is always going to have a slightly larger audience than that which is demanding.

We can do things through education, however, especially by beginning to educate kids when they are young enough that they don't even know what is happening to them aesthetically. We can make them aware that participating in the life of the creative mind is something natural. We can begin to corrupt them, if you will, toward a comprehension that aesthetics are a proper participation. We might be able to educate a society that could bring these things a little bit more into balance, a society that might prefer the arts that tell us something to the arts that remove us from participation. It may be that one day we will want to see more films that do not take us away from ourselves, but rather put us in greater contact with ourselves. It may be that some day we'll want television to educate us rather than turn our minds into mush. It is possible. It can happen. There are very few countries in which it can happen.

You mentioned word "elite," did you not? I don't know why "elite" has become almost as dirty a word as "liberal" in this country, but there is always going to be an elite. There is always going to be a group of people who appreciate some things more than others do. What I would like to do is see if we can't raise the entire level of participation—to get rid of this awful desire to homogenize the arts in our society down to a kind of safe mediocrity. The only artists who are severely punished in our society are those who try to extend beyond the safe and mediocre—those who try to break new grounds either aesthetically, intellectually, or emotionally. Those are the ones who are penalized. Those are the ones who take joy in the creative act.

If we could try to educate our people so that serious art was not penalized, people might begin to understand that they can get far more from an evening of theater that disturbs them and that haunts their thoughts for six months after the performance than they can get from a theater experience of which they recall nothing ten minutes after they leave the theater. Unfortunately, most people want theater and book experiences that pass right through them, from which they retain nothing. We can educate people so that they no longer want this. There will always be some people with their eyes in the stars and some people stuck down in the mud. There's nothing you can do about that. We might make the mud more interesting and the stars more accessible.

PARTICIPANT: You say that the creative artist is to present truth to . . .

ALBEE: Oh, I used that awful word again, I know you're going to question *truth*, aren't you?

PARTICIPANT: No, no, no, my question is: How do those of us who are on the receptive end of creative art distinguish between those who are bringing truth and those who are bringing their perception of truth?

ALBEE: Well, you are asking that question about truth. I knew you would. I should stop using the word *truth*, Edward. There are absolute truths somewhere, and I suspect that maybe, generally speaking, the serious creative artists have access to these truths that they are willing to express or that they have thought about consciously a little bit more than some other people may have. Some artists lie. Don't trust them at all. You can usually figure out which

185

ones are lying. There is a historical continuum of the art forms; they all interrelate; they all interlock. There is a history, just examine the history, the twenty-five-hundred-year history of the theater. Almost from the beginning, playwrights have had certain preoccupations of how people exist in their society, how people exist with each other, how people exist with themselves, whether they lie to themselves, whether they tell the truth, whether they deal honorably or dishonorably with themselves.

These are concerns and preoccupations that have concerned playwrights and all other creative artists throughout history. There seems to be some sense that there is an aesthetic access to truth—whatever that truth may be. Or maybe what they mean by truth is merely the absence of lying. Lying is far more easy to determine than what truth is.

The willingness to take the chance and participate in new ideas, to participate in things that run counter to what you believe you believe, to be willing to have new aesthetic experiences, new philosophical experiences in the arts, and to arrive at conclusions—these are the things that the arts can do. No, there are very few of us artists around who feel that we have access to "The Truth" and are the only ones who have access to "The Truth." Critics feel this way. Creative artists do not.

PARTICIPANT: How do we as a nation compare to Canada, or France, or some of these other countries that really support the arts in the amount of money that we've given to the arts?

ALBEE: In spite of the attempt of the government in each of the past eight years to destroy the National Endowment for the Arts, a few people in Congress have managed to sustain it at approximately $120 million a year, which is about forty cents per person in this country in support of the arts in the National Endowment. In West Germany, it is approximately five dollars a person, compared to about forty cents in this country. We lag behind many of the other participatory democracies in the support of the arts. We lag way behind. The attempts made constantly to cut these programs on a governmental level are shocking. This suggests to me only that our government, at least the present one, does not believe in the aesthetic education of the people. This is a great shame. We are lagging way behind. And we don't always necessarily put the best people to work even when we have the money to do it.

I'm very proud of the New York State Council of the Arts. It is the second largest arts organization in the United States. Its budget is something like forty million dollars a year in a state of only fourteen million people. It has a pretty good record and does a lot of good work in support of the arts. I

186

was on the council of the New York State Council of the Arts, one of thirty-five members. The only thing that puzzles and bothers me is that of those thirty-five members, I was the only creative artist on the council. The rest were apparatchiks, political powers, wealthy benefactors of the governor, and a few good administrators. We don't do enough. Very little of the council's money supports individual creative artists. You know it's not a largess to make life easy for the painters and dancers of this country, not at all. It is part of the aesthetic education of our people and we spend shockingly little money on it.

I have such a simple solution to the whole thing, by the way. I might as well share it with you. I have mentioned this to many senators and congressmen, and they look at me as if I were quite mad because the idea is so simple. Great Britain has a thing called a use tax on television sets. I know this will never happen in the Bush Administration because, read his lips, he's never going to raise taxes — until he gets elected, you know. The British use tax on television sets is twenty dollars a set. In other words, to use the airwaves everybody who owns a television set in Britain pays twenty bucks a year. If we had that in this country, with our at least a hundred million functioning television sets, we would have two billion dollars to support the arts if we used that use tax on television sets to support the arts. Painless. And my goodness, how we could contribute to the aesthetic education of the people in this country. There are so many simple ways of doing it.

But the arts, you see, are considered to be frivolous and ephemeral and decorative. Of course, we all know this is not true. The arts are enormously useful; artists wish to find consciousness. Why the arts are the first budget item to be cut as if they are nonessential, I will never figure out. This is not merely a parochial response on my part. I dare say that if I were sitting somewhere and someone made a speech like the one I made, I might begin to think that, yes, art support and arts education is enormously important. Even if I were not a creative artist, I might begin to think so. It is part of our education and our self-respect as a society, I think, that demands that we pay much more attention to the aesthetic education of the people through support of the arts.

PARTICIPANT: I was going to ask a question concerning the matter you just touched on, aesthetic education. You referred, in part, to what would happen in the broad medium. But I wonder if you want to make any comments about what you think is important, within a formal setting, within the schools or within the universities, for example.

ALBEE: I did mention, did I not, that I think it must begin so young.

Edward Albee

During the civil rights movement, for example, we forced people to behave a little more rationally and reasonably toward each other as adults. But it was only when we realized that if children were educated together, they would begin to comprehend each other, and we might even just begin to see the end of bigotry in this country. In the same way, I think that the aesthetic education of people can't begin at college. It must begin when they're so completely young — so young. I am shamed and shocked the more I travel around the country (and I even go to high schools sometimes to talk to students) to see the values that are being pounded into kids' heads — values of wealth, safe job, vanish into the society. The arts are frivolous and decorative and nonessential. I'm finding this view more and more prevalent in our society. Both parents must be capable and willing to begin the aesthetic education of their kids, and if they're not capable of doing it themselves, tolerating it when it does occur in schools. It is our responsibility to hire teachers who are capable of aesthetic education. Starting at college level won't do any good. The arts will, by that time, have begun to be thought of as something strange and exotic and unnecessary. We must bend the mind to comprehend aesthetic responsibilities so young, so enormously young. I can't get more specific about it than that; I just know that it has to begin at the very beginning.

PARTICIPANT: Aside from your courses at the University of Houston, what would you advise a young person who has a burning desire to be a playwright to do? What path would you advise him or her to take in pursuing that course?

ALBEE: First of all, I would tell them, be absolutely certain that being a playwright is something without which you cannot be a complete person. Be absolutely sure that this is not merely something you would like to do, but is what you *are* — that it is in your nature and without the practice of it you will be an incomplete person. Be sure of this because the arts are tough; the arts are ugly; the arts are painful; there's a lot of sadness in them. For all the wonder and all the joy that comes from creativity, a lot of bad exists, too. Be absolutely certain that without your participation in the arts you'll be an incomplete person. And once you decide that you must do it, do it.

Then I tell them, if I really think they want to hear it, you'll either be good or you won't. Educate yourself in the arts if you're going to be a playwright. Learn from the finest teachers you possibly can — learn from Chekov, learn from Pirandello, learn from Beckett, learn from Molière, learn from Shakespeare, learn from Sophocles. These are your teachers. Know everything you possibly can about your craft and about your art and also know everything you possibly can about the other crafts and the arts because they all do interrelate.

But most of all, be sure that you have to do it. That's the best advice that you can possibly give, because a lot of people think, "Hey, that sounds pretty good! Write plays, then go to the movies to write films, and it will be wonderful." Well, it's not. I was talking to a fairly well known playwright, John Guerr. Some of you may not know his name, but a lot of you know his work: *House of Blue Leaves* and various other plays. John told me that he had written fifteen plays by the time he was hired to write the screenplay for the film, *Atlantic City*. Until *Atlantic City*, John did not make a living from his writing, although he had an enormous reputation as an off-Broadway playwright up until that point. But he'd never made a living writing plays.

Do you know how many serious composers in the United States make a living by writing serious music? Three or four at the most. In New York City, where there are undoubtedly fifty thousand painters, do you know how many make a living off of their painting? Maybe a hundred. There are at least twenty-five thousand out-of-work actors in New York City. This gives us a number of very, very nice and attractive waiters and waitresses in our restaurants. While it is true that twenty-two thousand of those twenty-five thousand out-of-work actors probably deserve to be out of work because they aren't any good, there are still three thousand out of work who do not deserve to be. The arts aren't easy.

Ultimately, quite often after a person has died, excellence dies out. I am convinced that there are not many times when we suddenly discover a great composer or a great painter—certainly not a great playwright—fifty years after they have died. Usually talent dies out and especially in the theater, a hungry organization that wants novelty and constantly devours new plays. I can't imagine that there is an accomplished, serious, young playwright in the United States whose work will not be produced somewhere within five years or so after he writes it and begins to think of himself as a professional. But it's not the easiest thing in the world. Truth-telling seldom is.

PARTICIPANT: You describe the role of the creative artist as confronting the audience with truth and reality. There is also a paradox that includes the potential for depression, a kind of hopelessness, or on the other hand, a hope and an opportunity to advance. You have a powerful instrument in your control. Would you grant that the role of the artist might be inclined to turn the key just a bit one way or the other toward hopelessness or toward hope?

ALBEE: I've always thought that hopelessness existed in darkness, in the absence of examination of possibilities. I've never thought the soft gesture as effective as the tough gesture. I can think of very few serious creative artists whose ultimate message to the people is not an optimistic one, through self-awareness. Self-awareness can be tough, but I can think of very few pessimistic creative artists—the creative act itself is an act of extraordinary optimism. It assumes there is something to be communicated, and that people are willing to participate in the communication. People sometimes ask me, "Why are your plays so depressing?" I have to say, "Well, look around." When things stop being depressing, I will stop writing depressing plays. I don't go around lying about people. If people stop behaving this way, I'll stop writing about them behaving this way. Make my plays unnecessary.

All playwrights feel this way. All creative artists feel, "Make what I do absolutely unnecessary. Prove me wrong." In a utopian society, there would be no art because art would be unnecessary since it is instructive and corrective. There would be no need for it. I'm not holding my breath. I don't think that we are going to get there. It is not that the arts tell us too many depressing or awful things. The danger is that we are not willing to pay proper attention, so we can't struggle toward the light. We are going to be in true depression, which is self-deception and darkness.

PARTICIPANT: Can we return to critics? What do you want an art critic to do? Has one come close to it? And why haven't you tried your hand at that?

ALBEE: I can say almost without exception that I have learned more about how I practice my craft as a playwright, how good or how bad I am, from the reaction and opinion of fellow creative artists than I have from any critic. Obviously this leads one to the conclusion that for the health of our society and for the health of the arts, creative artists should be the critics. Creative artists have access to what's going on in the creative intelligence that other people don't have. We would be a much better society if painters were book critics, if playwrights were music critics, if composers were drama critics. We would have a far more adventuresome and interesting art structure in the United States.

Arthur Miller and I went to the *New York Times* more than twenty years ago and said, "Why not have two critics when you review a play? Why not have whoever you hired, in your infinite wisdom, to be the drama critic, but also have [and I think we slipped up here] somebody who knows something about the theater to give your reader half a chance?" But the *New York Times* was not interested in having the professional creative reaction to the professional creative experience. It was not interested in having its readers have that. The *New York Times* is one of our more responsible public organs. If the *Times* feels that way, why do you expect it to be any better anywhere else? Every once in awhile there are some good critics. But generally speaking, a critic usually tells me far more about how long my play is going to run than about whether I should have written it. He tells me far more about the nature of public tolerance of my ideas than about the value of my ideas. I love to be corrected when I am wrong. I love to be informed about how well or badly I'm practicing my craft. I dearly wish that there were more critics who could tell me.

It is not arrogance that leads me to say they are incapable of it. It is they are not equipped to analyze and discuss the validity of the creative act as a socially responsible effort to an audience. They're not hired for it. If they tried to do it, a lot of them would get fired. It is that simple. People don't have to put up with any of it. Critics are there only because the owners and publishers of the magazines and newspapers think that is the kind of criticism people want. If people decided they didn't want that kind of criticism, the owners and publishers, motivated by profit, would switch policies quickly. If somebody told the *New York Times* that everybody who read the paper would much prefer to read a playwright's opinion on theater in the United States you can quickly bet that Frank Rich would be fired in a second. Then some playwright whose opinion I detest would become critic.

PARTICIPANT: I would like to believe with you that playwrights tell hard truths about ourselves, but I often have a hard time putting my finger on what the truths are that are told in a great play. Take one of yours, say *Who's Afraid of Virginia Woolf?* that we all know, what are the hard truths about us in that play, and why are they not about George and Martha?

ALBEE: Well, let me see if I can remember exactly what I was after in that particular play. I believe that I wrote that play, and I figured this out afterwards, as a reply to [Eugene] O'Neill's play, *The Iceman Cometh*, which postulates that we must have what O'Neill calls in his "wonderful" way, "pipe dreams," or false illusions. O'Neill postulates in *The Iceman Cometh* that a person must have false illusions to survive—that people cannot accept the truth.

I think *Who's Afraid of Virginia Woolf?* was written to argue the opposite—to suggest that only if we rid ourselves of the false illusion, of the pipe dream, can we possibly build a complete and sensible life. In that particular play, George and Martha had constructed—I suppose through a certain

191

amount of time—societal and career pressure and other needs, a set of fictions about their lives that ended up controlling their lives. It was only through the destruction of these fictions, these false illusions, that they were able to see rock solid ground and make an intelligent decision about whether they were strong enough to rebuild. You can't build a new building on the wreckage of another one. You have to build it on solid ground. I guess the play was pretty much about that.

It is my private opinion that they were strong enough to do it. The play ended in 1962, and here it is 1988, twenty-six years later. I suspect that they are still married and doing rather well. I don't think they have invented a new fictional kid either. I suspect that was pretty much what the play was about, among other things. It was my view of what, I think, is the more valid way for society to maintain itself. Now, I'm right or I'm wrong. You take your chances.

PARTICIPANT: I was a student at Southwestern when you spent the semester there, and I remember how much the student body enjoyed having you there. At the same time, sometimes I feel pessimistic about the state of the arts in this country. I've studied in London for a year. For the price of a subway token, you could go to the National Gallery and spend all day there for nothing, and I understand that you can have your college education free there if you have the grades.

I then moved to New York City and found out that for the price of a subway token and five dollars you could go to the Metropolitan, and then if you sacrificed your monthly salary you might see an off-Broadway play.

At the same time, here in Texas, if you want to see a foreign film, you'd find that the only foreign film house in Austin is closed down, and when it was open, it only cost a dollar to get in. Sometimes I really wonder what is going to happen to us?

ALBEE: I found, and I still find, that it is very easy to participate in the arts without having a bunch of money even, for example, in New York City. Of course, you can sneak into any worthwhile play because there won't be many people there. Most of the serious young painters and sculptors are showing at galleries with free entry. Every museum in New York has a free day, by the way. And you don't have to spend thirty-five dollars even for a ticket to an off-Broadway play—unless you want to sit in the first ten rows. If you can't sneak in, you can always get standing room for about six bucks. It can be done. The access is there, and if you know your way around, it's not too tough. You can read the best new books in the world, because if they are good enough they're going to be remaindered even before they are published, and you can buy them for practically nothing at the serious bookstores in New York City.

The only problem arises when one lives in an environment without access to this stuff. Then I suppose it is a little more expensive — like the cost of the plane ticket to New York to see the play or see the work in the museums. There are economic problems with it all. I'm not trying to suggest that there aren't. Theater is infinitely too expensive. Films are too expensive. Books cost too much. Back in the days when I sold books at Bloomingdale's, in the 1950s, I was shocked when a hardcover book went up to five dollars. Now they are twenty and twenty-five dollars. I was so grateful when paperback books suddenly appeared in the United States. Then they were a dollar fifty, two dollars, and people could get great literature without spending very much money.

It is the possibility of access to the arts that is most important. Everybody wants that access for free. I would like it for free. I wish it would cost a great deal less to participate in the arts. If the government subsidized them properly and made it easier than it presently does for businesses and foundations to subsidize the arts, then they would be more likely to be free. But the most important thing is to ensure that the arts are accessible to people who want to participate in them and that these people are educated to participate in them. Worry if the museums vanish. Worry if all the serious movie houses close down. Worry if the people who come into the library can't take out the books. Worry if parents deny their children aesthetic education. Worry about that. Worry about the loss of opportunities of democracy in this country. Let's worry about the fact that things cost a little bit too much, but let's really keep our sight on the fact that there are forces that are less interested in people being aesthetically educated than we would like to think. There are forces of darkness in this society and we had really better watch out for them.

PARTICIPANT: In *The Closing of the American Mind*, Allan Bloom blames part of the problem in creativity and thinking in America today on the lack of classical literature in the schools and the lack of classical education in the home. Also you pointed out that creativity is getting in touch with and responding to the subconscious. Do you think that possibly two of the problems today might be the lack of discipline and the lack of time on the part of the young people?

ALBEE: I don't know if it is a lack of discipline or time. It certainly is a lack of being presented sufficiently with the opportunities to make valid choices. That is a question of values, is it not? What are the values that people feel kids should be educated toward? They certainly don't seem to include the aesthetic education. I'm absolutely convinced, although I can't prove it (I can't prove anything and I never pretended that I could), that a society that is properly educated aesthetically is probably better able to govern itself. I'm convinced of this. I'm convinced that the metaphor will permit us to govern ourselves more properly.

If people are not offered the opportunity of choice, they cannot make a choice. If people are not shown the possibilities, they are only going to deal with impossibilities. Unless students are forced to have jobs after school so they can't possibly do their homework, unless students are being educated by teachers who are incapable of educating anyone, unless students live in environments where they are discouraged from the life of the mind, I see no reason why they cannot obtain these things. Students must be educated to want to participate in the arts. This education demands a society that values these things. It demands an educational system capable of providing them.

I have very few answers for things. I would rather pose questions anytime that I think should be examined but to which I have no answers. If I limited anything I wrote or anything that I said concerning those questions to which I had the answers, I would be a very silent person. I would much rather raise a ruckus about things that I know are wrong and about which I expect someone else to provide the answers. It is my responsibility to keep shouting and making the noise.